THE DEATH OF EXPERTISE

THE DEATH OF EXPERTISE

The Campaign against Established Knowledge
and Why It Matters

Tom Nichols

OXFORD
UNIVERSITY PRESS

OXFORD

UNIVERSITY PRESS

Oxford University Press is a department of the University of Oxford. It furthers
the University's objective of excellence in research, scholarship, and education
by publishing worldwide. Oxford is a registered trade mark of Oxford University
Press in the UK and certain other countries.

Published in the United States of America by Oxford University Press
198 Madison Avenue, New York, NY 10016, United States of America.

Library of Congress Cataloging-in-Publication Data
Names: Nichols, Tom, 1960- author.
Title: The death of expertise : the campaign against established knowledge
and why it matters / Tom Nichols.
Description: New York, NY : Oxford University Press, [2017] |
Includes bibliographical references.
Identifiers: LCCN 2016037219 | ISBN 9780190469412 (hardcover) |
ISBN 9780190865979 (paperback)
Subjects: LCSH: Information society—Political aspects. | Knowledge, Theory
of—Political aspects. | Knowledge, Sociology of. | Expertise—Political aspects. |
Education, Higher—Political aspects. | Internet—Political aspects.
Classification: LCC HM851 .N54 2017 | DDC 303.48/33—dc23
LC record available at https://lccn.loc.gov/2016037219

7 9 8

Printed by Marquis, Canada

For
Lynn Marie Nichols
and
Hope Virginia Nichols
Expert wife and peerless daughter

CONTENTS

Preface to the Paperback Edition   ix

Preface   xix

Introduction: The Death of Expertise   1

1. Experts and Citizens   13

2. How Conversation Became Exhausting   40

3. Higher Education: The Customer Is Always Right   70

4. Let Me Google That for You: How Unlimited
   Information Is Making Us Dumber   105

5. The "New" New Journalism, and Lots of It   134

6. When the Experts Are Wrong   170

Conclusion: Experts and Democracy   209

Notes   239

Index   249

PREFACE TO THE PAPERBACK EDITION

I admit I was a bit anxious when the first copies of *The Death of Expertise* arrived. I was hopeful that the book would resonate with people who encouraged me to keep writing after they read a short article on the subject of experts and society I'd written some years earlier. But I was concerned that a wider audience might dismiss the book as just another curmudgeon's demand that everyone either listen to his advice or get off his lawn. (There's some of that. I can't deny it.) I also wondered if my central argument—about the unwillingness of ordinary citizens to listen to expert advice—was primarily an American phenomenon.

As soon as the book appeared, however, readers shared their stories with me. People in all walks of life told me of their own experiences about the dismissal of their skills or outright hostility to their knowledge and expertise. Nor was the book limited to an American readership; as of this writing, *The Death of Expertise* is available in eleven languages besides English, which I found a bit surprising. I had assumed, perhaps out of a kind of reverse-ethnocentrism, that Americans, ever sensitive to distinctions that impinge on their sense of egalitarianism, were among those mostly likely to exhibit their disdain for knowledge. Instead, I soon found myself talking with people from Japan, Ireland, South Korea, Italy, Australia, and many other countries about similar problems in their own societies.

Of course, my relief about the wide acceptance of the point of the book was immediately tempered by my alarm that the problem I was describing was far more prevalent than I had suspected. And that was not good news.

Doctors and teachers, of course, were enthusiastic constituencies for the book, but so were electricians and plumbers who told me stories of homeowners following them around and quizzing them about the details of their work, despite an obvious inability to understand the answers. Restaurant patrons who believe they understand the intricacies of fine cuisine were among some of the most reliable mainstays of these anecdotes, as were the usual vignettes of teenagers delivering impromptu lectures in high school and college classrooms. A wedding photographer told me how often someone would come to her as she was setting up and advise her—in complete ignorance—about what kind of lenses she should use.

Some of these stories are amusing, but others were quite depressing, and often involved injury or other misfortune. To take one of the more amazing items, I regret to report (and am sorry even to know about) the existence of the "poop cult," a dangerous fad invented by a woman in Ohio who claimed that all diseases are due to a fungus in the human gut and could be battled, according to one report, by drinking a "fermented slurry of salted cabbage that produces 'waterfalls' of diarrhea." While this might seem worth a brief laugh, it turns out that tens of thousands of people, including some with late-stage cancer, were taken in by this nonsense.

One such story has stayed with me. A pediatric surgeon in the Midwest told me of a family who demanded that he perform a risky operation on a small child. When he refused to take a scalpel to a toddler on demand, the parents informed him that they had done their own "research," that they were clients engaging him for a specific service, and that they did not need his advice. When he demurred, they went to another surgeon who agreed to do the job. The child, in the end, was gravely injured. While there are (as I discuss in these pages) doctors and other experts who make mistakes, this was the needless maiming of a child by adults who thought they knew better than doctors. It has made all of the other stories seem less funny to me ever since.

Still, one of the pleasures of writing a book about something experienced by so many people as part of their daily life is that it offers the readers the opportunity to become contributors. They have not only provided me with their own stories, but they made me think seriously about some of the places where I could have improved the argument. Did I let journalists off too easy, both for bias, and for making lazy mistakes in their stories? Perhaps. I could have said more about the misconduct of experts who lend themselves out as hired guns. And I definitely should have shone more of a spotlight on how meaningless "metrics" have taken the place of expert judgment, from classrooms to medical offices. Alas, there are only so many pages available (and only so much of your attention I can demand), but I am grateful to readers and reviewers for suggesting these as sources for yet more examination and debate.

I have also encountered a few misconceptions in the past few years about why I wrote the book, and I should clear up some of them. First and most important, the book and its central contentions had nothing to do with the 2016 presidential elections in the United States, or the "Brexit" vote in the United Kingdom to leave the European Union, or about any events since that time. I first wrote about "the death of expertise"—itself a phrase that has been around since at least the 1970s—in late 2013. Most of the manuscript was complete by the time Britain had voted to leave the EU and Donald Trump had gained the American presidency.

I did not know with any certainty that any of these things would happen. (In fact, despite being a card-carrying expert on politics, I was surprised both by Brexit and by Trump's win. It happens.) I had a bit more warning that the Italians were headed for a confused mess of an election in 2018 dominated by a political party founded by a professional comedian, but so did everyone else who follows European affairs. Obviously, these multiple shocks to several major political systems, including the astonishing capture of the U.S. presidency by a man whose campaign included populist rants against experts, drove a great deal of attention to the book. But they were not why I wrote it.

Often, I have been asked if the death of expertise is concentrated in a particular social or economic stratum. It is not. While it is easy to draw caricatures of lunch-pail philosophers or garrulous baristas, the reality is more complicated. The book was never intended as a jeremiad against millennials, or college students, or cable news viewers, or the elderly, or any other particular group. Hostility to expertise extends across race, class, education, gender, political affiliation, and region.

What varies across these populations is not the rejection of established knowledge, but the idiom of its expression. Affluent and educated anti-vaccine activists in California are just educated enough to use the language of science to doubt the work of scientists, while Bible Belt conspiracy theorists engage the language of religion to express distrust of those outside their communities who contradict their convictions. The Californians think the epidemiologist is either wrong or lying for profit, while the fundamentalists back East think paleontologists are conspiring to undermine their faith. Both are showing strains of the same malady, no matter how dissimilar they may seem otherwise.

Likewise, men and women doubt experts in different ways and for different reasons, as do the young and the old. As a generalization, men tend to invest a great deal of their self-image in knowing things, and therefore will often show unwarranted confidence in their own knowledge, while women will be more likely to doubt experts if they perceive them as threatening to their children or families. (This may be one reason why the anti-vaccine movement is heavily dominated by females.) Older people, meanwhile, often believe that their life experience overrules expertise, while younger people challenge authority as a natural part of being young. In short, readers who do not want to see themselves—or who are keen only to see others—in the pages of this book should thus be warned that I am an equal-opportunity critic. (And, as you will see in one of the later chapters, I do not carve out an exception for myself, either.)

Finally, this is not a book about politics, nor does it advocate any kind of partisan solution. But there is an undeniable political dimension here, with the death of expertise helping to fuel a kind of resentful, angry populism in the early 21st century that has made its way into the civic life of the world's democracies. I did not predict the rise of America's Trump or the UK's Brexiteers or the Italian Five Star Movement, any more than I could have predicted the new flat-earthers or lunar-landing doubters—and yes, they're back—but I knew that something like all of them were looming before us. I am still deeply concerned that we are headed into even darker days for logic, reason, and knowledge, and consequently for the survival of the kind of reasoned debate that sustains democratic societies.

This is a global problem. Many of the world's most advanced democracies now have movements whose voters seem to have no fundamental principle other than a kind of generalized defiance toward established knowledge. Citizens no longer seek expert views as part of making informed choices at the ballot box: mostly, they seem intent on punishing "experts" and "elites"—as I note in the book, two groups whom they incorrectly regard as one and the same—for failures both real and imagined. This is part of a larger flight from reason and responsibility, in which people in technologically modern, post-industrial nations not only dismiss the achievements of their societies but are increasingly prone to scapegoat experts for choices that should properly rest with voters. From overseas wars to economic tribulations, there is almost no sense that experts did not, and could not, make these decisions alone—or in some cases, at all.

Central to this collapse of reason is a stubborn insistence by a fair number of people that modern life is simply terrible, worse even than the lived experience of the recent past. We live in an age of peace and plenty, and yet many of our fellow citizens dismiss almost everything that made such an age possible. One reviewer, for example, took me to task by asking, with a complete lack of irony: "What have experts done for us in the past fifty years?" as though the world today was no better than one we left behind in the 1960s.

Even now, I find such a question shocking. I cannot speak for everyone who was alive at the time, but many of us remember the world of a half-century ago and the problems that experts and citizens faced together: the Cold War and its imminent threat of planetary destruction, a range of ghastly diseases that still included smallpox and polio, staggering levels of global and domestic violence, diagnoses of most forms of cancer as death sentences so terrifying that newspapers would not publish the word itself, and the relative rarity and expense of air conditioning. (That last one is a particular gripe from my own childhood.) It was a simpler time, to be sure, but one in which entire races of people and the female half of most populations were not equal members of their societies. To remember the mid-20th century fondly is to have a highly selective memory.

I still wrestle with the one question I've been asked more than any other: am I too pessimistic about the chance for recovery from this epidemic of know-nothingism? After all, I'm the one regularly telling my students and various audiences that the world works remarkably well, even in the places where it seems not to work at all. People across the globe (which is still round, despite the doubters) live longer than ever before. We have more access to medicine, food, information, and even to entertainment than at any time in history. The 21st century, as astonishing as it is to say it, is more peaceful than the 20th, even if we were to start our reckoning of the death toll only after the defeat of the totalitarians in 1945. Ordinary citizens may be disdainful of "expertise," but they benefit from it every day without even thinking of it. Each time we turn a tap and drink fresh, clean water, it is a triumph for a panoply of experts from chemists to city planners to, yes, even politicians and policymakers. We think of all this as the normal order of things.

And yet.

Despite all of these expert successes, from the cornucopia of the local pharmacy to the slashing of the world's nuclear arsenals, I worry that peace and affluence are conditions that actually produce a paradoxical resistance to expertise. It is striking how many people in the United States and other developed nations think that most of what happens around them, including the routine presence of stable institutions of government, is relatively easy. This is one of the most insidious beliefs that winds the mainspring of uninformed populism: that making policy and governing in technologically advanced, economically complex, and ethnically diverse societies isn't all that hard, and therefore anyone can do it.

Perhaps more disturbing is the peculiar Information Age notion that knowledge is now as omnipresent as sunlight, and that all we need do is bask in it with little additional effort on our part as citizens. Entire libraries are now not only free but easily accessible; high school graduation is now the norm rather than the exception; and college, despite its rising costs, is no longer an experience reserved for the wealthy. Local and global news pours into our ears and flashes before our eyes even as we walk through an airport. (Cheap and fast international travel is one of those "expert" things that was a lot harder to do fifty years ago, but I digress.) The collected works of everyone, from Vladimir Lenin to John Lennon, can fit on a device the size of a deck of cards. We can browse the great museums of the world in three-dimensional detail by staring at a screen.

Unfortunately, none of this is knowledge. It is the illusion of knowledge, an accumulation of trivia with perhaps a dusting of culture. It is more like wandering through a forest of useful facts and interesting ideas, with no guide to point out the thickets and brambles of half-truths, propaganda, and lies. There is a reason that successful autodidacts are rare: knowledge is not self-explanatory and education is not easy. Human beings learn by interaction with other human beings, and especially by putting aside their pride and ego long enough to accept instruction and to reflect on what they've learned. In turn, these students and apprentices one day pass along the skills or education they have gained as services to colleagues, clients, and customers—or as teachers to a new generation of students.

This ability to cage our egos long enough to learn something is where I remain a pessimist. We live in an age of resolute narcissism. I will leave it to others who have written better books on that subject than I could to explain how it happened, but this epidemic of narcissism is now enveloping our civic life in a miasma of resentment and stubborn ignorance. Decades of being told to focus on our own needs, combined with rising standards of living and the evaporation of both external and internal threats that once bound us together, have now left too many of us alone in front of our computers or televisions, insulated from any information that does not please us or affirm our pre-existing biases. We are swaddled in a sense of sullen, unfulfilled entitlement that makes self-correction and continued learning almost impossible.

As you will see when you (I hope) read the book, I noted that the great writer and essayist C.S. Lewis saw much of this coming over a half century ago, when he lamented the curdling of "democracy" into the misconception—a lie, if we are to be accurate—that all people are not just equal before the law, but are in fact equal in all respects. While I took this observation from Lewis's classic work *The Screwtape Letters*, I have since found myself thinking more and more often of a character from another Lewis novella, *The Great Divorce*.

In a parable written in the mid-1940s about a group of flawed human souls trapped in a dingy corner of Purgatory deciding whether to undertake the difficult journey onward to Heaven, Lewis describes "the Big Man," an angry, loud blowhard who is ever alert to any claim of superior status around him. When the denizens of the town, including the Big Man, gather at a bus stop, a smaller man nearby sniffs that he is used to better company. The bully overhears this and lashes out.

> "Huh!" said the Big Man: and then added with a glance at me, "Don't you stand any sauce from him, Mister. You're not afraid of him, are you?" Then, seeing I made no move, he rounded suddenly on the Short Man and said, "Not good enough for you, aren't we? Like your lip." Next moment he had fetched the Short Man one on the side of the face that sent him sprawling into the gutter. "Let him lay, let him lay," said the Big Man to no one in particular. "I'm a plain man that's what I am and I got to have my rights same as anyone else, see?"

No one likes being patronized. No one enjoys condescension. But we're now all in danger of becoming the Big Man, imagining only ourselves as authentic and plain in the midst of uppity, judgmental peers. We react to every slight, and count any disagreement or correction about anything, as a grave insult to our rights.

I am not sure how to remedy the spread of this kind of aggressive dysfunction. I wrote *The Death of Expertise* in part to raise the alarm that attacks on knowledge were no longer confined to hucksters, clueless know-it-alls, or overconfident undergraduates. Dismissing learning and expertise is now a habit of mind that is crippling the ability of millions of citizens in democratic nations to exercise even basic civic and social responsibilities in their communities.

We must somehow overcome this narcissistic isolation and the tribalized ignorance it produces. We must master just enough humility and goodwill to start asking each other questions rather than delivering perorations at each other. Otherwise, we court any number of avoidable disasters, after which we will inevitably turn, as we did after World War II, to experts to reconstruct our health, our economy, and the global order. The path that only takes us back to a respect for knowledge and ability through some sort of conflagration, however, is too dangerous a risk. (In the wake of a global pandemic or a nuclear conflict, there may be no path left at all.) I can only hope we recover our senses before then.

Tom Nichols
Summer, 2018

PREFACE

"The death of expertise" is one of those phrases that grandly announces its own self-importance. It's a title that risks alienating a lot of people before they even open the book, almost daring the reader to find a mistake in it somewhere just to take the author down a peg. I understand that reaction, because I feel much the same way about such sweeping pronouncements. Our cultural and literary life is full of premature burials of everything: shame, common sense, manliness, femininity, childhood, good taste, literacy, the Oxford comma, and so on. The last thing we all need is one more encomium for something we know isn't quite dead.

While expertise isn't dead, however, it's in trouble. Something is going terribly wrong. The United States is now a country obsessed with the worship of its own ignorance. It's not just that people don't know a lot about science or politics or geography; they don't, but that's an old problem. And really, it's not even a problem, insofar as we live in a society that works because of a division of labor, a system designed to relieve each of us of having to know about everything. Pilots fly airplanes, lawyers file lawsuits, doctors prescribe medication. None of us is a Da Vinci, painting the Mona Lisa in the morning and designing helicopters at night. That's as it should be.

No, the bigger problem is that we're *proud* of not knowing things. Americans have reached a point where ignorance, especially of anything related to public policy, is an actual virtue. To reject the advice of experts is to assert autonomy, a way for Americans to insulate their increasingly fragile egos from ever being told they're wrong about anything. It is a new Declaration of Independence: no longer do we hold *these* truths to be self-evident, we hold *all* truths to be self-evident, even the ones that aren't true. All things are knowable and every opinion on any subject is as good as any other.

This isn't the same thing as the traditional American distaste for intellectuals and know-it-alls. I'm a professor, and I get it: most people don't like professors. When I began my teaching career nearly three decades ago, it was at a college not far from my hometown, and so I would drop in now and then to say hello and visit a small tavern owned by my brother. One evening, after I left, a patron turned to my brother and said, "He's a professor, huh? Well, he seems like a good guy anyway." If you're in my profession, you get used to that.

But that's not why I wrote this book. Intellectuals who get outraged over zingers about the uselessness of intellectuals should find a different line of work. I've been a teacher, a political adviser, a subject-matter expert for both government and private industry, and a commenter on various media. I'm used to people disagreeing with me; in fact, I encourage it. Principled, informed arguments are a sign of intellectual health and vitality in a democracy.

Rather, I wrote this because I'm worried. We no longer have those principled and informed arguments. The foundational knowledge of the average American is now so low that it has crashed through the floor of "uninformed," passed "misinformed" on the way down, and is now plummeting to "aggressively wrong." People don't just believe dumb things; they actively resist further learning rather than let go of those beliefs. I was not alive in the Middle Ages, so I cannot say it is unprecedented, but within my living memory I've never seen anything like it.

That's not to say that this is the first time I've ever thought about this subject. Back in the late 1980s, when I was working in Washington, DC, I learned how quickly people in even casual conversation would immediately instruct me in what needed to be done in any number of areas, especially in my own areas of arms control and foreign policy. (As usual, it was what "they" should do, as in "they ought to . . . .") I was young and not yet a seasoned expert, but I was astonished at the way people who did not have the first clue about those subjects would confidently direct me on how best to make peace between Moscow and Washington.

To some extent, this was understandable. Politics invites discussion. And especially during the Cold War, when the stakes were global annihilation, people wanted to be heard. I accepted that this was just part of the cost of doing business in the public policy world. Over time, I found that other specialists in various policy areas had the same experiences, with laypeople subjecting them to ill-informed disquisitions on taxes, budgets, immigration, the environment, and many other subjects. If you're a policy expert, it goes with the job.

In later years, however, I started hearing the same stories from doctors. And from lawyers. And from teachers. And, as it turns out, from many other professionals whose advice is usually not contradicted easily. These stories astonished me: they were not about patients or clients asking sensible questions, but about those same patients and clients actively telling professionals why their advice was wrong. In every case, the idea that the expert knew what he or she was doing was dismissed almost out of hand.

Worse, what I find so striking today is not that people dismiss expertise, but that they do so with such frequency, on so many issues, and with such *anger*. Again, it may be that attacks on expertise are more obvious due to the ubiquity of the Internet, the undisciplined nature of conversation on social media, or the demands of the twenty-four-hour news cycle. But there is a self-righteousness and fury to this new rejection of expertise that suggest, at least to me, that this isn't just mistrust or questioning or the pursuit of alternatives: it is narcissism, coupled to a disdain for expertise as some sort of exercise in self-actualization.

This makes it all the harder for experts to push back and to insist that people come to their senses. No matter what the subject, the argument always goes down the drain of an enraged ego and ends with minds unchanged, sometimes with professional relationships or even friendships damaged. Instead of arguing, experts today are supposed to accept such disagreements as, at worst, an honest difference of opinion. We are supposed to "agree to disagree," a phrase now used indiscriminately as little more than a conversational fire extinguisher. And if we insist that not everything is a matter of opinion, that some things are right and others are wrong . . . well, then we're just being jerks, apparently.

It's possible, I suppose, that I am merely a symptom of generational change. I grew up in the 1960s and 1970s, an era when perhaps too much deference was paid to experts. These were the heady days when America was at the forefront of not only science but also international leadership. My parents were knowledgeable but uneducated people who, like most Americans, assumed that the same people who put a man on the moon were probably right about most other important things. I was not raised in an environment of utter obedience to authority, but in general, my family was typical in trusting that the people who worked in specialized fields, from podiatry to politics, knew what they were doing.

As critics of expertise rightly point out, in those days we were trusting the people who landed Neil Armstrong in the Sea of Tranquility, but who also landed a lot of less famous American men in places like Khe Sanh and the Ia Drang Valley in Vietnam. The public's trust, both in experts and political leaders, was not only misplaced but abused.

Now, however, we've gone in the other direction. We do not have a healthy skepticism about experts: instead, we actively resent them, with many people assuming that experts are wrong simply by virtue of being experts. We hiss at the "eggheads"—a pejorative coming back into vogue—while instructing our doctors about which medications we need or while insisting to teachers that our children's answers on a test are right even if they're wrong. Not only is everyone as smart as everyone else, but we all think we're the smartest people ever.

And we couldn't be more wrong.

I have many people to thank for their assistance with this book, and many more to absolve from any association with its views or conclusions.

I first wrote a post called "The Death of Expertise" for my personal blog, *The War Room*, back in 2013. That post was noticed by Sean Davis at *The Federalist*, and he contacted me about writing it up as an article. I am grateful to Sean and to *The Federalist* for giving the piece a home, where it was soon read by well over a million people from around the world. David McBride at Oxford University Press then saw the article, and in turn he contacted me about turning its main thesis into a book. His editorial guidance and advice were key to fleshing out the argument at greater length, and I am grateful to him and to Oxford, as well as to the anonymous reviewers of the proposal, for bringing the book to fruition.

I am fortunate to work at the US Naval War College, and many of my colleagues there, including David Burbach, David Cooper, Steve Knott, Derek Reveron, and Paul Smith, among others, provided comments and material. But the opinions and conclusions in this book are mine: they do not in any way represent the views of any other institution, nor of any agency of the US government.

Several friends and correspondents in various professions were kind enough to provide comments, read chapters, or to provide answers to a variety of questions outside my area of expertise, including Andrew Facini, Ron Granieri, Tom Hengeveld, Dan Kaszeta, Kevin Kruse, Rob Mickey, Linda Nichols, Brendan Nyhan, Will Saletan, Larry Sanger, John Schindler, Josh Sheehan, Robert Trobich, Michael Weiss, Salena Zito, and especially Dan Murphy and Joel Engel. I owe special thanks to David Becker, Nick Gvosdev, and Paul Midura for their comments on several drafts of the manuscript.

I am very grateful to the Harvard Extension School, for not only the opportunity to teach in the program, but also the many excellent student research assistants that Extension provides to its faculty. Kate Arline was an invaluable assistant on this project: she fielded even some of the oddest queries quickly and with aplomb. (Want to know how many fast-food joints have opened in America since 1959? Kate can find out.) Any of the factual errors or misinterpretations in this book, however, are mine and mine alone.

Writing a book can be a wonderful and engaging experience for the author, but less so for the people around him. My wife, Lynn, and my daughter, Hope, were as patient as ever with me while I worked on this volume, and I owe them a significant debt of gratitude for putting up with me while I was writing. This book is dedicated to both of them, with love.

Finally, I must thank the people who assisted me with this book but who, for obvious reasons, wish to remain anonymous. I am grateful to the many medical professionals, journalists, lawyers, educators, policy analysts, scientists, scholars, military experts, and others who shared their experiences and contributed their stories to this book. I could not have written it without them.

I hope in some way this book helps them and other experts in their work. But in the end, the clients of all professionals are the people of the society in which they live, and so I especially hope this book helps my fellow citizens in better using and understanding the experts on whom we all rely. More than anything, I hope this work contributes to bridging the rift between experts and laypeople that in the long run threatens not only the well-being of millions of Americans, but also the survival of our democratic experiment.

Introduction

The Death of Expertise

> There is a cult of ignorance in the United States, and there always
> has been. The strain of anti-intellectualism has been a constant
> thread winding its way through our political and cultural life, nur-
> tured by the false notion that democracy means that "my ignorance
> is just as good as your knowledge."
>
> Isaac Asimov

In the early 1990s, a small group of "AIDS denialists," including a
University of California professor named Peter Duesberg, argued
against virtually the entire medical establishment's consensus that
the human immunodeficiency virus (HIV) was the cause of Acquired
Immune Deficiency Syndrome. Science thrives on such counterintuitive challenges, but there was no evidence for Duesberg's beliefs,
which turned out to be baseless. Once researchers found HIV, doctors and public health officials were able to save countless lives
through measures aimed at preventing its transmission.

The Duesberg business might have ended as just another quirky
theory defeated by research. The history of science is littered with
such dead ends. In this case, however, a discredited idea nonetheless
managed to capture the attention of a national leader, with deadly
results. Thabo Mbeki, then the president of South Africa, seized on

the idea that AIDS was caused not by a virus but by other factors, such as malnourishment and poor health, and so he rejected offers of drugs and other forms of assistance to combat HIV infection in South Africa. By the mid-2000s, his government relented, but not before Mbeki's fixation on AIDS denialism ended up costing, by the estimates of doctors at the Harvard School of Public Health, well over three hundred thousand lives and the births of some thirty-five thousand HIV-positive children whose infections could have been avoided.[1] Mbeki, to this day, thinks he was on to something.

Many Americans might scoff at this kind of ignorance, but they shouldn't be too confident in their own abilities. In 2014, the *Washington Post* polled Americans about whether the United States should engage in military intervention in the wake of the 2014 Russian invasion of Ukraine. The United States and Russia are former Cold War adversaries, each armed with hundreds of long-range nuclear weapons. A military conflict in the center of Europe, right on the Russian border, carries a risk of igniting World War III, with potentially catastrophic consequences. And yet only one in six Americans—and fewer than one in four college graduates—could identify Ukraine on a map. Ukraine is the largest country entirely in Europe, but the median respondent was still off by about 1,800 miles.

Map tests are easy to fail. Far more unsettling is that this lack of knowledge did not stop respondents from expressing fairly pointed views about the matter. Actually, this is an understatement: the public not only expressed strong views, but respondents actually showed enthusiasm for military intervention in Ukraine *in direct proportion to their lack of knowledge about Ukraine*. Put another way, people who thought Ukraine was located in Latin America or Australia were the most enthusiastic about the use of US military force.[2]

These are dangerous times. Never have so many people had so much access to so much knowledge and yet have been so resistant to learning anything. In the United States and other developed nations, otherwise intelligent people denigrate intellectual achievement and reject the advice of experts. Not only do increasing numbers of lay-people lack basic knowledge, they reject fundamental rules of evidence and refuse to learn how to make a logical argument. In doing so, they risk throwing away centuries of accumulated knowledge and undermining the practices and habits that allow us to develop new knowledge.

This is more than a natural skepticism toward experts. I fear we are witnessing the *death of the ideal of expertise* itself, a Google-fueled, Wikipedia-based, blog-sodden collapse of any division between professionals and laypeople, students and teachers, knowers and wonderers—in other words, between those of any achievement in an area and those with none at all.

Attacks on established knowledge and the subsequent rash of poor information in the general public are sometimes amusing. Sometimes they're even hilarious. Late-night comedians have made a cottage industry of asking people questions that reveal their ignorance about their own strongly held ideas, their attachment to fads, and their unwillingness to admit their own cluelessness about current events. It's mostly harmless when people emphatically say, for example, that they're avoiding gluten and then have to admit that they have no idea what gluten is. And let's face it: watching people confidently improvise opinions about ludicrous scenarios like whether "Margaret Thatcher's absence at Coachella is beneficial in terms of North Korea's decision to launch a nuclear weapon" never gets old.

When life and death are involved, however, it's a lot less funny. The antics of clownish antivaccine crusaders like actors Jim Carrey and Jenny McCarthy undeniably make for great television or for a fun afternoon of reading on Twitter. But when they and other uninformed celebrities and public figures seize on myths and misinformation about the dangers of vaccines, millions of people could once again be in serious danger from preventable afflictions like measles and whooping cough.

The growth of this kind of stubborn ignorance in the midst of the Information Age cannot be explained away as merely the result of rank ignorance. Many of the people who campaign against established knowledge are otherwise adept and successful in their daily lives. In some ways, it is all *worse* than ignorance: it is unfounded arrogance, the outrage of an increasingly narcissistic culture that cannot endure even the slightest hint of inequality of any kind.

By the "death of expertise," I do not mean the death of actual expert abilities, the knowledge of specific things that sets some people apart from others in various areas. There will always be doctors and diplomats, lawyers and engineers, and many other specialists in various fields. On a day-to-day basis, the world cannot function without them. If we break a bone or get arrested, we call a doctor or a lawyer. When we travel, we take it for granted that the pilot knows how airplanes work. If we run into trouble overseas, we call a consular official who we assume will know what to do.

This, however, is a reliance on experts as technicians. It is not a *dialogue* between experts and the larger community, but the use of established knowledge as an off-the-shelf convenience as needed and only so far as desired. Stitch this cut in my leg, but don't lecture me about my diet. (More than two-thirds of Americans are overweight.) Help me beat this tax problem, but don't remind me that I should have a will. (Roughly half of Americans with children haven't bothered to write one.) Keep my country safe, but don't confuse me with the costs and calculations of national security. (Most US citizens do not have even a remote idea of how much the United States spends on its armed forces.)

All of these choices, from a nutritious diet to national defense, require a conversation between citizens and experts. Increasingly, it seems, citizens don't want to have that conversation. For their part, they'd rather believe they've gained enough information to make those decisions on their own, insofar as they care about making any of those decisions at all.

On the other hand, many experts, and particularly those in the academy, have abandoned their duty to engage with the public. They have retreated into jargon and irrelevance, preferring to interact with each other only. Meanwhile, the people holding the middle ground to whom we often refer as "public intellectuals"—I'd like to think I'm one of them—are becoming as frustrated and polarized as the rest of society.

The death of expertise is not just a rejection of existing knowledge. It is fundamentally a rejection of science and dispassionate rationality, which are the foundations of modern civilization. It is a sign, as the art critic Robert Hughes once described late twentieth-century America, of "a polity obsessed with therapies and filled with distrust of formal politics," chronically "skeptical of authority" and "prey to superstition." We have come full circle from a premodern age, in which folk wisdom filled unavoidable gaps in human knowledge, through a period of rapid development based heavily on specialization and expertise, and now to a postindustrial, information-oriented world where all citizens believe themselves to be experts on everything.

Any assertion of expertise from an actual expert, meanwhile, produces an explosion of anger from certain quarters of the American public, who immediately complain that such claims are nothing more than fallacious "appeals to authority," sure signs of dreadful "elitism," and an obvious effort to use credentials to stifle the dialogue required by a "real" democracy. Americans now believe that having equal rights in a political system also means that each person's opinion about anything must be accepted as equal to anyone else's. This is the credo of a fair number of people despite being obvious nonsense. It is a flat assertion of actual equality that is always illogical, sometimes funny, and often dangerous. This book, then, is about expertise. Or, more accurately, it is about the relationship between experts and citizens in a democracy, why that relationship is collapsing, and what all of us, citizens and experts, might do about it.

The immediate response from most people when confronted with the death of expertise is to blame the Internet. Professionals, especially, tend to point to the Internet as the culprit when faced with clients and customers who think they know better. As we'll see, that's not entirely wrong, but it is also too simple an explanation. Attacks on established knowledge have a long pedigree, and the Internet is only the most recent tool in a recurring problem that in the past misused television, radio, the printing press, and other innovations the same way.

So why all the fuss? What exactly has changed so dramatically for me to have written this book and for you to be reading it? Is this really the "death of expertise," or is this nothing more than the usual complaints from intellectuals that no one listens to them despite their self-anointed status as the smartest people in the room? Maybe it's nothing more than the anxiety about the masses that arises among professionals after each cycle of social or technological change. Or maybe it's just a typical expression of the outraged vanity of overeducated, elitist professors like me.

Indeed, maybe the death of expertise is a sign of progress. Educated professionals, after all, no longer have a stranglehold on knowledge. The secrets of life are no longer hidden in giant marble mausoleums, the great libraries of the world whose halls are intimidating even to the relatively few people who can visit them. Under such conditions in the past, there was less stress between experts and laypeople, but only because citizens were simply unable to challenge experts in any substantive way. Moreover, there were few public venues in which to mount such challenges in the era before mass communications.

Participation in political, intellectual, and scientific life until the early twentieth century was far more circumscribed, with debates about science, philosophy, and public policy all conducted by a small circle of educated males with pen and ink. Those were not exactly the Good Old Days, and they weren't that long ago. The time when most people didn't finish high school, when very few went to college, and when only a tiny fraction of the population entered professions is still within living memory of many Americans.

Social changes only in the past half century finally broke down old barriers of race, class, and sex not only between Americans in general but also between uneducated citizens and elite experts in particular. A wider circle of debate meant more knowledge but more social friction. Universal education, the greater empowerment of women and minorities, the growth of a middle class, and increased social mobility all threw a minority of experts and the majority of citizens into direct contact, after nearly two centuries in which they rarely had to interact with each other.

And yet the result has not been a greater respect for knowledge, but the growth of an irrational conviction among Americans that everyone is as smart as everyone else. This is the opposite of education, which should aim to make people, no matter how smart or accomplished they are, learners for the rest of their lives. Rather, we now live in a society where the acquisition of even a little learning is the endpoint, rather than the beginning, of education. And this is a dangerous thing.

WHAT'S AHEAD

In the chapters that follow, I'll suggest several sources of this problem, some of which are rooted in human nature, others that are unique to America, and some that are the unavoidable product of modernity and affluence.

In the next chapter, I'll discuss the notion of an "expert" and whether conflict between experts and laypeople is all that new. What does it even mean to be an expert? When faced with a tough decision on a subject outside of your own background or experience, whom would you ask for advice? (If you don't think you need any advice but your own, you're likely one of the people who inspired me to write this book.)

In chapter 2, I'll explore why conversation in America has become so exhausting not just between experts and ordinary citizens, but among everyone. If we're honest, we all would admit that any of us can be annoying, even infuriating, when we talk about things that mean a great deal to us, especially regarding beliefs and ideas to which we're firmly attached. Many of the obstacles to the working relationship between experts and their clients in society rest in basic human weaknesses, and in this chapter we'll start by considering the natural barriers to better understanding before we look more closely at the particular problems of the early twenty-first century.

We all suffer from problems, for example, like "confirmation bias," the natural tendency only to accept evidence that confirms what we already believe. We all have personal experiences, prejudices, fears, and even phobias that prevent us from accepting expert advice. If we think a certain number is lucky, no mathematician can tell us otherwise; if we believe flying is dangerous, even reassurance from an astronaut or a fighter pilot will not allay our fears. And some of us, as indelicate as it might be to say it, are not intelligent enough to know when we're wrong, no matter how good our intentions. Just as we are not all equally able to carry a tune or draw a straight line, many people simply cannot recognize the gaps in their own knowledge or understand their own inability to construct a logical argument.

Education is supposed to help us to recognize problems like "confirmation bias" and to overcome the gaps in our knowledge so that we can be better citizens. Unfortunately, the modern American university, and the way students and their parents treat it as a generic commodity, is now part of the problem. In chapter 3 I'll discuss why the broad availability of a college education—paradoxically—is making many people think they've become smarter when in fact they've gained only an illusory intelligence bolstered by a degree of dubious worth. When students become valued clients instead of learners, they gain a great deal of self-esteem, but precious little knowledge; worse, they do not develop the habits of critical thinking that would allow them to continue to learn and to evaluate the kinds of complex issues on which they will have to deliberate and vote as citizens.

The modern era of technology and communications is empowering great leaps in knowledge, but it's also enabling and reinforcing our human failings. While the Internet doesn't explain all of the death of expertise, it explains quite a lot of it, at least in the twenty-first century. In chapter 4, I'll examine how the greatest source of knowledge in human history since Gutenberg stained his fingers has become as much a platform for attacks on established knowledge as a defense against them. The Internet is a magnificent repository of knowledge, and yet it's also the source and enabler of a spreading epidemic of misinformation. Not only is the Internet making many of us dumber, it's making us meaner: alone behind their keyboards, people argue rather than discuss, and insult rather than listen.

In a free society, journalists are, or should be, among the most important referees in the great scrum between ignorance and learning. And what happens when citizens demand to be entertained instead of informed? We'll look at these unsettling questions in chapter 5.

We count on the media to keep us informed, to separate fact from fiction, and to make complicated matters comprehensible to people who do not have endless amounts of time and energy to keep up with every development in a busy world. Professional journalists, however, face new challenges in the Information Age. Not only is there, by comparison even to a half century ago, almost unlimited airtime and pages for news, but consumers expect all of that space to fill instantaneously and be updated continuously.

In this hypercompetitive media environment, editors and producers no longer have the patience—or the financial luxury—to allow journalists to develop their own expertise or deep knowledge of a subject. Nor is there any evidence that most news consumers want such detail. Experts are often reduced to sound bites or "pull quotes," if they are consulted at all. And everyone involved in the news industry knows that if the reports aren't pretty or glossy or entertaining enough, the fickle viewing public can find other, less taxing alternatives with the click of a mouse or the press of a button on a television remote.

Experts are not infallible. They have made terrible mistakes, with ghastly consequences. To defend the role of expertise in modern America is to invite a litany of these disasters and errors: thalidomide, Vietnam, the *Challenger*, the dire warnings about the dietary hazards of eggs. (Go ahead and enjoy them again. They're off the list of things that are bad for you.) Experts, understandably, retort that this is the equivalent of remembering one plane crash and ignoring billions of safely traveled air miles. That may be true, but sometimes airplanes *do* crash, and sometimes they crash because an expert screwed up.

In chapter 6, I'll consider what happens when experts are wrong. Experts can be wrong in many ways, from outright fraud to well-intentioned but arrogant overconfidence in their own abilities. And sometimes, like other human beings, they just make mistakes. It is important for laypeople to understand, however, how and why experts can err, not only to make citizens better consumers of expert advice but also to reassure the public about the ways in which experts try and police themselves and their work. Otherwise, expert errors become fodder for ill-informed arguments that leave specialists resentful of attacks on their profession and laypeople fearful that the experts have no idea what they're doing.

Finally, in the conclusion I'll raise the most dangerous aspect of the death of expertise: how it undermines American democracy. The United States is a republic, in which the people designate others to make decisions on their behalf. Those elected representatives cannot master every issue, and they rely on experts and professionals to help them. Despite what most people think, experts and policymakers are not the same people, and to confuse the two, as Americans often do, corrodes trust among experts, citizens, and political leaders.

Experts advise. Elected leaders decide. In order to judge the performance of the experts, and to judge the votes and decisions of their representatives, laypeople must familiarize themselves with the issues at hand. This does not mean that every American must engage in deep study of policy, but if citizens do not bother to gain basic literacy in the issues that affect their lives, they abdicate control over those issues whether they like it or not. And when voters lose control of these important decisions, they risk the hijacking of their democracy by ignorant demagogues, or the more quiet and gradual decay of their democratic institutions into authoritarian technocracy.

Experts, too, have an important responsibility in a democracy, and it is one they've shirked in recent decades. Where public intellectuals (often in tandem with journalists) once strove to make important issues understandable to laypeople, educated elites now increasingly speak only to each other. Citizens, to be sure, reinforce this reticence by *arguing* rather than *questioning*—an important difference—but that does not relieve experts of their duty to serve society and to think of their fellow citizens as their clients rather than as annoyances.

Experts have a responsibility to educate. Voters have a responsibility to learn. In the end, regardless of how much advice the professionals might provide, only the public can decide the direction of the important policy choices facing their nation. Only voters can resolve among the choices that affect their families and for their country, and only they bear the ultimate responsibility for those decisions.

But the experts have an obligation to help. That's why I wrote this book.

1

Experts and Citizens

WASHINGTON, DC—Citing years of frustration over their advice being misunderstood, misrepresented or simply ignored, America's foremost experts in every field collectively tendered their resignation Monday.

The Onion

A NATION OF EXPLAINERS

We've all met them. They're our coworkers, our friends, our family members. They are young and old, rich and poor, some with education, others armed only with a laptop or a library card. But they all have one thing in common: they are ordinary people who believe they are actually troves of knowledge. Convinced that they are more informed than the experts, more broadly knowledgeable than the professors, and more insightful than the gullible masses, they are the explainers who are more than happy to enlighten the rest of us about everything from the history of imperialism to the dangers of vaccines.

We accept such people and put up with them not least because we know that deep down, they usually mean well. We even have a certain affection for them. The 1980s television sitcom *Cheers*, for example, immortalized the character of Cliff Clavin, the Boston mailman and barfly who was an expert on everything. Cliff, like his real-life counterparts, prefaced every statement with "studies have shown" or "it's a known fact." Viewers loved Cliff because everyone knew some-one like him: the cranky uncle at a holiday dinner, the young student home from that crucial first year of college.

We could find such people endearing because they were quirky exceptions in a country that otherwise respected and relied on the views of experts. But something has changed over the past few decades. The public space is increasingly dominated by a loose assortment of poorly informed people, many of them autodidacts who are disdain-ful of formal education and dismissive of experience. "If experience is necessary for being president," the cartoonist and author Scott Adams tweeted during the 2016 election, "name a political topic I can't mas-ter in one hour under the tutelage of top experts," as though a discus-sion with an expert is like copying information from one computer drive to another. A kind of intellectual Gresham's Law is gathering momentum: where once the rule was "bad money drives out good," we now live in an age where misinformation pushes aside knowledge.

This is a very bad thing. A modern society cannot function with-out a social division of labor and a reliance on experts, professionals, and intellectuals. (For the moment, I will use these three words inter-changeably.) No one is an expert on everything. No matter what our aspirations, we are bound by the reality of time and the undeniable limits of our talent. We prosper because we specialize, and because we develop both formal and informal mechanisms and practices that allow us to trust each other in those specializations.

In the early 1970s, the science fiction writer Robert Heinlein issued a dictum, often quoted since, that "specialization is for insects." Truly capable human beings, he wrote, should be able to do almost anything from changing a diaper to commanding a warship. It is a noble sentiment that celebrates human adaptability and resilience, but it's wrong. While there was once a time when every homesteader lumbered his own trees and built his own house, this not only was inefficient, but produced only rudimentary housing.

There's a reason we don't do things that way anymore. When we build skyscrapers, we do not expect the metallurgist who knows what goes into a girder, the architect who designs the building, and the glazier who installs the windows to be the same person. That's why we can enjoy the view from a hundred floors above a city: each expert, although possessing some overlapping knowledge, respects the professional abilities of many others and concentrates on doing what he or she knows best. Their trust and cooperation lead to a final product greater than anything they could have produced alone.

The fact of the matter is that we cannot function without admitting the limits of our knowledge and trusting in the expertise of others. We sometimes resist this conclusion because it undermines our sense of independence and autonomy. We want to believe we are capable of making all kinds of decisions, and we chafe at the person who corrects us, or tells us we're wrong, or instructs us in things we don't understand. This natural human reaction among individuals is dangerous when it becomes a shared characteristic among entire societies.

IS THIS NEW?

Is knowledge in more danger, and are conversation and debate really all that more difficult today than they were fifty or a hundred years ago? Intellectuals are always complaining about the denseness of their fellow citizens, and laypeople have always distrusted the pointy-heads and experts. How new is this problem, and how seriously should we take it?

Some of this conflict in the public square is just so much predictable noise, now amplified by the Internet and social media. The Internet gathers factoids and half-baked ideas, and it then splays all that bad information and poor reasoning all over the electronic world. (Imagine what the 1920s would have sounded like if every crank in every small town had his own radio station.) Maybe it's not that people are any dumber or any less willing to listen to experts than they were a hundred years ago: it's just that we can hear them all now.

Besides, a certain amount of conflict between people who know some things and people who know other things is inevitable. There were probably arguments between the first hunters and gatherers over what to have for dinner. As various areas of human achievement became the province of professionals, disagreements were bound to grow and to become sharper. And as the distance between experts and the rest of the citizenry grew, so did the social gulf and the mistrust between them. All societies, no matter how advanced, have an undercurrent of resentment against educated elites, as well as persistent cultural attachments to folk wisdom, urban legends, and other irrational but normal human reactions to the complexity and confusion of modern life.

Democracies, with their noisy public spaces, have always been especially prone to challenges to established knowledge. Actually, they're more prone to challenges to established *anything*: it's one of the characteristics that makes them "democratic." Even in the ancient world, democracies were known for their fascination with change and progress. Thucydides, for example, described the democratic Athenians of the fifth century B.C. as a restless people "addicted to innovation," and centuries later, St. Paul found that the Athenians "spent their time doing nothing but talking about and listening to the latest ideas." This kind of restless questioning of orthodoxy is celebrated and protected in a democratic culture.

The United States, with its intense focus on the liberties of the individual, enshrines this resistance to intellectual authority even more than other democracies. Of course, no discussion about "how Americans think" is complete without an obligatory nod to Alexis de

Tocqueville, the French observer who noted in 1835 that the denizens of the new United States were not exactly enamored of experts or their smarts. "In most of the operations of the mind," he wrote, "each American appeals only to the individual effort of his own understanding." This distrust of intellectual authority was rooted, Tocqueville theorized, in the nature of American democracy. When "citizens, placed on an equal footing, are all closely seen by one another," he wrote, they "are constantly brought back to their own reason as the most obvious and proximate source of truth. It is not only confidence in this or that man which is destroyed, but the disposition to trust the authority of any man whatsoever."

Such observations have not been limited to early America. Teachers, experts, and professional "knowers" have been venting about a lack of deference from their societies since Socrates was forced to drink his hemlock. In more modern times, the Spanish philosopher José Ortega y Gasset in 1930 decried the "revolt of the masses" and the unfounded intellectual arrogance that characterized it:

> Thus, in the intellectual life, which of its essence requires and presupposes qualification, one can note the progressive triumph of the pseudo-intellectual, unqualified, unqualifiable, and, by their very mental texture, disqualified.
>
> I may be mistaken, but the present-day writer, when he takes his pen in hand to treat a subject which he has studied deeply, has to bear in mind that the average reader, who has never concerned himself with this subject, if he reads does so with the view, not of learning something from the writer, but rather, of pronouncing judgment on him when he is not in agreement with the commonplaces that the said reader carries in his head.[1]

In terms that would not sound out of place in our current era, Ortega y Gasset attributed the rise of an increasingly powerful but increasingly ignorant public to many factors, including material affluence, prosperity, and scientific achievements.

The American attachment to intellectual self-reliance described by Tocqueville survived for nearly a century before falling under a series of assaults from both within and without. Technology, universal secondary education, the proliferation of specialized expertise, and the emergence of the United States as a global power in the mid-twentieth century all undermined the idea—or, more accurately, the myth—that the average American was adequately equipped either for the challenges of daily life or for running the affairs of a large country.

Over a half century ago, the political scientist Richard Hofstadter wrote that "the complexity of modern life has steadily whittled away the functions the ordinary citizen can intelligently and competently perform for himself."

In the original American populistic dream, the omnicompetence of the common man was fundamental and indispensable. It was believed that he could, without much special preparation, pursue the professions and run the government.

Today, he knows that he cannot even make his breakfast without using devices, more or less mysterious to him, which expertise has put at his disposal; and when he sits down to breakfast and looks at his morning newspaper, he reads about a whole range of issues and acknowledges, if he is candid with himself, that he has not acquired competence to judge most of them.[2]

Hofstadter argued—and this was back in 1963—that this overwhelming complexity produced feelings of helplessness and anger among a citizenry that knew itself increasingly to be at the mercy of smarter elites. "What used to be a jocular and usually benign ridicule of intellect and formal training has turned into a malign resentment of the intellectual in his capacity as expert," Hofstadter warned. "Once the intellectual was gently ridiculed because he was not needed; now he is fiercely resented because he is needed too much."

Fifty years later, the law professor Ilya Somin pointedly described how little had changed. Like Hofstadter before him, Somin wrote in 2015 that the "size and complexity of government" have made it "more difficult for voters with limited knowledge to monitor and evaluate the government's many activities. The result is a polity in which the people often cannot exercise their sovereignty responsibly and effectively." More disturbing is that Americans have done little in those intervening decades to remedy the gap between their own knowledge and the level of information required to participate in an advanced democracy. "The low level of political knowledge in the American electorate," Somin correctly notes, "is still one of the best-established findings in social science."[3]

SO IT'S NOT NEW. IS IT EVEN A PROBLEM?

People who specialize in particular subjects are prone to think that others should be as interested in it as they are. But really, who *needs* to know all this stuff? Most experts in international affairs would have difficulty passing a map test outside of their area of specialization, so what's the harm if the average person has no idea how to nail the exact location of Kazakhstan? After all, when the Rwandan genocide broke out in 1994, future secretary of state Warren Christopher had to be shown the location of Rwanda. So why should the rest of us walk around carrying that kind of trivia in our heads?

No one can master that much information. We do our best, and when we need to find something out, we consult the best sources we can find. I remember asking my high school chemistry teacher (a man I was certain knew everything) for the atomic number of a certain element off the top of his head, in part to challenge him but mostly because I was too lazy to look it up myself. He raised an eyebrow and said that he didn't know. He then gestured over his shoulder at the periodic table of elements posted on the wall and said, "This is why scientists use charts, Tom."

Without doubt, some of these expert complaints about laypeople are unfair. Even the most attentive parent, the most informed shopper, or the most civic-minded voter cannot keep up with the flood of news about everything from childhood nutrition to product safety to trade policy. If ordinary citizens could absorb all of that information, they wouldn't need experts in the first place.

The death of expertise, however, is a different problem than the historical fact of low levels of information among laypeople. The issue is not indifference to established knowledge; it's the emergence of a positive *hostility* to such knowledge. This is new in American culture, and it represents the aggressive replacement of expert views or established knowledge with the insistence that every opinion on any matter is as good as every other. This is a remarkable change in our public discourse.

This change is not only unprecedented but dangerous. The distrust of experts and the more general anti-intellectual attitudes that go with it are problems that should be getting better, but instead are getting worse. When Professor Somin and others note that the public's ignorance is no worse than it was a half century ago, this in itself should be a cause for alarm, if not panic. Holding the line isn't good enough. In fact, the line may not be holding at all: the death of expertise actually threatens to *reverse* the gains of years of knowledge among people who now assume they know more than they actually do. This is a threat to the material and civic well-being of citizens in a democracy.

It would be easy to dismiss a distrust of established knowledge by attributing it to the stereotype of suspicious, uneducated yokels rejecting the big-city ways of the mysterious eggheads. But again the reality is far more unsettling: campaigns against established knowledge are being led by people who should know better.

In the case of vaccines, for example, low rates of participation in child vaccination programs are actually not a problem among small-town mothers with little schooling. Those mothers have to accept vaccinations for their kids because of the requirements in the public schools. The parents more likely to resist vaccines, as it turns out, are found among educated San Francisco suburbanites in Marin County. While these mothers and fathers are not doctors, they are educated just enough to believe they have the background to challenge established medical science. Thus, in a counterintuitive irony, educated parents are actually making worse decisions than those with far less schooling, and they are putting everyone's children at risk.

Indeed, ignorance has become hip, with some Americans now wearing their rejection of expert advice as a badge of cultural sophistication. Consider, for example, the raw milk movement, a fad among gourmands who advocate the right to ingest untreated dairy products. In 2012, the *New Yorker* reported on this trend, noting that "raw milk stirs the hedonism of food lovers in a special way."

> Because it is not heated or homogenized and often comes from animals raised on pasture, it tends to be richer and sweeter, and, sometimes, to retain a whiff of the farm—the slightly discomfiting flavor known to connoisseurs as "cow butt." "Pasteurization strips away layers of complexity, layers of aromatics," Daniel Patterson, a chef who has used raw milk to make custard and eggless ice cream at Coi, his two-Michelin-star restaurant in San Francisco, said.[4]

Chef Patterson is an expert in the preparation of food, and there's no arguing with his, or anyone else's, palate. But while pasteurization may affect the taste of milk, it also strips away pathogens that can kill human beings.

The raw milk movement is not some on-the-edge experience plumped by a few exotic chefs. Raw milk adherents argue not only that untreated dairy products taste good, but also that they are healthier and better for human beings. After all, if raw vegetables are better for us, why not raw everything? Why not eat the way nature intended us to and go back to a purer, simpler time?

It may have been a simpler time, but it was also a time when people routinely died of food-borne diseases. Still, it's a free country, and if fully informed adult gastronomes want to risk a trip to the hospital for the scent of a cow's nether regions in their coffee, that's their choice. I'm not one to judge this too harshly, since my favorite dishes include raw shellfish and steak tartare, items whose menu disclaimers always make me feel as if I'm ordering contraband. Still, while raw meat and raw shellfish carry risks, they are not dietary staples, and especially not for children, for whom raw milk is outright hazardous.

In short order, doctors at the Centers for Disease Control (CDC) tried to get involved, to no avail. The CDC issued a report in 2012 that noted that raw dairy products were 150 times more likely than pasteurized products to cause food-borne illness. A Food and Drug Administration expert put it as bluntly as possible, calling the consumption of raw dairy the food equivalent of Russian roulette. None of this has swayed people who not only continue to ingest untreated products but who insist on giving it to the consumers who have no choice or ability to understand the debate: their children.

Why listen to doctors about raw milk? After all, they've gotten other things wrong. When it comes to food, for example, Americans for decades have been told to limit their consumption of eggs and certain kinds of fats. Government experts told people to limit their intake of red meat, increase the role of grains in their diet, and in general to stay away from anything that tastes good. (That last one,

I admit, is how I interpreted those recommendations.) Years later, it turned out that eggs are not only harmless, they might even be good for you. Margarine turned out to be worse for us than butter. And a few glasses of wine each day might be better than teetotaling.

So there it is: the doctors were wrong. Is it time to break out the bacon cheeseburgers and pour another martini?

Not quite. The debate about eggs isn't over, but to focus on one aspect of the American diet is to miss the point. The doctors may have been mistaken about the specific impact of eggs, but they're not wrong that a steady diet of fast food, washed down with a sugary soda or a six-pack of beer, isn't good for you. Some folks seized on the news about eggs (much as they did on a bogus story about chocolate being a healthy snack that made the rounds earlier) to rationalize *never* listening to doctors, who clearly have a better track record than the average overweight American at keeping people alive with healthier diets.

At the root of all this is an inability among laypeople to understand that experts being wrong on occasion about certain issues is not the same thing as experts being wrong consistently on everything. The fact of the matter is that experts are more often right than wrong, especially on essential matters of fact. And yet the public constantly searches for the loopholes in expert knowledge that will allow them to disregard all expert advice they don't like.

In part, this is because human nature—as we'll see—tends to search for those loopholes in everything. But equally if not more important is that when experts and professionals are wrong, the consequences can be catastrophic. Raise the issue of medical advice, for example, and you will almost certainly find someone who will throw out the word "thalidomide" as though it is a self-explanatory rejoinder. It's been decades since the introduction of thalidomide, a drug once thought safe that was given to pregnant women as a sedative. No one realized at the time that thalidomide also caused horrendous birth defects, and pictures of children with missing or deformed limbs haunted the public imagination for many years afterward. The drug's name has become synonymous with expert failure to this day.

No one is arguing, however, that experts can't be wrong (a subject we'll discuss in this book). Rather, the point is that they are less likely to be wrong than nonexperts. The same people who anxiously point back in history to the thalidomide disaster routinely pop dozens of drugs into their mouths, from aspirin to antihistamines, which are among the thousands and thousands of medications shown to be safe by decades of trials and tests conducted by experts. It rarely occurs to the skeptics that for every terrible mistake, there are countless successes that prolong their lives.

Sometimes, second-guessing the professionals can turn into an obsession, with tragic results. In 2015, a Massachusetts accountant named Stephen Pasceri lost his seventy-eight-year-old mother to cardiovascular disease. Mrs. Pasceri had a long history of health trouble, including emphysema, and died after an operation to repair a heart valve. Pasceri, however, was convinced that one of his mother's doctors, Michael Davidson—the director of endovascular cardiac surgery at a top Boston hospital and a professor at Harvard Medical School—had ignored warnings about a particular drug given to Pasceri's mother. In a literal case of the death of expertise, the accountant showed up at the hospital and shot the doctor to death. He then killed himself after leaving behind a flash drive with his "research" about the drug.

Obviously, Stephen Pasceri was a disturbed man, unhinged by the death of his mother. But a few minutes of conversations with professionals in any field will yield similar, if less dramatic, stories. Doctors routinely tussle with patients over drugs. Lawyers will describe clients losing money, and sometimes their freedom, because of unheeded advice. Teachers will relate stories of parents insisting that their children's exam answers are right even when they're demonstrably wrong. Realtors tell of clients who bought houses against their experienced advice and ended up trapped in a money pit.

No area of American life is immune to the death of expertise. The American public's declining capabilities in science and mathematics are enabling multiple public health crises from obesity to childhood diseases. Meanwhile, in the worlds of politics and public policy—where at least some familiarity with history, civics, and geography is crucial to informed debate—attacks on established knowledge have reached frightening proportions.

THE RISE OF THE LOW-INFORMATION VOTER

Political debate and the making of public policy are not science. They are rooted in conflict, sometimes conducted as respectful disagreement but more often as a hockey game with no referees and a standing invitation for spectators to rush onto the ice. In modern America, policy debates sound increasingly like fights between groups of ill-informed people who all manage to be wrong at the same time. Those political leaders who manage to be smarter than the public (and there seem to be fewer of those lately) wade into these donnybrooks and contradict their constituents at their own peril.

There are many examples of these brawls among what pundits and analysts gently refer to now as "low-information voters." Whether about science or policy, however, they all share the same disturbing characteristic: a solipsistic and thin-skinned insistence that every opinion be treated as truth. Americans no longer distinguish the phrase "you're wrong" from the phrase "you're stupid." To disagree is to disrespect. To correct another is to insult. And to refuse to acknowledge all views as worthy of consideration, no matter how fantastic or inane they are, is to be closed-minded.

The epidemic of ignorance in public policy debates has real consequences for the quality of life and well-being of every American. During the debate in 2009 over the Affordable Care Act, for example, at least half of all Americans believed claims by opponents like former Republican vice presidential nominee Sarah Palin that the legislation included "death panels" that would decide who gets health care based on a bureaucratic decision about a patient's worthiness to live. (Four years later, almost a third of surgeons apparently continued to believe this.)[5] Nearly half of Americans also thought the ACA established a uniform government health plan. Love it or hate it, the program does none of these things. And two years after the bill passed, at least 40 percent of Americans weren't even sure the program was still in force as a law.

Legislation is complicated, and it is perhaps unreasonable to ask Americans to grasp the details of a bill their own representatives seemed unable to understand. Then-House Speaker Nancy Pelosi, wilting under a barrage of perfectly reasonable questions in 2011, finally said in exasperation that the debate was simply too complicated and too riven by conflict, and therefore Congress would have to first pass the bill "so that you can find out what is in it, away from the fog of the controversy," a remarkable suggestion that the public should allow a proposal to become law before knowing its full contents.

Taxes are another good example of how public ignorance influences national debates. Everybody hates taxes. Everybody complains about them. And every spring, the hideous complexity of the US tax code produces a fair amount of anxiety among honest citizens who, at best, end up guessing at the right answers when trying to pay their levy.

The sad reality, however, is that the average American has no real idea how his or her money is spent. Polls upon polls show not only that Americans generally feel government spends too much, and taxes them too highly, but also that they are consistently wrong about who pays taxes, how much they pay, and where the money goes. This, despite the fact that information about the budget of the United States is more accessible than the days when the government would have to mail a document the size of a cinder block to the few voters who wanted to see it.

Or consider foreign aid. This is a hot-button issue among some Americans, who deride foreign aid as wasted money. Americans routinely believe, on average, that more than 25 percent of the national budget is given away as largesse in the form of foreign aid. In reality, that guess is not only wrong, but wildly wrong: foreign aid is a small fraction of the budget, less than three-quarters of 1 percent of the total expenditures of the United States of America.

Only 5 percent of Americans know this. One in ten Americans, meanwhile, think that more than *half* of the US budget—that is, several trillion dollars—is given away annually to other countries.[6] Most think that no matter how much it is, it's given as a check worth cold cash. That's also wrong. Foreign aid, in fact, might even qualify as a jobs program, since much of it is given in the form of products, from food to military aircraft, actually purchased by the government from Americans and then sent to other nations.

To argue that foreign aid is a waste of money is a comprehensible political position. I and other experts might say that such a blanket objection is unwise, but it is at least a position rooted in principle rather than based on an error of fact. To object to foreign aid because of a mistaken belief that it constitutes a quarter of the US budget, however, almost immediately defeats any sensible discussion right at the outset.

This level of ignorance can get pretty expensive. Americans tend to support national missile defenses against nuclear attack, for example, in part because many believe the United States already has them. (This is a public misconception going back decades, long before the United States fielded the small number of interceptors now operational in Alaska.) Whether such systems will work or whether they should be built are now largely irrelevant questions. What began as a program aimed at the Soviet Union during the Cold War in the 1980s is now enshrined in the popular imagination and supported by both Republicans and Democrats to the tune of billions of dollars.

The overall problem here isn't among people who have genuine concerns about possible side effects from vaccines, or who might be conflicted about whether to build defenses against nuclear attack. Reasoned skepticism is essential not only to science but also to a healthy democracy. Instead, the death of expertise is more like a national bout of ill temper, a childish rejection of authority in all its forms coupled to an insistence that strongly held opinions are indistinguishable from facts.

Experts are supposed to clear up this kind of confusion or at least to serve as guides through the thicket of confusion issues. But who are the real "experts"? Before we move on to discuss the sources of the campaign against established knowledge, and why we're in such a pickle at a time when citizens should be more informed and engaged than ever before, we need to think about how we divide "experts" or "intellectuals" from the rest of the population.

"Expert" is an overused label, of course: every business proclaims itself "the yard care experts" or the "carpet cleaning experts," and while that has some meaning, surgeons and carpet cleaners are not the same kind of expert. "Intellectual" and "academic" are, more than ever, terms of derision in America. Let's untangle some of this before we proceed.

EXPERTS AND CITIZENS

So who's an expert? What constitutes "expertise"?

A lot of people declare that they're experts or intellectuals, and sometimes they are. On the other hand, self-identification can be worse than misleading. People who claim to be experts are sometimes only about as self-aware as people who think they're good kissers.

Dictionaries aren't much help here. Most define experts in a rather circular way, as people who have "comprehensive" and "authoritative" knowledge, which is another way of describing people whose command of a subject means that the information they provide the rest of us is true and can be trusted. (How do we know it can be trusted? Because experts tell us so.) As Justice Potter Stewart once said of pornography, expertise is one of those things that's difficult to define, but we usually know it when we see it.

There are lots of experts in the world. Some are easy to spot: medical doctors, engineers, and airline pilots are experts, as are film directors and concert pianists. Athletes and their coaches are experts. But so are plumbers, police officers, and carpenters. For that matter, your local mail carrier is an expert, at least in his own field; if you need a blood test interpreted, you should ask a doctor or a nurse, but if you'd like to know exactly how a letter from your friend in Brazil got to your door in Michigan, you might ask someone who's been handling that responsibility for years.

Specialized knowledge is inherent in every occupation, and so here I will use the words "professionals," "intellectuals," and "experts" interchangeably, in the broader sense of people who have mastered particular skills or bodies of knowledge and who practice those skills or use that knowledge as their main occupation in life. This helps us to distinguish the "professional pilot" from the weekend flyer, or even a "professional gambler" from the hapless mark who occasionally hands money to a casino.

Put another way, experts are the people who know considerably more on a subject than the rest of us, and are those to whom we turn when we need advice, education, or solutions in a particular area of human knowledge. Note that this does not mean that experts know all there is to know about something. Rather, it means that experts in any given subject are, by their nature, a minority whose views are more likely to be "authoritative"—that is, correct or accurate—than anyone else's.

And even among experts, there are experts. A doctor with a newly minted MD is far more qualified than any layperson to diagnose and treat a disease, but when faced by a puzzling case he or she may in turn defer to a specialist. A practicing attorney and a Supreme Court justice are both lawyers, but the one in the black robes in Washington is more likely to be an expert on constitutional issues than the one handling wills and divorces for a small community. Of course, experience counts, too. In 2009, when a USAir flight in New York City was crippled on takeoff by striking a flock of birds, there were two pilots in the cockpit, but the more expert captain, with many more hours of flying time, said "my aircraft" and guided the jet to a water ditching in the Hudson River. Everyone aboard survived.

One reason claims of expertise grate on people in a democracy is that specialization is necessarily exclusive. When we study a certain area of knowledge or spend our lives in a particular occupation, we not only forego expertise in other jobs or subjects, but also trust that other people in the community know what they're doing in their area as surely as we do in our own. As much as we might want to go up to the cockpit after the engine flames out to give the pilots some helpful tips, we assume—in part, because we have to—that they're better able to cope with the problem than we are. Otherwise, our highly evolved society breaks down into islands of incoherence, where we spend our time in poorly informed second-guessing instead of trusting each other.

So how do we distinguish these experts among us, and how do we identify them? True expertise, the kind of knowledge on which others rely, is an intangible but recognizable combination of education, talent, experience, and peer affirmation. Each of these is a mark of expertise, but most people would rightly judge how all of them are combined in a given subject or professional field when deciding whose advice to trust.

Formal training or education is the most obvious mark of expert status, and the easiest to identify, but it is only a start. For many professions, credentials are necessary for entry into a field: teachers, nurses, and plumbers all have to have certification of some kind to exercise their skills, as a signal to others that their abilities have been reviewed by their peers and meet a basic standard of competence. While some of the most determined opponents of established knowledge deride this as mere "credentialism," these degrees and licenses are tangible signs of achievement and important markers that help the rest of us separate hobbyists (or charlatans) from true experts.

To be fair, some of these credentials are new inventions, and some of them might not matter very much. In some cases, credentials are made up by states and localities as revenue gimmicks, while others affirm no skill other than passing a test once and then never again. Lawyers in modern America complete a law degree, but in earlier times young men merely "read law" and then had to pass admittance to their state's bar. While this less formal system produced men of greatness like Abraham Lincoln—who became a well-regarded and competent attorney it also produced lesser lights such as Henry Billings Brown, the Supreme Court justice who wrote the majority opinion in the "separate but equal" *Plessy v. Ferguson* decision. (Brown attended courses in law at both Harvard and Yale but did not graduate from either of them.)

Still, credentials are a start. They carry the imprimatur of the institutions that bestow them, and they are a signal of quality, just as consumer brands tend to promote (and, hopefully, to protect) the quality of their products. Look carefully at an actual college degree, and note what most of them actually say: that the bearer has been examined by the faculty and admitted to the degree, which in turn is backed by a committee of schools in that region or a body representing a particular profession. Those faculties, and the associations who accredit their courses of study, are in effect vouching for the graduate's knowledge of a particular subject. The name of the school or institution, no less than the degree holder, is on the line, at least as an initial affirmation of capability.

There is no denying that good colleges have graduated a lot of people without a lick of common sense. Lesser institutions have likewise produced geniuses. But as the saying goes, while the race may not always be to the swift, that's the way to bet. The track record for genius production from MIT or Georgia Tech is demonstrably higher than for less competitive schools or self-educated inventors. Still, MIT has also produced people who not only can't balance a checkbook, but who aren't very good engineers. What makes the experts, especially the prominent leaders in their specialization, stand apart from others with similar credentials?

One difference is aptitude or natural talent. Talent is indispensable to an expert. (As Ernest Hemingway once said about writing, "Real seriousness in regard to writing is one of two absolute necessities. The other, unfortunately, is talent.") The person who studied Chaucer in college is going to know more than most other people about English literature, in some purely factual way. But the scholar who has a real talent for the study of medieval literature not only knows more, but can explain it coherently and perhaps even generate new knowledge on the subject.

Talent separates those who have gained a credential from people who have a deeper feel or understanding of their area of expertise. Every field has maze-bright achievers who, as it turns out, are not good at their jobs. There are brilliant law students who freeze in front of a jury. Some of the high scorers on a police examination have no street smarts and will never develop them. A fair number of new holders of doctorates from top universities will never write another thing of consequence after laboring through a dissertation. These people may have cleared the wickets of entry to a profession, but they're not very good at it, and their expertise will likely never exceed the natural limitation of their own abilities.

This is where experience helps to separate the credentialed from the incompetent. Sometimes, markets themselves winnow out untalented or unskilled would-be experts. While professional stockbrokers make mistakes, for example, most manage to make a living. Amateur day-traders, however, almost never make money. *Business Insider* CEO and former Wall Street analyst Henry Blodgett once called amateur day-trading "the dumbest job there is" and that most people who engage it "would make more money working at Burger King."[7] Eventually, they run out of cash. Likewise, bad teachers over time will tend to get bad evaluations, lousy lawyers will lose clients, and untalented athletes will fail to make the cut.

Every field has its trials by fire, and not everyone survives them, which is why experience and longevity in a particular area or profession are reasonable markers of expertise. Indeed, asking about "experience" is another way of asking the age-old question: "What have you done *lately*?" Experts stay engaged in their field, continually improve their skills, learn from their mistakes, and have visible track records. Over the span of their career, they get better, or at least maintain their high level of competence, and couple it to the wisdom—again, an intangible—that comes from time.

There are many examples of the role of experience in expertise. Experienced law enforcement officers often have an instinct for trouble that their younger colleagues miss, an intuition they can explain only as a sense that something "isn't right." Doctors or pilots who've experienced and survived multiple crises in the operating theater or the cockpit are less likely to be panicked by adversity than their newer colleagues. Veteran teachers are less intimidated by challenging or difficult students. Stand-up comedians who've done a lot of gigs on the road do not fear hecklers, and even know how to use them as raw material for more laughs.

These are not always quantifiable skills. Here's an example from my own education and field of study.

After college, I went on to the Harriman Institute at Columbia University for further study in the politics of the Soviet Union. This was part of my own credentialing: I wanted to teach and work in Soviet affairs, and Columbia was one of the best schools in that field at the time. The director of the institute was a professor named Marshall Shulman, a well-known Sovietologist who had also served in Jimmy Carter's White House as an advisor on Soviet matters.

Like all Sovietologists, Shulman studied the Soviet press very carefully for indications of policy positions within the Kremlin. This process was an almost Talmudic exercise in textual analysis, and it was a mystery to those of us who had never done it. How, we students asked him, did he make sense of any of the stilted prose of Soviet newspapers, or divine any meaning from such turgid passages? How could a thousand formulaic stories on the heroic struggles of collective farms illuminate the secrets of one of the most closed systems on earth? Shulman shrugged and said, "I can't really explain it. I just read *Pravda* until my nose twitches."

At the time, I thought that this was one of the stupidest things I'd ever heard. I even started to wonder if I'd made a poor life choice investing in further education. What Shulman meant, however, is that he'd spent years reading Soviet periodicals, and thus he had become so attuned to their method of communication that he could spot changes or irregularities when they passed before his trained and experienced eye.

Although skeptical, I did the same throughout my schooling and into the early years of my career. I read Soviet materials almost daily and tried to see the patterns in them that were previously invisible to me. Eventually, I came to understand what Shulman meant. I can't say that my nose ever twitched or my ears wiggled, but I realized that reading things from a foreign country in a foreign language was a specific kind of expertise. It could not be distilled into a course or a test. There was no quick means to develop it as a skill: it took time, practice, and advice from more experienced experts in the same field.

Another mark of true experts is their acceptance of evaluation and correction by other experts. Every professional group and expert community has watchdogs, boards, accreditors, and certification authorities whose job is to police its own members and to ensure not only that they live up to the standards of their own specialty, but also that their arts are practiced only by people who actually know what they're doing.

This self-policing is central to the concept of professionalism and is another way how we can identify experts. Every specialized group creates barriers to entry into their profession. Some of these barriers are more reasonable and honest than others, but usually they are grounded in the need to ensure that the name of the profession isn't devalued by incompetence or fraud. I could gather together a handful of colleagues, hang a shingle outside my home, and call it the "Tom Nichols Institute of High-Energy Physics," but the fact of the matter is that I don't know a thing about high-energy physics. That's why my notional institute would never be accredited by real physicists, who would not take kindly to me printing up phony degrees and who in short order would seek to close me down to protect the meaning of the word "physicist."

Expert communities rely on these peer-run institutions to maintain standards and to enhance social trust. Mechanisms like peer review, board certification, professional associations, and other organizations and professions help to protect quality and to assure society—that is, the expert's clients—that they're safe in accepting expert claims of competence. When you take an elevator to the top floor of a tall building, the certificate in the elevator does not say "good luck up there"; it says that a civic authority, relying on engineers educated and examined by other engineers, have looked at that box and know, with as much certainty as anyone can, that you'll be safe.

Experience and professional affirmation matter, but it's also true that there is considerable wisdom in the old Chinese warning to beware a craftsman who claims twenty years of experience when in reality he's only had one year of experience twenty times. There are bad dentists who were lousy at pulling teeth when they graduated from dentistry school and who do not get much better at it before retirement. There are teachers who induce narcolepsy in their students on the first day of their class just as they do on their last. But we should remember two important things about experts, even ones who might not be the best in their field.

First, while our clumsy dentist might not be the best tooth puller in town, he or she is better at it than *you*. We don't all need the dean of the dentistry school for a crown or a simple cavity. You might be able to get lucky once and pull a tooth, but you're not educated or experienced enough to do it without a great deal of risk. Most people won't even cut their own hair. (Beauticians, after all, handle all kinds of chemicals and sharp objects, and they are another group that requires training and licensing.) Few of us are going to risk taking out our own teeth or those of our loved ones.

Second, and related to this point about relative skill, experts will make mistakes, but they are far less likely to make mistakes than a layperson. This is a crucial distinction between experts and everyone else, in that experts know better than anyone the pitfalls of their own profession. As the renowned physicist Werner Heisenberg once put it, an expert "is someone who knows some of the worst mistakes that can be made in his subject and how to avoid them." (His fellow physicist Niels Bohr had a different take: "An expert is someone who has made all the mistakes which can be made in a very narrow field.")

Both of these points should help us to understand why the pernicious idea that "everyone can be an expert" is so dangerous. It's true in a relative sense that almost anyone with particular skills can develop specialized knowledge to which others, in most circumstances, must defer. Trouble, however, rears its head when people start to believe that knowing a little bit about something means "expertise." It's a thin line between the hobbyist who knows a lot about warships from reading *Jane's Fighting Ships* and an actual expert on the capabilities of the world's naval vessels, but that line nonetheless exists.

Knowing things is not the same as understanding them. Comprehension is not the same thing as analysis. Expertise is a not a parlor game played with factoids.

And while there are self-trained experts, they are rare exceptions. More common are the people seeking quick entry into complicated fields but who have no idea how poor their efforts are. They are like the moderately entertaining karaoke singers who think they have a chance to become the next winner of *American Idol*, or the scratch golfers who think they might take a shot at going pro. Doing something well is not the same thing as becoming a trusted source of advice or learning about a subject. (Notice that the same people who think they can become singers never think they can become voice coaches.)

This lack of self-awareness and intellectual limits can produce some awkward interactions between experts and laypeople. Some years ago, for example, I had a call from a gentleman who insisted that he had some important work that might be of use in our curriculum at the Naval War College. He'd been referred to me by a former student at another school, and he very much wanted me to read an important article about the Middle East. I asked who wrote the piece. Well, he answered, he did. He was a businessman, and he'd "read a lot." I asked if he'd had any training in the subject, visited the region, or read any of the languages of the Middle East. He had no such background, he admitted, and then said, "But after all, you can become an expert reading a book a month, right?"

Wrong.

American culture tends to fuel these kinds of romantic notions about the wisdom of the common person or the gumption of the self-educated genius. These images empower a certain kind of satisfying social fantasy, in which ordinary people out-perform the stuffy professor or the nerdy scientist through sheer grit and ingenuity.

There are plenty of examples of this in American popular culture, especially in films that depict remarkably bright young people out-smarting businesses, universities, and even governments. In 1997, for example, Ben Affleck and Matt Damon scripted a film called *Good Will Hunting*, about a janitor who turns out to be a secret prodigy. In what is now an iconic scene, Damon growls out a chowdery Boston working-man's accent and faces down an effete, ponytailed Ivy League graduate student in a bar:

> You're a first-year grad student; you just got finished reading some Marxian historian, Pete Garrison probably. You're gonna be convinced of that 'til next month when you get to James Lemon. Then you're going to be talking about how the economies of Virginia and Pennsylvania were entrepreneurial and capitalist way back in 1740.
>
> That's gonna last until next year. You're gonna be in here regurgitating Gordon Wood, talkin' about, you know, the pre-revolutionary utopia and the capital-forming effects of military mobilization.... You got that from Vickers, "Work in Essex County," page 98, right? Yeah, I read that too. Were you gonna plagiarize the whole thing for us? Do you have any thoughts of your own on this matter?
>
> You dropped 150 grand on a [expletive] education you could have got for a dollar fifty in late charges at the public library.

Later, the young man fences with his psychotherapist about the works of Howard Zinn and Noam Chomsky. Stilted and silly, these moments nonetheless resonated with moviegoers at the time. Damon and Affleck went home with Oscars for the screenplay, and no doubt they encouraged at least some viewers to believe that reading enough books is almost like going to school.

In the end, expertise is difficult to define, and experts are sometimes hard to tell from dilettantes. Still, we should be able to distinguish between people who have a passing acquaintance with a subject and people whose knowledge is definitive. No one's knowledge is complete, and experts realize this better than anyone. But education, training, practice, experience, and acknowledgment by others in the same field should provide us with at least a rough guide to dividing experts from the rest of society.

One of the most basic reasons experts and laypeople have always driven each other crazy is because they're all human beings. That is, they all share similar problems in the way they absorb and interpret information. Even the most educated people can make elementary mistakes in reasoning, while less intelligent people are prone to overlook the limitations in their own abilities. Expert or layperson, our brains work (or sometimes don't) in similar ways: we hear things the way we want to hear them, and we reject facts we don't like. Those problems are the subject of the next chapter.

2

How Conversation Became Exhausting

A few centuries earlier ... humans still knew pretty well when a thing was proved and when it was not; and if it was proved they really believed it.

C. S. Lewis, *The Screwtape Letters*

Yeah, well, you know, that's just, like, your opinion, man.

"The Dude," *The Big Lebowski*

I'D LIKE AN ARGUMENT, PLEASE

Conversation in the twenty-first century is sometimes exhausting and often maddening, not only between experts and laypeople, but among everyone else, too. If in a previous era too much deference was paid to experts, today there is little deference paid to anyone at all. Even among laypeople in their daily interactions, disagreement and debate have devolved into grueling exchanges of contradiction, random factoids, and shaky sources few of the participants themselves understand. Years of better education, increased access to data, the explosion of social media, and lowered barriers to entry into the public arena were supposed to improve our abilities to deliberate and decide. Instead, these advances seem to have made all of this worse rather than better.

Public debate over almost everything devolves into trench warfare, in which the most important goal is to establish that the other person is wrong. Sensible differences of opinion deteriorate into a bad high school debate in which the objective is to win and facts are deployed like checkers on a board—none of this rises to the level of chess—mostly to knock out other facts. Like the customer in Monty Python's legendary "Argument Clinic" sketch, we find ourselves merely gainsaying whatever the other person said last. ("This isn't an argument," the angry customer tells the professional arguer. "Yes, it is," he responds. "No, it isn't! It's just contradiction!" "No, it isn't." "Yes, it is!")

Here, we need to start with the obvious and universal problem: you and me. Or more accurately, the way you and I think. From biology to social psychology, we fight an uphill battle in trying to understand each other.

We all have an inherent and natural tendency to search for evidence that already meshes with our beliefs. Our brains are actually wired to work this way, which is why we argue even when we shouldn't. And if we feel socially or personally threatened, we will argue until we're blue in the face. (Perhaps in the Internet age, the expression on social media should be "until our fingers are numb.") Experts are no exception here; like everyone else, we want to believe what we want to believe.

In our personal lives, we tend to be a bit more forgiving, because we are social animals who want acceptance and affection from those closest to us. In our intimate social circles, most of us think we're competent and trustworthy, and we want others to see us that way, too. We all want to be taken seriously and to be respected. In practice, this means we don't want anyone to think we're dumb, and so we pretend to be smarter than we are. Over time, we even come to believe it.

Of course, there's also the basic problem that some people just aren't very bright. And as we'll see, the people who are the most certain about being right tend to be the people with the least reason to have such self-confidence. But it is too facile simply to dismiss the exasperating nature of modern discussion as only a function of the stupidity of others. (That's not to say it isn't sometimes true.) Most people simply are not that intellectually limited, at least not if measured by basic indicators such as rates of literacy or completion of high school.

The fact of the matter is that the pitfalls of discussion and debate aren't limited to mistakes made by the least intelligent among us. We all fall prey to a series of problems, including the way we all try to resolve problems and questions in ways that make us feel better about ourselves and our friends. The many influences on the death of expertise, including higher education, the media, and the Internet, are all enablers of these basic human traits. All of these challenges to better communication between experts and citizens can be overcome with education, rigor, and honesty, but only if we know how they're plaguing us in the first place.

MAYBE WE'RE ALL JUST DUMB

Let's confront the most painful possibility first. Perhaps experts and laypeople have problems talking with each other because the ordinary citizen is just unintelligent. Maybe the intellectual gulf between the educated elites and the masses is now so large that they simply cannot talk to each other except to exchange expressions of mutual contempt. Maybe conversations and arguments fail because one—or both—of the parties is just stupid.

These are fighting words. No one likes to be called stupid: it's a judgmental, harsh word that implies not only a lack of intelligence, but a willful ignorance almost to the point of moral failure. (I have used it, more than I should. So have you, most likely.) You can call people with whom you disagree misinformed, mistaken, incorrect, or almost anything else. But don't call them stupid.

Fortunately, the use of "stupid" is not only rude, it's mostly inaccurate. By any measure Americans are smarter, or at least no less intelligent, than they were several decades ago. Nor was the early twentieth century a Periclean Age of culture and learning. In 1943, incoming college freshmen—only 6 percent of whom could list the original thirteen colonies—named Abraham Lincoln as the first president and the one who "emaciated [sic] the slaves." The *New York Times* saw those results and took a moment from reporting on World War II to lament the nation's "appallingly ignorant" youth.[1]

Whether people in the twenty-first century can keep up with the gap between their education and the speed of change in the world is another matter entirely. Grade school students in 1910 and 2010 both had to learn how to calculate the sides of a triangle, but today's students must use that knowledge to comprehend the existence of a permanent international space station, whereas their great-great-grandparents likely had never seen a car, much less an airplane. And nothing can prevent willful detachment, in any era. No amount of education can teach someone the name of their member of Congress if they don't care in the first place.

With that said, there's still the problem of at least some people thinking they're bright when in fact they're not very bright at all. We've all been trapped at a party or a dinner when the least-informed person in the room holds court, never doubting his or her own intelligence and confidently lecturing the rest of us with a cascade of mistakes and misinformation. It's not your imagination: people spooling off on subjects about which they know very little and with completely unfounded confidence really happens, and science has finally figured it out.

This phenomenon is called "the Dunning-Kruger Effect," named for David Dunning and Justin Kruger, the research psychologists at Cornell University who identified it in a landmark 1999 study. The

Dunning-Kruger Effect, in sum, means that the dumber you are, the more confident you are that you're not actually dumb. Dunning and Kruger more gently label such people as "unskilled" or "incompetent." But that doesn't change their central finding: "Not only do they reach erroneous conclusions and make unfortunate choices, but their incompetence robs them of the ability to realize it."[2]

In fairness to the "unskilled," we all tend to overestimate ourselves. Ask people where they think they rate on any number of talents, and you will encounter the "above average effect," in which everyone thinks they're ... well, above average. This, as Dunning and Kruger dryly note, is "a result that defies the logic of descriptive statistics." It is nonetheless so recognizable a human failing that the humorist Garrison Keillor famously created an entire town dedicated to this principle, the mythical Lake Wobegone, where "all the children are above average" in his radio show *A Prairie Home Companion*.

As Dunning later explained, we all overestimate ourselves, but the less competent do it more than the rest of us.

A whole battery of studies conducted by myself and others have confirmed that people who don't know much about a given set of cognitive, technical, or social skills tend to grossly overestimate their prowess and performance, whether it's grammar, emotional intelligence, logical reasoning, firearm care and safety, debating, or financial knowledge. College students who hand in exams that will earn them Ds and Fs tend to think their efforts will be worthy of far higher grades; low-performing chess players, bridge players, and medical students, and elderly people applying for a renewed driver's license, similarly overestimate their competence by a long shot.[3]

Students who study for a test, older people trying to maintain their independence, and medical students looking forward to their careers would rather be optimistic than underestimate themselves. Other than in fields like athletic competition, where incompetence is manifest and undeniable, it's normal for people to avoid saying they're bad at something.

As it turns out, however, the more specific reason that unskilled or incompetent people overestimate their abilities far more than others is because they lack a key skill called "metacognition." This is the ability to know when you're not good at something by stepping back, looking at what you're doing, and then realizing that you're doing it wrong. Good singers know when they've hit a sour note; good directors know when a scene in a play isn't working; good marketers know when an ad campaign is going to be a flop. Their less competent counterparts, by comparison, have no such ability. They think they're doing a great job.

Pair such people with experts, and, predictably enough, misery results. The lack of metacognition sets up a vicious loop, in which people who don't know much about a subject do not know when they're in over their head talking with an expert on that subject. An argument ensues, but people who have no idea how to make a logical argument cannot realize when they're failing to make a logical argument. In short order, the expert is frustrated and the layperson is insulted. Everyone walks away angry.

Even more exasperating is that there is no way to educate or inform people who, when in doubt, will make stuff up. Dunning described the research done at Cornell as something like "a less flamboyant version of Jimmy Kimmel's bit," and it proved the comedian's point that when people have no idea what they're talking about, it does not deter them from talking anyway.

In our work, we ask survey respondents if they are familiar with certain technical concepts from physics, biology, politics, and geography. A fair number claim familiarity with genuine terms like *centripetal force* and *photon*. But interestingly, they also claim some familiarity with concepts that are entirely made up, such as the *plates of parallax*, *ultra-lipid*, and *cholarine*. In one study, roughly 90 percent claimed some knowledge of at least one of the nine fictitious concepts we asked them about.

Even worse, "the more well-versed respondents considered themselves in a general topic, the more familiarity they claimed with the meaningless terms associated with it in the survey." This makes it tough to argue with these "incompetent individuals," because when compared with the experts, "they were less able to spot competence when they saw it."

In other words, the least-competent people were the least likely to know they were wrong or to know that others were right, the most likely to try to fake it, and the least able to learn anything.

Dunning and Kruger have several explanations for this problem. In general, people don't like to hurt each other's feelings, and in some workplaces, people and even supervisors might be reluctant to correct incompetent friends or colleagues. Some activities, like writing or speaking, do not have any evident means of producing immediate feedback. You can only miss so many swings in baseball before you have to admit you might not be a good hitter, but you can mangle grammar and syntax every day without ever realizing how poorly you speak.

The problem of the "least competent" is an immediate challenge to discussions between experts and laypeople, but there's not much we can do about a fundamental characteristic of human nature. Not everyone, however, is incompetent, and almost no one is incompetent at everything. What kinds of errors do more intelligent or agile-minded people make in trying to comprehend complicated issues? Not surprisingly, ordinary citizens encounter pitfalls and biases that befall experts as well.

CONFIRMATION BIAS: BECAUSE YOU KNEW THIS ALREADY

"Confirmation bias" is the most common—and easily the most irritating—obstacle to productive conversation, and not just between experts and laypeople. The term refers to the tendency to look for information that only confirms what we believe, to accept facts that only strengthen our preferred explanations, and to dismiss data that challenge what we already accept as truth. We all do it, and you can be certain that you and I and everyone who's ever had an argument with anyone about anything has infuriated someone else with it.

For example, if we think left-handed people are evil (it's where the word *sinister* comes from, after all), every left-handed murderer proves our point. We'll see them everywhere in the news, since those are the stories we will choose to remember. No amount of data on how many more right-handed killers are on Death Row will sway us. Every lefty is proof; every righty is an exception. Likewise, if we've heard Boston drivers are rude, the next time we're visiting Beantown we'll remember the ones who honked at us or cut us off. We will promptly ignore or forget the ones who let us into traffic or waved a thank you. (For the record, in 2014 the roadside assistance company AutoVantage rated Houston the worst city for rude drivers. Boston was fifth.)

In the 1988 film *Rain Man*, the autistic character Ray is a perfect, if extreme, example of confirmation bias. Ray is a savant whose mind is like a computer: it can do complex calculations at great speed, and it contains a giant repository of unrelated facts. But Ray, due to his condition, cannot arrange those facts into a coherent context. Whatever Ray's mind remembers is more important than all the other facts in the world.

Thus, when Ray and his brother have to fly from Ohio to California, Ray panics. Every US airline has, at some point, suffered a terrible disaster and Ray can remember the dates and body counts *of every single one*. Focused on these terrifying exceptions, Ray refuses to get on any of the available flights. When the exasperated brother asks which company Ray will trust, he quietly names Australia's national airline. "Qantas," he says. "Qantas never crashed." Of course, Qantas does not fly domestically within the United States, and so Ray and his brother set off to drive cross-country, which is vastly more dangerous than flying. But because Ray has no databank of awe-inducing car crashes in his head, he gladly gets in the car.

We're all a little bit like Ray. We focus on the data that confirm our fears or fuel our hopes. We remember things that make an impression on us and ignore less dramatic realities. And when we argue with each other, or when we consult the advice of an expert, most of us have a hard time letting go of those memories, no matter how irrational it may be to focus on them.

To some extent, this is a problem not of general intelligence but of education. People simply do not understand numbers, risk, or probability, and few things can make discussion between experts and laypeople more frustrating than this "innumeracy," as the mathematician John Allen Paulos memorably called it. For people who believe flying is dangerous, there will never be enough safe landings to outweigh the fear of the one crash. "Confronted with these large numbers and with the correspondingly small probabilities associated with them," Paulos wrote in 2001, "the innumerate will inevitably respond with the non sequitur, 'Yes, but what if you're that one,' and then nod knowingly, as if they've demolished your argument with their penetrating insight."[4]

Human beings can get quite creative with the "but what if I'm the one unlucky case" argument. Back in the early 1970s, I visited an uncle who lived in rural Greece. He was a tough, athletic man, but he had a terrible fear of flying, which was preventing him from going to London to seek medical treatment for a serious ailment. My father tried to assure him with the fatalistic suggestion that while everyone has a time they have to leave the earth one way or another, it's likely not his time to go. My uncle, like so many people who fear flying, resorted to a common objection: "Yes, but what if it's the *pilot's* time to go?"

None of us is perfectly rational, and most of us fear situations in which we are not in control. My uncle was an uneducated man born in a village in Greece in the early years of the twentieth century. I am an educated man of the twenty-first century with a good grasp of statistics and history—and yet I'm not much better about flying on those nights I've been buckled into the seat of a jetliner during some bumpy approaches into Providence. At moments like that, I try to think about the thousands of aircraft on approach all over the world, and the incredibly small chance that my plane will hit the Disaster Lottery. Usually, I fail miserably: all the flights that may be safely landing from Vancouver to Johannesburg are completely irrelevant to me as I grip the arms of my seat while my aircraft skims the house-tops of Rhode Island.

The late science fiction writer and medical doctor Michael Crichton used an example from the early days of the AIDS epidemic in the early 1980s to show how people are so often convinced that they will always draw the shortest straw. The disease was poorly understood at the time, and a friend called Crichton for reassurance. Instead, she ended up nettled at the doctor's insistence on logic:

> I try to explain about risk. Because I have recently noticed how few people really understand the risks they face. I watch people keep guns in their houses, drive without seatbelts, eat artery-clogging French food, and smoke cigarettes, yet they never worry about these things. Instead they worry about AIDS. It's kind of crazy.
>
> "Ellen. Do you worry about dying in a car crash?"

"No, never."

"Worry about getting murdered?"

"No."

"Well, you're much more likely to die in a car accident, or be murdered by a stranger, than to get AIDS."

"Thanks a lot," Ellen says. She sounds annoyed. "I'm so glad I called you. You're really reassuring, Michael."[5]

A decade later, AIDS was better understood and the hysteria faded. In later years, however, new health risks like Ebola, SARS, and other rare afflictions have caused similar irrational reactions, all of them a concern to innumerate Americans who worry more about an exotic disease than about talking on their mobile phones while driving home after having a few drinks at the local pub.

Notice, too, how this bias almost never works in the other direction. Few of us are certain of being the exception in a *good* way. We'll buy a lottery ticket, fantasize about it for a moment, and then put it in our pocket and forget about it. No one heads to a car dealership or a realtor with tomorrow's Powerball number.

We are gripped by irrational fear rather than irrational optimism because confirmation bias is, in a way, a kind of survival mechanism. Good things come and go, but dying is forever. Your brain doesn't much care about all those other people who survived a plane ride or a one-night stand: they're not you. Your intellect, operating on limited or erroneous information, is doing its job, trying to minimize any risk to your life, no matter how small. When we fight confirmation bias, we're trying to correct for a basic function—a feature, not a bug—of the human mind.

Whether the question is mortal peril or one of life's daily dilemmas, confirmation bias comes into play because people must rely on what they already know. They cannot approach every problem as though their minds are clean slates. This is not the way memory works, and more to the point, it would hardly be an effective strategy to begin every morning trying to figure everything out from scratch.

Scientists and researchers tussle with confirmation bias all the time as a professional hazard. They, too, have to make assumptions in order to set up experiments or explain puzzles, which in turn means they're already bringing some baggage to their projects. They have to make guesses and use intuition, just like the rest of us, since it would waste a lot of time for every research program to begin from the assumption that no one knows anything and nothing ever happened before today.[6] "Doing before knowing" is a common problem in setting up any kind of careful investigation: after all, how do we know what we're looking for if we haven't found it yet?[7]

Researchers learn to recognize this dilemma early in their training, and they don't always succeed in defeating it. Confirmation bias can lead even the most experienced experts astray. Doctors, for example, will sometimes get attached to a diagnosis and then look for evidence of the symptoms they suspect already exist in a patient while ignoring markers of another disease or injury. (Television's fictional diagnostician Dr. House would tell his medical students, "It's *never* lupus," which, of course, led to an episode where the most arrogant doctor in the world had to contend with his failure to spot the one case in which it was, in fact, lupus.) Even though every researcher is told that "a negative result is still a result," no one really wants to discover that their initial assumptions went up in smoke.

This is how, for example, a 2014 study of public attitudes about gay marriage went terribly wrong. A graduate student claimed he'd found statistically unassailable proof that if opponents of gay marriage talked about the issue with someone who was actually gay, they were likelier to change their minds. His findings were endorsed by a senior faculty member at Columbia University who had signed on as a coauthor of the study. It was a remarkable finding that basically amounted to proof that reasonable people can actually be talked out of homophobia.

The only problem was that the ambitious young researcher had falsified the data. The discussions he claimed he was analyzing never took place. When others outside the study reviewed it and raised alarms, the Columbia professor pulled the article. The student, who was about to start work on a bright future as a faculty member at Princeton, found himself out of a job.

Why didn't the faculty and reviewers who should have been keeping tabs on the student find the fraud right at the start? Because of confirmation bias. As the journalist Maria Konnikova later reported in the *New Yorker*, the student's supervisor admitted that he wanted to believe in its findings. He and other scholars *wanted* the results to be true, and so they were less likely to question the methods that produced their preferred answer. "In short, confirmation bias—which is especially powerful when we think about social issues—may have made the study's shakiness easier to overlook," Konnikova wrote in a review of the whole business.[8] Indeed, it was "enthusiasm about the study that led to its exposure," because other scholars, hoping to build on the results, found the fraud only when they delved into the details of research they thought had already reached the conclusion they preferred.

This is why scientists, when possible, run experiments over and over and then submit their results to other people in a process called "peer review." This process—when it works—calls upon an expert's colleagues (his or her peers) to act as well-intentioned but rigorous devil's advocates. This usually takes place in a "double-blind" process, meaning that the researcher and the referees are not identified to each other, the better to prevent personal or institutional biases from influencing the review.

This is an invaluable process. Even the most honest and self-aware scholar or researcher needs a reality check from someone less personally invested in the outcome of a project. (The proposal for the book you're reading right now was peer-reviewed: that doesn't mean that the scholars who read it agreed with it, but that they were asked to consider the arguments and present whatever objections or advice they might have.) The ability to serve as a referee is often the role of a senior expert, since the ability to find and to recognize evidence that challenges or even disconfirms a hypothesis is something that takes quite a while to learn. Scholars and researchers spend a good part of their careers trying to master it as one of their core skills.

These reviews and revisions are invisible to laypeople because they all take place before the final product is released. The public only becomes aware of these processes when they go wrong—and when peer review goes wrong, it can go horribly wrong. The whole enterprise, instead of producing expert assurances of quality, can turn into fakery, backscratching, score settling, favoritism, and all the other petty behavior to which human beings are prone. In the case of the gay-marriage study, the fraud was discovered and the system worked, albeit not in time to stop the article's initial publication.

In modern life outside of the academy, however, arguments and debates have no external review. Facts come and go as people find convenient at the moment. Thus, confirmation bias makes attempts at reasoned argument exhausting because it produces arguments and theories that are *nonfalsifiable*. It is the nature of confirmation bias itself to dismiss all contradictory evidence as irrelevant, and so *my* evidence is always the rule, *your* evidence is always a mistake or an exception. It's impossible to argue with this kind of explanation, because by definition it's never wrong.

An additional problem here is that most laypeople have never been taught, or they have forgotten, the basics of the "scientific method." This is the set of steps that lead from a general question to a hypothesis, testing, and analysis. Although people commonly use the word "evidence," they use it too loosely; the tendency in conversation is to use "evidence" to mean "things which I perceive to be true," rather than "things that have been subjected to a test of their factual nature by agreed-upon rules."

At this point, laypeople might object to all this as just so much intellectual hokum. Why does the average person need all this scholarly self-awareness? There's always common sense. Why isn't that good enough?

Most of the time, laypeople actually do not need any of this scholarly apparatus. In day-to-day matters, common sense serves us well and is usually better than needlessly complicated explanations. We don't need to know, for example, exactly how fast a car can go in a rainstorm before the tires begin to lose contact with the road. Somewhere there's a mathematical formula that would allow us to know the answer with great precision, but our common sense needs no such formula to tell us to slow down in bad weather, and that's good enough.

When it comes to untangling more complicated issues, however, common sense is not sufficient. Cause and effect, the nature of evidence, and statistical frequency are far more intricate than common sense can handle. Many of the thorniest research problems often have counterintuitive answers that by their nature defy our common sense. (Simple observation, after all, told early humans that the sun revolved around the earth, not the other way around.) The simple tools of common sense can betray us and make us susceptible to errors both great and small, which is why laypeople and experts so often talk past each other even on relatively trivial issues like superstitions and folk wisdom.

WIVES' TALES, SUPERSTITION, AND CONSPIRACY THEORIES

"Old wives' tales" and other superstitions are classic examples of confirmation bias and nonfalsifiable arguments. Many superstitions have some kind of grounding in experience. While it's a superstition that you shouldn't walk under ladders, for example, it's also true that it's *dangerous* to walk under a ladder. Whether you'll have bad luck all day by annoying a house painter is a different matter, but it's just dumb to walk under his ladder.

Superstitions are especially prone to confirmation bias, and they survive because common sense and confirmation bias sometimes reinforce each other. Are black cats unlucky? Cats, black or otherwise, by their nature tend to get underfoot, but we might only remember the black ones who trip us up. I actually live with a lovely black cat named Carla, and I can confirm that she is, on occasion, a menace to my navigation of the stairs. A superstitious person might nod here knowingly; the fact that Carla is also the *only* cat in the house, of course, or whether other cat owners have tumbled over their tabbies will mean nothing.

The most extreme cases of confirmation bias are found not in the wives' tales and superstitions of the ignorant, but in the conspiracy theories of more educated or intelligent people. Unlike superstitions, which are simple, conspiracy theories are horrendously complicated. Indeed, it takes a reasonably smart person to construct a really interesting conspiracy theory, because conspiracy theories are actually highly complex explanations. They are also challenging intellectual exercises both for those who hold them and those who would disprove them. Superstitions are generally easy enough to disprove. Any statistician can verify that my cat is probably no more or less dangerous than any other on a staircase. Deep down, we know it anyway, which is why superstitions tend to be little more than harmless habits.

Conspiracy theories, by contrast, are frustrating precisely because they are so intricate. Each rejoinder or contradiction only produces a more complicated theory. Conspiracy theorists manipulate all tangible evidence to fit their explanation, but worse, they will also point to the *absence* of evidence as even stronger confirmation. After all, what better sign of a really effective conspiracy is there than a complete lack of any trace that the conspiracy exists? Facts, the absence of facts, contradictory facts: everything is proof. Nothing can ever challenge the underlying belief.

These kinds of overcomplicated explanations violate the famous concept of "Occam's Razor" (sometimes spelled "Ockham"), named for the medieval monk who advocated the straightforward idea that we should always begin from the simplest explanation for anything we see. We should only work our way up toward more complicated explanations if we need them. This is also called the "law of parsimony," meaning that the most likely explanation is the one that requires the fewest number of logical leaps or shaky assumptions.

Imagine, for example, that we hear a noise, followed by someone swearing loudly in the next room. We run to the room and see a man, alone, holding his foot and jumping around with a grimace on his face. There's an empty crate and broken bottles of beer all over the floor. What happened?

Most of us will derive a simple explanation that the man dropped the crate on the floor, hurt his foot, and yelped an expletive. We heard the crash and we've seen people swear when injured. We have a good grasp of what other people look like when they're in pain, and the fellow is obviously hurting. It does not take many assumptions to create a reasonable explanation. It might not be a complete explanation, but it's a sensible first cut, given the available evidence.

But wait. Maybe the man is an alcoholic, and he's swearing because he's angry that he dropped the crate and the beer is now gone. Or maybe he's a temperance advocate, and he smashed the beer to the floor himself while cursing its vile existence. And perhaps he's holding his foot and jumping around because he is from a little-known culture in the far Canadian Arctic where people's faces are usually covered by parkas and they therefore express sorrow (or joy, or anger) by holding their feet and jumping. Or maybe he's a foreigner who thinks that certain pungent Anglo-Saxon words actually mean "Help, I dropped a crate of beer on my foot."

This is where the law of parsimony comes in. Any one of those oddball and highly unlikely possibilities could be true, but it would be ridiculous to jump right to such immensely complicated theorizing when we have a far more direct and serviceable explanation staring us right in the face. We have no idea if the man is a teetotaler or a drunk, whether he's from Canada or Cleveland, or whether his native language is English. While we can conduct some eventual investigation to find out whether any of those things are true, to *start* from any of those assumptions violates both logic and human experience.

If conspiracy theories are so complicated and ridiculous, why do they have such a hold on the popular imagination in so many societies? And make no mistake: they are in fact very popular and have been for centuries. Modern America is no exception. In the 1970s, for example, the novelist Robert Ludlum excelled at creating such conspiracies in a hugely popular series of novels, including one about a circle of political killers who were responsible for the assassination of President Franklin Roosevelt. (But wait, you say: FDR wasn't assassinated. *Exactly.*) Ludlum sold millions of books and created the fictional superassassin Jason Bourne, who was the main character in a string of lucrative movies in the twenty-first century. Books, films, and television shows from *The Manchurian Candidate* in the 1960s to *The X-Files* thirty years later have had millions of fans.

In modern American politics, conspiracy theories abound. President Obama is a secret Muslim who was born in Africa. President Bush was part of the plot to attack America on 9/11. The Queen of England is a drug dealer. The US government is spraying mind-controlling chemicals in the air through the exhaust ports of jet aircraft. The Jews control everything—except when the Saudis or Swiss bankers are controlling everything.

One reason we all love a good conspiracy thriller is that it appeals to our sense of heroism. A brave individual against a great conspiracy, fighting forces that would defeat the ordinary person, is a trope as old as the many legends of heroes themselves. American culture in particular is attracted to the idea of the talented amateur (as opposed, say, to the experts and elites) who can take on entire governments—or even bigger organizations—and win. James Bond didn't confront the evil superconspiracy of SPECTRE until the British author Ian Fleming realized he needed something bigger than communism for Bond to fight when his novels started to move to the Hollywood screen for American audiences.

More important and more relevant to the death of expertise, however, is that conspiracy theories are deeply attractive to people who have a hard time making sense of a complicated world and who have no patience for less dramatic explanations. Such theories also appeal to a strong streak of narcissism: there are people who would choose to believe in complicated nonsense rather than accept that their own circumstances are incomprehensible, the result of issues beyond their intellectual capacity to understand, or even their own fault.

Conspiracy theories are also a way for people to give context and meaning to events that frighten them. Without a coherent explanation for why terrible things happen to innocent people, they would have to accept such occurrences as nothing more than the random cruelty either of an uncaring universe or an incomprehensible deity. These are awful choices, and even thinking about them can induce the kind of existential despair that leads a character in the nineteenth-century classic *The Brothers Karamazov* to make a famous declaration about tragedy: "If the sufferings of children go to make up the sum of the sufferings necessary to buy truth, then I protest that the truth is not worth such a price."

The only way out of this dilemma is to imagine a world in which our troubles are the fault of powerful people who had it within their power to avert such misery. In such a world, a loved one's incurable disease is not a natural event: it is the result of some larger malfeasance by industry or government. Revelations of the horrid behavior of a celebrity are not evidence that someone we admired is evil: it is a plot to smear a beloved figure. Even the loss of our favorite sports team might be a fix. ("I don't want to see the Buffalo Bills winning the Super Bowl," the chief villain in *The X-Files* said in a 1996 episode. "As long as I'm alive, that doesn't happen.") Whatever it is, *somebody* is at fault, because otherwise we're left blaming only God, pure chance, or ourselves.

Just as individuals facing grief and confusion look for reasons where none may exist, so, too, will entire societies gravitate toward outlandish theories when collectively subjected to a terrible national experience. Conspiracy theories and the flawed reasoning behind them, as the Canadian writer Jonathan Kay has noted, become especially seductive "in any society that has suffered an epic, collectively felt trauma. In the aftermath, millions of people find themselves casting about for an answer to the ancient question of why bad things happen to good people."[9] This is why conspiracy theories spiked in popularity after World War I, the Russian Revolution, the assassination of John F. Kennedy, and the terror attacks of September 2001, among other historical events.

Today, conspiracy theories are reactions mostly to the economic and social dislocations of globalization, just as they were to the aftermath of war and the advent of rapid industrialization in the 1920s and 1930s. This is not a trivial obstacle when it comes to the problems of expert engagement with the public: nearly 30 percent of Americans, for example, think "a secretive elite with a globalist agenda is conspiring to eventually rule the world," and 15 percent think media or government add secret "mind-controlling" technology to TV broadcasts. (Another 15 percent aren't quite sure about the television issue.) Nearly half of all respondents think it at least likely that Princess Diana of the United Kingdom was murdered in

THE DEATH OF EXPERTISE

a plot. "At these rates," as Kay rightly points out, "we can't speak of conspiracy thinking as a fringe phenomenon, nor one that has only a negligible impact on the civic sphere and cultural values."

Conspiracy theories are not harmless. At their worst, conspiracy theories can produce a moral panic in which innocent people get hurt. In the early 1980s, for example, hysteria swept the United States when many parents became convinced that Satanic sex cults were operating inside children's day-care centers. Faux "experts" helped to fuel the panic, interpreting every confused utterance from a toddler as confirming abuse of the weirdest kind. It goes without saying that child abuse exists, but a grandiose theory—which likely reflected the fears and guilty feelings of working parents more than anything else—took hold of the American imagination, damaging numerous lives forever and temporarily clouding better approaches to a very real but far more limited problem.[10]

If trying to get around confirmation bias is difficult, trying to deal with a conspiracy theory is impossible. Someone who believes that the oil companies are suppressing a new car that can run on seaweed is unlikely to be impressed by your new Prius or Volt. (That's the efficient car the industrial barons will *allow* you to have.) The people who think alien bodies were housed at Area 51 won't change their minds if they take a tour of the base. (The alien research lab is underground, you see.)

Arguing at length with a conspiracy theorist is not only fruitless but sometimes dangerous, and I do not recommend it. It's a treadmill of nonsense that can exhaust even the most tenacious teacher. Such theories are the ultimate bulwark against expertise, because of course every expert who contradicts the theory is *ipso facto* part of the conspiracy. As the writer Jef Rouner has put it,

> You have to remember that the sort of person who readily subscribes to conspiracy theories already fears that there are vast,

powerful forces maliciously allied against the areas of life that mean the most to them. Any denial of the threat increases the power of the threat by virtue of its being allowed to operate undetected.[11]

That's a place in a conversation where none of us wants to be.

Fortunately, these large-scale cases of irrationality are far and few between. The more prosaic and common unwillingness to accept expert advice, however, is rooted in the same kind of populist suspicion of those perceived as smarter or more educated than the general public. The damage might be less dramatic, but it is no less tangible, and sometimes quite costly.

STEREOTYPES AND GENERALIZATIONS

"You can't generalize like that!" Few expressions are more likely to arise in even a mildly controversial discussion. People resist generalizations—boys tend to be like *this*, girls tend to be like *that*—because we all want to believe we're unique and that we cannot be pigeonholed that easily.

What most people usually mean when they object to "generalizing," however, is not that we shouldn't generalize, but that we shouldn't *stereotype*, which is a different issue. The problem in casual discourse is that people often don't understand the difference between stereotypes and generalizations, and this makes conversation, especially between experts and laypeople, arduous and exhausting. (I realize, of course, that I am generalizing here. But bear with me.)

The difference matters. Stereotyping is an ugly social habit, but generalization is at the root of every form of science. Generalizations are probabilistic statements, based in observable facts. They are not, however, explanations in themselves—another important difference from stereotypes. They're measurable and verifiable. Sometimes generalizations can lead us to posit cause and effect, and in some cases we might even observe enough to create a theory or a law that under constant circumstances is always true.

It is a generalization, for example, to say that "people in China are usually shorter than people in America." That may or may not be true. People who mistake this for a stereotype will immediately rush to find exceptions, and discussion will quickly run into a ditch: "I think Chinese people tend to be shorter than Americans." "You can't generalize like that! Chinese-born basketball player Yao Ming is seven and a half feet tall!"

The existence of an unusually tall Chinese basketball player proves nothing either way. We can settle this question only by going to the United States and China, measuring people, and seeing how often our assumption is true. If it's the case that Chinese people overall are shorter than Americans, then we've only noted something that is factually true enough times that we would not be wrong to assert it as a general but not infallible rule.

The hard work of explanation comes after generalization. *Why* are Americans taller than the Chinese? Is it genetic? Is it the result of a different diet? Are there environmental factors at work? There are answers to this question somewhere, but whatever they are, it's still not wrong to say that Americans tend to be taller than the Chinese, no matter how many slam-dunking exceptions we might find.

To say that *all* Chinese people are short, however, is to stereotype. The key to a stereotype is that it is impervious to factual testing. A stereotype brooks no annoying interference with reality, and it relies on the clever use of confirmation bias to dismiss all exceptions as irrelevant. (Racists have mastered this mode of argument: "All Romanians are thieves except this one lady I work with, but she's different.") Stereotypes are not *predictions*, they're *conclusions*. That's why it's called "prejudice": it relies on pre-judging.

The tangle comes when we make generalizations that are negative or rooted in arguable criteria. No one can really dispute a generalization about height; it's something easily measurable in ways we all accept. Nor do we impute any sort of moral or political character to height. "Tall, aren't you?" a femme fatale says to the literary detective Phillip Marlowe in the 1939 novel *The Big Sleep*. "I didn't mean to be," Marlowe replies. It's witty precisely because we know being short or tall isn't something we control or for which we have to apologize.

Negative generalizations, however, raise hackles, especially when they are based on arguable definitions. To say that "Russians are more corrupt than Norwegians," for example, is true but only if we adopt a shared definition of "corrupt." By Western definitions, Russia is plagued by corruption, but it's also a perfectly reasonable objection to note that one culture's "corruption" is another culture's "favors." This is why generalizations need to be as carefully formulated as possible if they are to serve as basis for future research. There is a clear difference between "Russians in official positions are more willing to break established rules in conducting government business than Norwegians in similar offices" as opposed to a broader statement that "Russians are more corrupt than Norwegians."

If we apply those narrower filters, we have a statement that is far less inflammatory and measurably true. Again, however, we have no idea why it's generally true. We know only that if we apply the same criteria consistently—that is, if we watch the same Russian and Norwegian officials process the same transactions enough times— we can establish something that is more often true than false. It may be that Russian laws are outdated and impossible to follow even for the most honest bureaucrat. (That's a bit of a stretch, but there's an element of truth in it, and it is an argument made quite often by actual Russians.) That's where more research comes in: to establish the *why* after confirming the *what*.

Of course, in daily conversation, none of this matters very much. These things may be true in some narrow, definable sense, but who wants to hear things that, if given without context, sound only like inflammatory assertions? Conversations among laypeople, and between laypeople and experts, can get difficult because human emotions are involved, especially if they are about things that are true in general but might not apply to any one case or circumstance.

That's why one of the most important characteristics of an expert is the ability to remain dispassionate, even on the most controversial issues. Experts must treat everything from cancer to nuclear war as problems to be solved with detachment and objectivity. Their distance from the subject enables open debate and consideration of alternatives, in ways meant to defeat emotional temptations, including fear, that lead to bias. This is a tall order, but otherwise conversation is not only arduous but sometimes explosive.

I'M OK, YOU'RE OK—SORT OF

There are other social and psychological realities that hobble our ability to exchange information. No matter how much we might suffer from confirmation bias or the heavy hand of the Dunning-Kruger Effect, for example, we don't like to tell people we know or care about that they're wrong. (At least not to their face.) Likewise, as much as we enjoy the natural feeling of being right about something, we're sometimes reluctant to defend our actual expertise. And overall we find it hard to separate the information, erroneous or otherwise, that serves as the foundations of our political and social beliefs from our self-image and our conceptions about who we are.

In 2014, for example, an international study reached a surprising conclusion: people will go to great lengths to give each other a fair hearing and to weigh all opinions equally, even when everyone involved in the conversation knows there are substantial differences in competence between them. The authors of the study (which included people from China, Iran, and Denmark) suggest that this is an "equality bias" built into us based on a human need to be accepted as part of a group. When two people were involved in repeated discussions and decision making—and establishing a bond between the participants was a key part of the study—researchers found that the less capable people advocated for their views more than might have been expected, and that the more competent member of the conversation deferred to those points of view even when they were demonstrably wrong.[12]

At first, this sounds like nothing more than good manners and a desire for acceptance. Each party wanted to stay relevant to the other, rather than risk disrupting the relationship. The less competent person wanted to be respected and involved by not being seen as wrong or uninformed. The more competent person, meanwhile, did not want to alienate anyone by being consistently right.

This might make for a pleasant afternoon, but it's a lousy way to make decisions. As Chris Mooney, a *Washington Post* science writer, noted, this kind of social dynamic might grease the wheels of human relationships, but it can do real harm where facts are at stake. The study, he wrote, underscored "that we need to recognize experts more, respect them, and listen to them. But it also shows how our evolution in social groups binds us powerfully together and enforces collective norms, but can go haywire when it comes to recognizing and accepting inconvenient truths."[13]

Why can't people simply accept these differences in knowledge or competence? This is an unreasonable question, since it amounts to saying "Why don't people just accept that other people are smarter than they are?" (Or, conversely, "Why don't smart people just explain why other people are dumber than they are?") The reality is that social insecurity trips up both the smart and the dumb. We all want to be liked.

In a similar vein, few of us want to admit to being lost in a conversation, especially when so much information is now so easily accessible. Social pressure has always tempted even intelligent, well-informed people to pretend to know more than they do, but this impulse is magnified in the Information Age. Karl Taro Greenfeld, a novelist and writer, described this kind of anxiety in a meditation on why people attempt to "fake cultural literacy."

> What we all feel now is the constant pressure to know enough, at all times, lest we be revealed as culturally illiterate. So that we can survive an elevator pitch, a business meeting, a visit to the office kitchenette, a cocktail party, so that we can post, tweet, chat, comment, text as if we have seen, read, watched, listened. What matters to us, awash in petabytes of data, is not necessarily having actually consumed this content firsthand but simply knowing that it exists—and having a position on it, being able to engage in the chatter *about* it. We come perilously close to performing a pastiche of knowledgeability that is really a new model of know-nothingness.[14]

People skim headlines or articles and share them on social media, but they do not read them. Nonetheless, because people want to be perceived by others as intelligent and well informed, they fake it as best they can.

As if all of this weren't enough of a challenge, the addition of politics makes things even more complicated. Political beliefs among both laypeople and experts work in much the same way as confirmation bias. The difference is that beliefs about politics and other subjective matters are harder to shake, because our political views are deeply rooted in our self-image and our most cherished beliefs about who we are as people.

As Konnikova put it in her examination of the fraudulent gay-marriage study, confirmation bias is more likely to produce "persistently false beliefs" when it stems "from issues closely tied to our conception of self." These are the views that brook no opposition and that we will often defend beyond all reason, as Dunning noted:

> Some of our most stubborn misbeliefs arise not from primitive childlike intuitions or careless category errors, but from the very values and philosophies that define *who we are* as individuals. Each of us possesses certain foundational beliefs—narratives about the self, ideas about the social order—that essentially cannot be violated: To contradict them would call into question our very self-worth. As such, these views demand fealty from other opinions.

Put another way, what we believe says something important about how we see ourselves as people. We can take being wrong about the kind of bird we just saw in our backyard, or who the first person was to circumnavigate the globe, but we cannot tolerate being wrong about the concepts and facts that we rely upon to govern how we live our lives.

Take, for example, a fairly common American kitchen-table debate: the causes of unemployment. Bring up the problem of joblessness with almost any group of laypeople and every possible intellectual problem will rear its head. Stereotypes, confirmation bias, half-truths, and statistical incompetence all bedevil this discussion.

Consider a person who holds firmly, as many Americans do, to the idea that unemployed people are just lazy and that unemployment benefits might even encourage that laziness. Like so many examples of confirmation bias, this could spring from personal experience. Perhaps it proceeds from a lifetime of continuous employment, or it may be the result of knowing someone who's genuinely averse to work. Every "help wanted" sign—which confirmation bias will note and file away—is further proof of the laziness of the unemployed. A page of job advertisements or a chronically irresponsible nephew constitutes irrefutable evidence that unemployment is a personal failing rather than a problem requiring government intervention.

Now imagine someone else at the table who believes that the nature of the American economy itself forces people into unemployment. This person might draw from experience as well: he or she may know someone who moved to follow a start-up company and ended up broke and far from home, or who was unjustly fired by a corrupt or incompetent supervisor. Every corporate downsizing, every racist or sexist boss, and every failed enterprise is proof that the system is stacked against innocent people who would never choose unemployment over work. Unemployment benefits, rather than subsidizing indolence, are a lifeline and perhaps the only thing standing between an honest person and complete ruin.

There's a real argument to be had, of course, about the degree to which any of this is true, but these two people—admittedly, drawn as caricatures for our purposes here—are not going to be the ones to have it. It's unarguable that unemployment benefits suppress the urge to work in at least *some* people; it's also undeniable that *some* corporations have a history of ruthlessness at the expense of their workers, whose reliance on benefits is reluctant and temporary. This conversation can go on forever, because both the Hard Worker on one side and the Kind Heart on the other can adduce anecdotes, carefully vetted by their own confirmation bias, that are always true but are in no way dispositive.

There's no way to win this argument, because in the end, there are no answers that will satisfy everyone. Laypeople want a definitive answer from the experts, but none can be had because there is not one answer but many, depending on circumstances. When do benefits encourage sloth? How often are people thrown out of work against their will, and for how long? These are nuances in a broad problem, and where our self-image is involved, nuance isn't helpful. Unable to see their own biases, most people will simply drive each other crazy arguing rather than accept answers that contradict what they already think about the subject. The social psychologist Jonathan Haidt summed it up neatly when he observed that when facts conflict with our values, "almost everyone finds a way to stick with their values and reject the evidence."[15]

This tendency is in fact so strong that a fair number of people, regardless of political affiliation, will shoot the messenger rather than hear something they don't like. A 2015 study, for example, tested the reactions of both liberals and conservatives to certain kinds of news stories, and it found that "just as conservatives discount the scientific theories that run counter to their worldview, liberals will do exactly the same."[16] Even more disturbing, the study found that when exposed to scientific research that challenged their views, both liberals and conservatives reacted by doubting the *science*, rather than themselves. "Just reading about these polarizing topics," one of the authors noted, "is having a negative effect on how people feel about science."

This is why, as we'll see later in this book, the only way to resolve these debates in terms of policy choices is to move them from the realm of research to the arena of politics and democratic choice. If democracy is to mean anything at all, then experts and laypeople have to solve complicated problems together. First, however, they have to overcome the widening gulf between them. More education seems like an obvious solution, but in the next chapter we'll see that education, at least at the college level, is now part of the problem.

3

Higher Education
The Customer Is Always Right

Those persons whom nature has endowed with genius and virtue should be rendered by liberal education worthy to receive and able to guard the sacred deposit of the rights and liberties of their fellow citizens.

Thomas Jefferson

Mr. Braddock: Would you mind telling me what those four years of college were for? What was the point of all that hard work?

Benjamin: You got me.

The Graduate

THOSE MAGICAL SEVEN YEARS

Higher education is supposed to cure us of the false belief that everyone is as smart as everyone else. Unfortunately, in the twenty-first century the effect of widespread college attendance is just the opposite: the great number of people who have been in or near a college think of themselves as the educated peers of even the most accomplished scholars and experts. College is no longer a time devoted to learning and personal maturation; instead, the stampede of young Americans into college and the consequent competition for their tuition dollars have produced a consumer-oriented experience in which students learn, above all else, that the customer is always right.

Before World War II, most people did not finish high school and few went to college. In this earlier time, admissions to top schools were dominated by privileged families, although sometimes young men and a very few women could scrape up the money for tuition or earn a scholarship. It was an exclusive experience often governed as much by social class as by merit. Still, college attendance was an indication of potential, and graduation was a mark of achievement. A university degree was rare, serving as one of the signposts dividing experts and knowers from the rest of society.

Today, attendance at postsecondary institutions is a mass experience. As a result of this increased access to higher education, the word "college" itself is losing meaning, at least in terms of separating educated people from everyone else. "College graduate" today means a lot of things. Unfortunately, "a person of demonstrated educational achievement" is not always one of them.

Bashing colleges and universities is an American tradition, as is bashing the faculty, like me, who teach in them. Stereotypes abound, including the stuffy (or radical, or irrelevant) professor in front of a collection of bored children who themselves came to campus for any number of activities except education. "College boy" was once a zinger aimed by older people at young men, with the clear implication that education was no substitute for maturity or wisdom.

But this book isn't about why colleges are screwed up. I don't have enough pages for that. Rather, it is about why fewer people respect learning and expertise, and this chapter, in turn, is about how colleges and universities paradoxically became an important part of that problem.

I say this while remaining a defender of the American university system, including the much-maligned liberal arts. I am personally a beneficiary of wider access to higher education in the twentieth century and the social mobility it provided. The record of these institutions is unarguable: universities in the United States are still the leading intellectual powerhouses in the world. I continue to have faith in the ability of America's postsecondary schools to produce both knowledge and knowledgeable citizens.

Still, the fact of the matter is that many of those American higher educational institutions are failing to provide to their students the basic knowledge and skills that form expertise. More important, they are failing to provide the ability to *recognize* expertise and to engage productively with experts and other professionals in daily life. The most important of these intellectual capabilities, and the one most under attack in American universities, is critical thinking: the ability to examine new information and competing ideas dispassionately, logically, and without emotional or personal preconceptions.

This is because attendance at a postsecondary institution no longer guarantees a "college education." Instead, colleges and universities now provide a full-service experience of "going to college." These are not remotely the same thing, and students now graduate believing they know a lot more than they actually do. Today, when an expert says, "Well, I went to college," it's hard to blame the public for answering, "Who hasn't?" Americans with college degrees now broadly think of themselves as "educated" when in reality the best that many of them can say is that they've continued on in some kind of classroom setting after high school, with wildly varying results.

The influx of students into America's postsecondary schools has driven an increasing commodification of education. Students at most schools today are treated as *clients*, rather than as students. Younger people, barely out of high school, are pandered to both materially and intellectually, reinforcing some of the worst tendencies in students who have not yet learned the self-discipline that once was essential to the pursuit of higher education. Colleges now are marketed like multiyear vacation packages, rather than as a contract with an institution and its faculty for a course of educational study. This commodification of the college experience itself as a product is not only destroying the value of college degrees but is also undermining confidence among ordinary Americans that college means anything.

This is a deeper problem than the usual stunts, fads, and intellectual silliness on campuses that capture the public imagination from time to time. There will always be a certain amount of foolishness to a lot of campus life. As a Tufts University professor, Dan Drezner, has written, "One of the purposes of college is to articulate stupid arguments in stupid ways and then learn, through interactions with fellow students and professors, exactly how stupid they are."[1] College life, especially at the most elite schools, is insulated from society, and when young people and intellectuals are walled off from the real world, strange things can happen.

Some of this is just so much expensive inanity, harmless in itself. Parents of students at Brown University, for example, are shelling out some serious money so their children can take part in things like "Campus Nudity Week." (One female Brown participant said in 2013 that "the negative feedback" about the event "has helped prepare her for life after college." One can only hope.) In the end, however, I'm not all that worried about naked students amok in the streets of Providence. Instead, my concerns about colleges and how they've accelerated the death of expertise rest more with what happens—or isn't happening—in the classroom.

At its best, college should aim to produce graduates with a reasonable background in a subject, a willingness to continue learning for the rest of their lives, and an ability to assume roles as capable citizens. Instead, for many people college has become, in the words of a graduate of a well-known party school in California, "those magical seven years between high school and your first warehouse job." College is no longer a passage to educated maturity and instead is only a delaying tactic against the onset of adulthood—in some cases, for the faculty as well as for the students.

Part of the problem is that there are too many students, a fair number of whom simply don't belong in college. The new culture of education in the United States is that everyone should, and must, go to college. This cultural change is important to the death of expertise, because as programs proliferate to meet demand, schools become diploma mills whose actual degrees are indicative less of *education* than of *training*, two distinctly different concepts that are increasingly conflated in the public mind. In the worst cases, degrees affirm neither education nor training, but attendance. At the barest minimum, they certify only the timely payment of tuition.

This is one of those things professors are not supposed to say in polite company, but it's true. Young people who might have done better in a trade sign up for college without a lot of thought given to how to graduate, or what they'll do when it all ends. Four years turns into five, and increasingly six or more. A limited course of study eventually turns into repeated visits to an expensive educational buffet laden mostly with intellectual junk food, with very little adult supervision to ensure that the students choose nutrition over nonsense.

The most competitive and elite colleges and universities have fewer concerns in this regard, as they can pick and choose from applicants as they wish and fill their incoming classes with generally excellent students. Their students will get a full education, or close to it, and then usually go on to profitable employment. Other institutions, however, end up in a race to the bottom. All these children, after all, are going to go to college somewhere, and so schools that are otherwise indistinguishable on the level of intellectual quality compete to offer better pizza in the food court, plushier dorms, and more activities besides the boring grind of actually going to class.

Not only are there too many students, there are too many professors. The very best national universities, the traditional sources of university faculty, are promiscuously pumping out PhDs at a rate far higher than any academic job market can possibly absorb. Lesser schools that have no business offering advanced degrees—and many of which barely qualify as glorified high schools even at the undergraduate level—offer doctorates of such low quality that they themselves would never hire their own graduates. Scads of unemployed PhDs, toting mediocre dissertations in any number of overly esoteric subjects, roam the academic landscape literally willing to teach for food.

Even the term "professor" has been denatured by overuse. Once a rare title, American postsecondary institutions now use it at will. Anyone who teaches in anything above the level of a high school is now a professor, from the head of a top department at a major research university to a part-time instructor in a local community college. And just as every teacher is a "professor," so, too, is every small college now a "university," a phenomenon that has reached ridiculous proportions. Tiny local schools that once catered to area residents have reemerged as "universities," as though they now have a particle collider behind the cafeteria.

The emergence of these faux universities is in part a response to an insatiable demand for degrees in a culture where everyone thinks they should go to college. This, in turn, has created a destructive spiral of credential inflation. Schools and colleges cause this degree inflation the same way governments cause monetary inflation: by printing more paper. A high school diploma was once the requirement for entering the trades or beginning a profession. But everybody has one of those now, including people who can't even read. Consequently, colleges serve to verify the completion of high school, and so a master's degree now fills the requirement once served by a bachelor's degree. Students are going broke running around in this educational hamster wheel, without learning very much.[2]

How to solve all this is a crucial question for the future of American education. In 2016, a Democratic Party presidential candidate, Senator Bernie Sanders, said that a college degree today is the equivalent of what a high school degree was fifty years ago—and that therefore everyone should go to college just as everyone now attends high school. In reality, treating colleges as remedial high schools is a large part of how we got here in the first place. The larger point, however, is that the cumulative result of too many "students," too many "professors," too many "universities," and too many degrees is that college attendance is no longer a guarantee that people know what they're talking about.

The failures of the modern university are fueling attacks on the very knowledge those same institutions have worked for centuries to create and to teach to future generations. Intellectual discipline and maturation have fallen by the wayside. The transmission of important cultural learning—including everything from how to construct a logical argument to the foundational DNA of American civilization—is no longer the mission of the customer-service university.

WELCOME, CLIENTS!

College is supposed to be an uncomfortable experience. It is where a person leaves behind the rote learning of childhood and accepts the anxiety, discomfort, and challenge of complexity that leads to the acquisition of deeper knowledge—hopefully, for a lifetime. A college degree, whether in physics or philosophy, is supposed to be the mark of a truly "educated" person who not only has command of a particular subject, but also has a wider understanding of his or her own culture and history. It's not supposed to be easy.

This is no longer how college is viewed in modern America either by the providers or by the consumers of higher education. College as a client-centered experience caters to adolescents instead of escorting them away from adolescence. Rather than disabusing students of their intellectual solipsism, the modern university ends up reinforcing it. Students can leave campus without fully accepting that they've met anyone more intelligent than they are, either among their peers or their teachers. (This assumes that they even bother to make any distinction between peers and teachers at all.) They accept their degree as a receipt for spending several years around a lot of interesting people they and their families have paid for a service.

This is not to say that today's students are intellectually incompetent. Most of the young people at competitive schools have already mastered the rituals of test taking, recommendations, extracurricular activities, and other college-bound merit badges. Unfortunately, once they defeat the admissions maze and arrive at college, they then spend the next four years being undereducated but overly praised. They might even suspect as much, and as a result they risk developing a toxic combination of insecurity and arrogance that serves them poorly once they're beyond the embrace of their parents and the walls of their schools.

Meanwhile, at less competitive schools, students have far fewer worries during the application process. As the economic writer Ben Casselman pointed out in 2016, most college applicants "never have to write a college entrance essay, pad a résumé or sweet-talk a potential letter-writer," because more than three-quarters of American undergraduates attend colleges that accept at least half their applicants. Only 4 percent attend schools that accept 25 percent or less, and fewer than 1 percent attend elite schools that accept fewer than 10 percent of their applicants.[3] Students at these less competitive institutions then struggle to finish, with only half completing a bachelor's degree within six years.

Many of these incoming students are not qualified to be in college and need significant remedial work. The colleges know it, but they accept students who are in over their heads, stick them in large (but cost-efficient) introductory courses, and hope for the best. Why would schools do this and obviously violate what few admissions standards they might still enforce? As James Piereson of the Manhattan Institute wrote in 2016, "Follow the money." The fact of the matter is that "private colleges—at least those below the elite levels—are desperate for students and willing to accept deeply unqualified ones if it means more tuition dollars."[4] Some finish, some don't, but for a few years the institution gets paid either way, and somewhere a young person can say he or she has at least "some college."

Even without these financial pressures, the stampede toward college by unprepared students is also due to a culture of affirmation and self-actualization that forbids confronting children with failure. As Robert Hughes wrote in 1995, America is a culture in which "children are coddled not to think they're dumb."[5] A junior high school teacher in Maryland captured the essence of this problem two decades later in a 2014 article she published in the *Washington Post* after she decided to quit her profession. She said that her school administration gave her two instructions that to her were "defining slogans for public education." One was that students were not allowed to fail. The other foreshadowed the client-centered approach to college: "If they have D's or F's, there is something that you are not doing for them."[6]

I have encountered this myself numerous times, and not just among children or young college undergraduates. I have had graduate students tell me that if they did not get an A in my class, their lesser grade would be evidence of poor instruction on my part. I have also had students who've nearly failed my class ask me for—and, in some cases, *demand*—a recommendation for a graduate program or a professional school. College students may not be dumber than they were thirty years ago, but their sense of entitlement and their unfounded self-confidence have grown considerably.

Parenting obviously plays a major role here. Overprotective parents have become so intrusive that a former dean of first-year students at Stanford wrote an entire book in which she said that this "helicopter parenting" was ruining a generation of children. These are the parents who defend and coddle their children even into high school and college, doing their homework for them—the Stanford dean politely calls this "overhelping"—and in general participating in every aspect of their child's life.[7] Some are worse than others: there are even parents now moving to the same town as their children's colleges to be near them while they attend school. This is not "helicopter parenting" but more like "close air-support jet fighter parenting."

Another problem, paradoxically enough, is affluence. This sounds like a remarkable claim at a time when so many parents and young people are worrying about how to meet educational costs. But the fact of the matter is that more people than ever before are going to college, mostly by tapping a virtually inexhaustible supply of ruinous loans. Buoyed by this government-guaranteed money, and in response to aggressive marketing from tuition-driven institutions, teenagers from almost all of America's social classes now shop for colleges the way the rest of us shop for cars.

The campus visit is a good example of the shopping ritual that teaches children to choose colleges for any number of reasons besides an education. Each spring and summer, the highways fill with children and their parents on road trips to visit schools not to which the young clients have been accepted, but to which they are considering applying. These are not just rich kids touring the Ivy League; friends with teenage children regularly tell me about hitting the road to visit small colleges and state schools I've never even heard of. Every year, these parents ask me for my advice, and every year, I tell them it's a bad idea. Every year, they thank me for my input and do it anyway. By the end of the process, the entire family is cranky and exhausted, and the question of what the schools actually teach seems almost an afterthought.

Usually, the youngsters like most of the schools, because, to a teenager stuck in high school, all colleges seem like pretty great places. Some choices, of course, quickly drop off the radar. An ugly town, a dingy campus, a decrepit dormitory, and that's that. Other times, prospective students fall in love with a school and then spend months agonizing like anxious suitors, hoping that a school they chose while they were barely past their sixteenth birthdays will give them the nod and change the course of their lives.

The idea that adolescents should first think about why they want to go to college at all, find schools that might best suit their abilities, apply only to those schools, and then visit the ones to which they're *accepted* is now alien to many parents and their children. Ask the parents why they drove their daughter all over Creation to visit schools she may have no desire to attend or to which she has no chance of admittance, and the answer rarely varies: "Well, she wanted to see it." The sentence few of them add is: "And we chose to spend the money to do it." College applications, at fifty bucks a pop or more, aren't cheap, but it's a lot more expensive to go road-tripping from Amherst to Atlanta.

This entire process means not only that children are in charge, but that they are already being taught to value schools for some reason other than the education it might provide them. Schools know this, and they're ready for it. In the same way the local car dealership knows exactly how to place a new model in the showroom, or a casino knows exactly how to perfume the air that hits patrons just as they walk in the door, colleges have all kinds of perks and programs at the ready as selling points, mostly to edge out their competitors over things that matter only to kids.

Driven to compete for teenagers and their loan dollars, educational institutions promise an experience rather than an education. (I am leaving aside for-profit schools here, which are largely only factories that create debt and that in general I exclude from the definition of "higher education.") There's nothing wrong with creating an attractive student center or offering a slew of activities, but at some point it's like having a hospital entice heart patients to choose it for a coronary bypass because it has great food.

Children and young adults are more empowered in this process at least in part because loan programs have shifted control over tuition from parents to students. There is also the more general trend, however, that parents for some decades have abdicated more and more decisions about many things to their children. Either way, it is hard to disagree with the *Bloomberg* columnist Megan McArdle's observation that decisions over the whole business have migrated from parents to children, with predictable results when "students are more worried about whether their experience is unpleasant than are parents."[8]

Undergraduate institutions play to these demands in every way. For example, some schools now try to accommodate the anxiety every high school student faces about living with strangers. Once upon a time, learning to live with a roommate was part of the maturing process but one that was understandably dreaded by children still living with their parents. No longer, as a faculty member at Arizona State wrote in 2015:

> At many colleges, new students already have been introduced to their roommates on social media and live in luxurious apartment-like dorms. That ensures they basically never have to share a room or a bathroom, or even eat in the dining halls if they don't want to. Those were the places where previous generations learned to get along with different people and manage conflicts when they were chosen at random to live with strangers in close and communal quarters.[9]

If a student chooses to go to Arizona State because he or she likes the idea of never eating in a dining hall, something is already wrong with the entire process. Many young people, of course, have made worse choices for even sillier reasons.

Students are young and parents love their kids. Fair enough. But when the entire carnival of applications and admissions is over, the faculty have to teach students who have walked into their classrooms with expectations completely unrelated to the actual requirements of gaining a college education. Today, professors do not instruct their students; instead, the students instruct their professors, with an authority that comes naturally to them. A group of Yale students in 2016, for example, demanded that the English department abolish its Major English Poets course because it was too larded with white European males: "We have spoken," they said in a petition. "We are speaking. Pay attention."[10] As a professor at an elite school once said to me, "Some days, I feel less like a teacher and more like a clerk in an expensive boutique."

And why shouldn't he? These are children who have been taught to address adults by their first names since they were toddlers. They have been given "grades" meant to raise their self-esteem rather than to spur achievement. And they have matriculated after being allowed to peruse colleges as though they were inspecting a condo near a golf course. This stream of small but meaningful adult concessions to children and their self-esteem corrodes their ability to learn, and it inculcates a false sense of achievement and overconfidence in their own knowledge that lasts well into adulthood.

When I first arrived at Dartmouth at the end of the 1980s, I was told a story about a well-known (and, at the time, still-living) member of the faculty that in a small way illustrates this problem and the challenge it presents to experts and educators. The renowned astrophysicist Robert Jastrow gave a lecture on President Ronald Reagan's plan to develop space-based missile defenses, which he strongly supported. An undergraduate challenged Jastrow during the question-and-answer period, and by all accounts Jastrow was patient but held to his belief that such a program was possible and necessary. The student, realizing that a scientist at a major university was not going to change his mind after a few minutes of arguing with a sophomore, finally shrugged and gave up.

"Well," the student said, "your guess is as good as mine."

Jastrow stopped the young man short. "No, no, no," he said emphatically. "*My* guesses are much, *much* better than yours."

Professor Jastrow has since passed away, and I never got the chance while I was in Hanover to ask him what happened that day. But I suspect that he was trying to teach some life lessons that are increasingly resisted by college students and citizens alike: that admission to college is the beginning, not the end, of education and that respecting a person's *opinion* does not mean granting equal respect to that person's *knowledge*. Whether national missile defenses are a wise policy is still debatable. What hasn't changed, however, is that the guesses of an experienced astrophysicist and a college sophomore are not equivalently good.

This is more than some Ivy League smart-alecks cracking wise with their professors. To take a less rarified example, a young woman in 2013 took to social media for help with a class assignment. (Where she lives or where she was studying is unclear, but she described herself as a future doctor.) She apparently was tasked with researching the deadly chemical substance Sarin, and, as she explained to thousands on Twitter, she needed help because she had to watch her child while doing her assignment. In minutes, her request was answered by Dan Kaszeta, the director of a security consulting firm in London and a top expert in the field of chemical weapons, who volunteered to help her.

What happened next transfixed many readers. (Jeffrey Lewis, an arms expert in California, captured and posted the exchange online.) "I can't find the chemical and physical properties of sarin gas [*sic*] someone please help me," the student tweeted. Kaszeta offered his help. He corrected her by noting that Sarin isn't a gas and that the word should be capitalized. As Lewis later wryly noted, "Dan's help [met] with a welcome sigh of relief from our beleaguered student."

Actually, it met with a string of expletives. The student lectured the expert in a gale-force storm of outraged ego: "yes the [expletive] it is a gas you ignorant [expletive]. sarin is a liquid & can evaporate . . . shut the [expletive] up." Kaszeta, clearly stunned, tried one more time: "Google me. I'm an expert on Sarin. Sorry for offering to help." Things did not improve before the exchange finally ended.

One smug Dartmouth kid and one angry Twitter user could be outliers, and they're certainly extreme examples of trying to deal with students. But faculty both in the classroom and on social media report that incidents where students take correction as an insult are occurring more frequently. Unearned praise and hollow successes build a fragile arrogance in students that can lead them to lash out at the first teacher or employer who dispels that illusion, a habit that proves hard to break in adulthood.

CAN'T I JUST EMAIL YOU?

Client servicing and the treatment of expertise as a product are evident in colleges today, even in the smallest things. Consider, for example, the influence of email, which encourages all kinds of odd behavior that students would usually hesitate to display in person.

Even if we leave aside the occasional bad decision after a weekend of drinking and partying to write something and hit "send," email encourages a misplaced sense of intimacy that erodes the boundaries necessary to effective teaching. As we'll see in the next chapter, this is a characteristic of interactions over electronic media in general, but the informality of communication between teachers and students is one more example of how college life in particular now contributes to the eroding respect for experts and their abilities.

Email became common on campuses in the early 1990s, and within a decade, professors noticed the changes wrought by instant communications. In 2006, the *New York Times* asked college educators about their experiences with student email, and their frustration was evident. "These days," the *Times* wrote, "students seem to view [faculty] as available around the clock, sending a steady stream of e-mail messages . . . that are too informal or downright inappropriate." As a Georgetown theology professor told the *Times*, "The tone that they would take in e-mail was pretty astounding. 'I need to know this and you need to tell me right now,' with a familiarity that can sometimes border on imperative."[11]

Email, like social media, is a great equalizer, and it makes students comfortable with the idea of messages to teachers as being like any communication with a customer-service department. This has a direct impact on respect for expertise, because it erases any distinction between the students who ask questions and the teachers who answer them. As the *Times* noted,

> While once professors may have expected deference, their expertise seems to have become just another service that students, as consumers, are buying. So students may have no fear of giving offense, imposing on the professor's time or even of asking a question that may reflect badly on their own judgment.
>
> Kathleen E. Jenkins, a sociology professor at the College of William and Mary in Virginia, said she had even received e-mail requests from students who missed class and wanted copies of her teaching notes.

When faced with these kinds of faculty complaints about email, one Amherst sophomore said, "If the only way I could communicate with my professors was by going to their office or calling them, there would be some sort of ranking or prioritization taking place. Is this question worth going over to the office?"

To which a faculty member might respond: *that's exactly the point.* Professors are not intellectual valets or on-call pen pals. They do not exist to resolve every student question instantly—including, as one UC Davis professor reported, advice about whether to use a binder or a subject notebook. One of the things students are supposed to learn in college is self-reliance, but why bother looking something up when the faculty member is only a few keystrokes away?

Education is designed to cure students of all this, not to encourage it. For many reasons, including the risk to their jobs, professors are sometimes hesitant to take charge, especially if they are untenured or adjunct faculty. Some of them, of course, treat children as their equals because they have absorbed the idea that the students really are their peers, a mistake that hurts both teaching and learning. Some educators even repeat the old saw that "I learn as much from my students as they learn from me!" (With due respect to my colleagues in the teaching profession who use this expression, I am compelled to say: if that's true, *then you're not a very good teacher.*)

The solution to this reversal of roles in the classroom is for teachers to reassert their authority. To do so, however, would first require overturning the entire notion of education as client service. Tuition-conscious administrators would hardly welcome such a counterrevolution in the classroom, but in any case, it would likely be deeply unpopular with the clients.

For many years, Father James Schall at Georgetown University would shock his political philosophy students at the very first class meeting by handing out an essay he'd written called "What a Student Owes His Teacher." Here's a sample:

Students have obligations to teachers. I know this sounds like strange doctrine, but let it stand.

The first obligation, particularly operative during the first weeks of a new semester, is a moderately good will toward the teacher, a trust, a confidence that is willing to admit to oneself that the teacher has probably been through the matter, and, unlike the student, knows where it all leads. I do not want here to neglect the dangers of the ideological professor, of course, the one who imposes his mind on what is. But to be a student requires a certain modicum of humility.

Thus, the student owes the teacher trust, docility, effort, thinking.[12]

Schall made that essay required reading for many years before retiring. One can only imagine the howls of outrage it would provoke now on most campuses to tell students they need to work harder, have more perspective about their own talents, and trust their teachers. Many faculty members today might agree with Schall, but they cannot risk aggravating the students, because, as everyone in any service industry knows, the customer is always right.

Students, well intentioned or otherwise, are poorly served by the idea that students and teachers are intellectual and social equals and that a student's opinion is as good as a professor's knowledge. Rather than disabusing young people of these myths, college too often encourages them, with the result that people end up convinced they're actually smarter than they are. As the social psychologist David Dunning has noted, "The way we traditionally conceive of ignorance—as an absence of knowledge—leads us to think of education as its natural antidote. But education, even when done skillfully, can produce illusory confidence."[13]

Just imagine how difficult things get when education isn't done skillfully.

THE GENERIC UNIVERSITY

An administrator at a small college—excuse me, a "university"—could well read this chapter and protest that I am unfairly excoriating businesses for acting like businesses. Higher education, after all, is an industry, and it is no sin if the corporations in it compete with each other. The business analogy, however, fails when the schools themselves do not deliver what they've promised: an education.

The game begins long before a prospective student fills out an application. Even as colleges have moved toward intellectually low-impact programs surrounded by lifestyle improvements and nonacademic activities, they have attempted simultaneously to inflate their importance and burnish their brands. My earlier comment about the proliferation of "universities" was not a stray observation: it's actually happening, and it has been going on since at least the 1990s. Like so much else associated with the current maladies of higher education, it is a change driven by money and status.

One reason these small schools become universities is to appeal to students who want to believe they're paying for something in a higher tier—that is, for a regional or national "university," rather than a local college.[14] State colleges and community colleges are lower-status institutions, when compared with four-year universities, in the eyes of college-bound high school students. Hence, many of them have tried to distinguish themselves with an attempted rebranding as "universities."

A more prosaic motivation behind this name game is to find new funding streams by grafting graduate programs onto small colleges. The competition to pull in more money and the consequent proliferation of graduate programs have thus forced these new "universities" into a degree-granting arms race. Not only are schools adding graduate programs in professional degrees like business administration, but many of them are bloating their undergraduate programs with additional coursework for a master's degree.

Faced with this competitive pressure from other schools doing likewise, some of these fledgling universities then step up their game and add doctoral programs. And because these small schools cannot support a doctoral program in an established field, they construct esoteric interdisciplinary fields that exist only to create new credentials. It's not hard to see how this ends up creating degrees that do not actually signal a corresponding level of knowledge.

All of this borders on academic malpractice. The creation of graduate programs in colleges that can barely provide a reasonable undergraduate education cheats both graduates and undergrads. Small colleges do not have the resources—including the libraries, research facilities, and multiple programs—of large universities, and repainting the signs at the front gates cannot magically create that kind of academic infrastructure. Turning Smallville College into Generic University might look good on the new stationery, but it is the kind of move that can push what might have been a serviceable local college into a new status as a half-baked university.

This rebranding dilutes the worth of all postsecondary degrees. When everyone has attended a university, it gets that much more difficult to sort out actual achievement and expertise among all those "university graduates." Americans are burying themselves in a blizzard of degrees, certificates, and other affirmations of varying value. People eager to misinform their fellow citizens will often say that they have graduate education and that they are therefore to be taken seriously. The only thing more disheartening than finding out these folks are lying about possessing multiple degrees is to find out that they're telling the truth.

Students will likely object that the demands of their major are a lot more work than I'm giving credit for here. Perhaps, but that depends on the major itself. The requirements of a degree in a STEM field (science, technology, engineering, mathematics), a demanding foreign language, or a rigorous degree in the humanities can be a different matter than a major in communications or visual arts or—as much as it pains me to say it—political science. Every campus has "default majors," chosen when a student has no real idea what to do, some of which are off-ramps from more demanding programs after students learn the limits of their abilities.

At the risk of being misunderstood, I should clarify a few points. First, it's not news to me or anyone else in higher education that even the best schools have "gut" courses, the class a student can pass by exchanging oxygen for carbon dioxide for a set number of weeks. Perhaps it might be shocking for a professor to admit this, but there's nothing wrong with easy or fun courses. I would even defend at least some of them as necessary. There *should* be classes where students can experiment with a subject, take something enjoyable, and get credit for learning something.

The problem comes when all the courses start to look like gut courses. They exist in the sciences, the humanities, and the social sciences, and their numbers, at least by my subjective judgment, are growing. No field is immune, and a look through the offerings of many programs around the country—as well as a compilation of the grades given in them—suggests that what were once isolated professorial vices are now common departmental habits.

I should also note that I am not making an argument here for slimming colleges down to a bunch of STEM departments with a smattering of English or history majors. I deplore those kinds of arguments, and I have long objected to what I see as an assault on the liberal arts. Too often, those who denigrate the liberal arts are in reality advocating for nothing less than turning colleges into trade schools. Art history majors always take the cheap shots here, even though many people don't realize that a lot of art history majors go on to some pretty lucrative careers. In any case, I don't want to live in a civilization where there are no art history majors or, for that matter, film studies, philosophy, or sociology majors.

The question is how many students in these majors are actually learning anything, or whether there need to be so many students taking these subjects at third-string institutions—especially if supported by taxpayer dollars. There is no way around the reality that students are too often wasting their money and obtaining the illusion of an education by gravitating toward courses or majors that either shouldn't exist or whose enrollments should be restricted to the small number of students who intend to pursue them seriously and with rigor. This, too, is one of the many things faculty are not supposed to say out loud, because to resentful parents and hopeful students, it sounds like baseless elitism.

It might be elitism, but it's not baseless. Many small schools were once called "teacher's colleges" and served that purpose well. Their history or English departments fulfilled the perfectly useful function of producing history and English teachers. Today, however, these tiny "universities" offer anthropology or the philosophy of science as though their students are slated for graduate study at Stanford or Chicago. These majors are sometimes built around the interests of the few faculty members who teach them, or offered as a way to fatten the catalog of a school that otherwise might not seem intellectually sturdy enough to prospective students.

There's nothing wrong with personal fulfillment or following your bliss—if you can afford it. If a small college has a history course that interests you, by all means, take it. It might be terrific. But students who choose majors with little thought about where their school stands, what academic resources it can offer in that program, or where it places graduates from those programs will risk leaving campus (whenever they finally finish) with less knowledge than they've been led to believe, a problem at the core of a lot of needless arguments with people who are deeply mistaken about the quality of their own education.

When rebranded universities offer courses and degree programs as though they are roughly equivalent to their better-known counterparts, they are not only misleading prospective students but also undermining later learning. The quality gap between programs risks producing a sense of resentment: if you and I both have university degrees in history, why is your view about the Russian Revolution any better than mine? Why should it matter that your degree is from a top-ranked department, but mine is from a program so small it has a single teacher? If I studied film at a local state college, and you went to the film program at the University of Southern California, who are you to think you know more than I? We have the same degree, don't we?

These kinds of comparisons and arguments about the differences between colleges and their various degrees and programs get under the skin pretty quickly. The student who gained admission to a top school and finished a degree there resents the leveling that comes with an indifferent comparison to his or her fellow major from an unknown public "university." (If all schools are equally good, why are some harder to get into than others?) Meanwhile, the student who worked day and night to get the same degree bridles at the implication that his or her achievement means less without a pedigree. (If everything except the Ivy League is junk, why are all these other programs fully accredited?)

There's plenty of bad faith in these arguments, which are often little more than social one-upmanship. A lousy student who attended a good school is still a lousy student; a diligent student from a small institution is no less intelligent for the lack of a famous pedigree. The fact remains, however, that taking a course at a regional college with an overworked adjunct is usually a lot different than studying at a top university with an accomplished scholar. It might be true, but saying so immediately generates huffy cries of snobbery, and everyone walks away angry.

We may not like any of these comparisons, but they matter in sorting out expertise and relative knowledge. It's true that great universities can graduate complete dunderheads. Would-be universities, however, try to punch above their intellectual weight for all the wrong reasons, including marketing, money, and faculty ego. In the end, they are doing a disservice to both their students and society. Studying the same thing might give people a common language for further discussion of a subject, but it does not automatically make them peers.

Colleges and universities also mislead their students about their own competence through grade inflation. Collapsing standards so that schoolwork doesn't interfere with the fun of going to college is one way to ensure a happy student body and relieve the faculty of the pressure of actually failing anyone. As *Bloomberg's* McArdle wrote, this attempt to lessen the unpleasant impact of actually having to attend college on the customers should be no surprise when classroom seats are a commodity rather than a competitively earned privilege.

> You see the results most visibly in the lazy rivers and rock-climbing walls and increasingly luxurious dorms that colleges use to compete for students, but such a shift does not limit itself to extraneous amenities. Professors marvel at the way students now shamelessly demand to be given good grades, regardless of their work ethic, but that's exactly what you would expect if the student views themselves as a consumer, and the product as a credential, rather than an education.

Or as a *Washington Post* writer Catherine Rampell describes it, college is now a deal in which "students pay more in tuition, and expect more in return—better service, better facilities and better grades."[15] Less is demanded of students now than even a few decades ago. There is less homework, shorter trimester and quarter systems, and technological innovations that make going to college more fun but less rigorous. When college is a business, you can't flunk the customers.

College isn't always rock climbing and kayaking, but there can be no doubt that the trend is toward deemphasizing grades by inflating them. As a University of Chicago study found in 2011, "it does not take a great deal of effort to demonstrate satisfactory academic performance in today's colleges and universities."

> Forty-five percent of students reported that in the prior semester they did not have a single course that required more than twenty pages of writing over the entire semester; 32 percent did not have even one class that assigned more than forty pages of reading per week. Unsurprisingly, many college students today decide to invest time in other activities in college.[16]

Some of those "other activities" are noble and enriching. Many others are the sorts of things parents would probably just as soon not know about.

When it comes to the death of expertise, the effect of lighter workloads and easier grades should be obvious: students graduate with a high GPA that doesn't reflect a corresponding level of education or intellectual achievement. (Again, I am leaving aside certain kinds of degrees here, and talking about the bulk of majors taken in the United States today.) "I was a straight-A student at a university" does not mean what it did in 1960 or even 1980. A study of two hundred colleges and universities up through 2009 found that A was the most commonly given grade, an increase of nearly 30 percent since 1960 and over 10 percent just since 1988. Grades in the A and B range together now account for more than 80 percent of all grades in all subjects, a trend that continues unabated.[17]

In other words, all the children are now above average. In 2012, for example, the most frequently given grade at Harvard was a straight A. At Yale, more than 60 percent of all grades are either A- or A. That can happen now and then in a particular class, but that's almost impossible across an entire university in any normal grade distribution, even among the brightest students.

Every institution, when confronted with these facts, blames every other institution around it. The problem, of course, is that no one university or program can take a stand against grade inflation without harming its own students: the first faculty to deflate their grades instantly make their students seem less capable than those from other institutions. This, as Rampell correctly noted, means that the default grade is no longer the "gentleman's C" of the 1950s, but a "gentleman's A," now bestowed more as an entitlement for course completion than as a reward for excellence.

Princeton, Wellesley, and Harvard, among others, established committees to look into the problem of grade inflation. Princeton adopted a policy that tried to limit the faculty's ability to give A grades in 2004, an experiment that was rolled back by the faculty itself less than a decade later. At Wellesley, humanities departments tried to cap the average grade at a B+ in their courses; those courses lost a fifth of their enrollments and the participating departments lost nearly a third of their majors.

Experienced educators have grappled with this problem for years. I am one of them, and like my colleagues, I have not found a solution. The two most important facts about grade inflation, however, are that it exists and that it suffuses students with unwarranted confidence in their abilities. Almost every institution of higher education is complicit in what is essentially collusion on grades, driven on one side by market pressures to make college fun, to make students attractive to employers, and to help vulnerable professors escape the wrath of dissatisfied students, and on the other by irresponsible notions about the role of self-esteem in education.

RATE ME GENTLY

Another way colleges and universities enhance the notion that students are clients, and thus devalue respect for expertise, is to encourage the students to evaluate the educators standing in front of them as though they are peers. Student evaluations came out of the movement for more "relevance" and student involvement after the 1960s. They are still with us, and in an era where businesses, including education, are obsessed with "metrics," they are used and abused more than ever.

I am actually a supporter of some limited use of student evaluations. I will immodestly say that mine have been pretty good since the day I began teaching—I have won awards for teaching at both the Naval War College and the Harvard Extension School—and so I have no personal axe to grind here. I'm also a former academic administrator who had to review the evaluations of other faculty as part of my duties overseeing a department. I've read thousands of these evaluations over the years, from students at all levels, and they're a worthwhile exercise if they're handled properly. Nonetheless, the whole idea is now out of control, with students rating professional men and women as though they're reviewing a movie or commenting on a pair of shoes.

Evaluations usually fall into a gray area, where most teachers are competent and most students generally like the courses. Where evaluations are most useful is in spotting trends: a multiyear look at evaluations can identify both the best and the worst teachers, especially if the readers are adept at decoding how students write such reports.

("She's boring," for example, often means "she actually expected me to read the book she assigned instead of just entertaining me.") In my own classes, I use them to spot things in my courses that are working as well as what might be missing the mark, such as books or lectures that I should drop or keep, or to let me know if my own sense of whether I had an especially good or weak term was shared by the students.

Still, there's something wrong with a system that asks a student how much they liked their education. College isn't a restaurant. (I sometimes hear a Yelp review as I'm reading these evaluations: "The basic statistics course was served a bit cold, but it was substantial, while my partner chose a light introduction to world religions that had just a hint of spice.") Evaluating teachers creates a habit of mind in which the layperson becomes accustomed to judging the expert, despite being in an obvious position of having inferior knowledge of the subject material.

Student evaluations are also a hypersensitive indicator, influenced by the tiniest and most irrelevant things, from the comfort of the seats to the time of day the course is offered. A certain number of them have to be ignored. And some of them are just strange, to the point where professors will exchange stories of the worst or weirdest evaluations they've gotten. One of my colleagues once gave a detailed lecture on British naval history, for example, and a military student's only comment was that the teacher needed to press his shirt. A top historian I knew was regularly ridiculed on evaluations for being short. I was once told by an undergraduate that I was a great professor but that I needed to lose some weight. (That one was accurate.) Another student disliked me so much that he or she said on my evaluation that they would pray for me.

As entertaining as these evaluations are, they all encourage students to think of themselves as the arbiters of the talent of the teachers. And when education is about making sure clients are happy, a college's reliance on evaluations forces weaker or less secure teachers to become dancing bears, striving to be loved or at least liked, so that more students will read the reviews and keep the class (and the professor's contract) alive for the next term. This creates and sustains a vicious circle of pandering and grade inflation.

Students should be involved in their education as more than observers or receptacles for information. Engagement and debate are the lifeblood of a university, and professors are not above criticism of either their ideas or their teaching ability. But the industrial model of education has reduced college to a commercial transaction, where students are taught to be picky consumers rather than critical thinkers. The ripple effect on expertise and the fuel this all provides to attacks on established knowledge defeat the very purpose of a university.

COLLEGE IS NOT A SAFE SPACE

Young men and women are not as irresponsible as we sometimes portray them in the media or the pop culture or in our mind's eye, for that matter. We laugh at college movie comedies and fondly remember our own irresponsible moments as students, and then we sternly lecture our children never to be like us. We applaud student activism if we like the cause, and we deplore it if we disagree. Adults always have a tendency to be sour critics of the generation that follows them.

None of this, however, excuses colleges for allowing their campuses to turn into circuses. It was probably inevitable that the anti-intellectualism of American life would invade college campuses, but that is no reason to surrender to it. And make no mistake: campuses in the United States are increasingly surrendering their intellectual authority not only to children, but also to activists who are directly attacking the traditions of free inquiry that scholarly communities are supposed to defend.

I have plenty of strong opinions on what I see as assaults on free inquiry, but I'm not going to air them here. There are dozens of books and articles out there about how colleges and universities have become havens of political correctness, where academic freedom is suffocated under draconian codes enforced by ideologues among the students and the faculty. I see no point in rehearsing those arguments here.

When it comes to the death of expertise, however, it is important to think about the way the current fads on campus, including "safe spaces" and speech codes, do in fact corrode the ability of colleges to produce people capable of critical thought. (And remember, "critical thinking" isn't the same thing as "relentless criticism.") In the same way that shopping for schools teaches young men and women to value a school for reasons other than an education, these accommodations to young activists encourage them to believe, once again, that the job of a college student is to enlighten the professors instead of the other way around.

There are so many examples of this it is almost unfair to point to any one policy or controversy at any particular university. The problem is endemic to American universities and has recurred, in waves of varying strength, since the early 1960s. What is different today, and especially worrisome when it comes to the creation of educated citizens, is how the protective, swaddling environment of the modern university infantilizes students and thus dissolves their ability to conduct a logical and informed argument. When feelings matter more than rationality or facts, education is a doomed enterprise. Emotion is an unassailable defense against expertise, a moat of anger and resentment in which reason and knowledge quickly drown. And when students learn that emotion trumps everything else, it is a lesson they will take with them for the rest of their lives.

Colleges are supposed to be the calm environment in which educated men and women determine what's true and what's false, and where they learn to follow a model of scholarly inquiry no matter where it takes them. Instead, many colleges have become hostages to students who demand that their feelings override every other consideration. They no doubt believe in their right to make this demand because their lives, up until then, have been lived that way, in a therapeutic culture that leaves no thought unexpressed and no feeling invalidated.

Still, student activism is a normal part of college life. Adolescents are *supposed* to be passionate; it's part of being a teen or a twenty-something. I'm still old-fashioned enough that I expect educated men and women to be leaders among the voters by virtue of a better education, and so I applaud tomorrow's voters exercising their political reasoning in debate and discussion.

Unfortunately, the new student activism is regressing back to the old student activism of a half century ago: intolerance, dogmatism, and even threats and violence. Ironically (or perhaps tragically), students are mobilizing extreme language and demands over increasingly small things. While Baby Boomers might well claim that they were busting up the campus for peace in 1967, there's some truth to the notion that young men about to be drafted and sent to an Asian jungle were understandably emotional about the subject. Members of minority groups who were not fully citizens in the eyes of the law until the early 1960s justifiably felt they were out of less spectacular options than protest, even if nothing excuses the violence that ensued.

Today, by contrast, students explode over imagined slights that are not even remotely in the same category as fighting for civil rights or being sent to war. Students now build majestic Everests from the smallest molehills, and they descend into hysteria over pranks and hoaxes. In the midst of it all, the students are learning that emotion and volume can always defeat reason and substance, thus building about themselves fortresses that no future teacher, expert, or intellectual will ever be able to breach.

At Yale in 2015, for example, a house master's wife had the temerity to tell minority students to ignore Halloween costumes they thought offensive. This provoked a campuswide temper tantrum that included professors being shouted down by screaming students. "In your position as master," one student howled in a professor's face, "it is your job to create a place of comfort and home for the students. . . . Do you understand that?!"

Quietly, the professor said, "No, I don't agree with that," and the student unloaded on him:

> "Then why the [expletive] did you accept the position?! Who the [expletive] hired you?! You should step down! If that is what you think about being a master you should step down! *It is not about creating an intellectual space! It is not! Do you understand that? It's about creating a home here.* You are not doing that!"[18] [emphasis added]

Yale, instead of disciplining students in violation of their own norms of academic discourse, apologized to the tantrum throwers. The house master eventually resigned from his residential post, while staying on as a faculty member. His wife, however, resigned her faculty position and left college teaching entirely.

To faculty everywhere, the lesson was obvious: the campus of a top university is not a place for intellectual exploration. It is a luxury home, rented for four to six years, nine months at a time, by children of the elite who may shout at faculty as if they're berating clumsy maids in a colonial mansion.

A month after the Yale fracas, protests at the University of Missouri flared up after a juvenile incident in which a swastika was drawn on a bathroom wall with feces. Exactly what Missouri's flagship public university was supposed to do, other than to wash the wall, was unclear, but the campus erupted anyway. "Do you know what systemic oppression is?!" a student yelled at the flustered Mizzou president. "Google it!" she hollered. Student journalists were harassed and threatened, in one case by a faculty member with a courtesy appointment, ironically enough, in the journalism school. After a few more days of these theatrics, the university's president resigned. (The chancellor and a professor who had refused to cancel classes after the protests both followed suit.)

Missouri, however, isn't Yale. It does not have a nearly inelastic demand for its services. Applications and donations soon took a hit in the wake of the protests and resignations.[19] Some months later, the adjunct journalism professor who had confronted a student was fired. When the smoke cleared, the university was left with fewer faculty, administrators, applicants, and donations, all because a group of students, enabled by an even smaller group of faculty, reversed the roles of teachers and learners at a major public university.

Interestingly, this is a subject that often unites liberal and conservative intellectuals. The British scholar Richard Dawkins, something of a scourge to conservatives because of his views on religion, was perplexed by the whole idea of "safe spaces," the places American students demand as a respite from any form of political expression they might find "triggering." Dawkins minced no words: "A university is not a 'safe space,'" he said on Twitter. "If you need a safe space, leave, go home, hug your teddy and suck your thumb until ready for university."

Likewise, after the Yale and Missouri events, an *Atlantic* writer, Conor Friedersdorf, noted that "what happens at Yale does not stay there" and that tomorrow's elites were internalizing values not of free expression but of sheer intolerance. "One feels for these students," Friedersdorf later wrote. (I do not, but Friedersdorf is more understanding than I am.) "But if an email about Halloween costumes has them skipping class and suffering breakdowns, either they need help from mental-health professionals or they've been grievously ill-served by debilitating ideological notions they've acquired about what ought to cause them pain."[20]

Meanwhile, a libertarian columnist and University of Tennessee law professor, Glenn Reynolds, suggested a more dramatic solution.

> To be a voter, one must be able to participate in adult political discussions. It's necessary to be able to listen to opposing arguments and even—as I'm doing right here in this column—to change your mind in response to new evidence.
>
> So maybe we should raise the voting age to 25, an age at which, one fervently hopes, some degree of maturity will have set in. It's bad enough to have to treat college students like children. But it's intolerable to be *governed* by spoiled children. People who can't discuss Halloween costumes rationally don't deserve to play a role in running a great nation.[21]

It's a safe bet that no one's going to amend the Constitution in response to Professor Reynolds's suggestion, but his comments, like those of other observers, point to the bizarre paradox in which college students are demanding to run the school while at the same time insisting that they be treated as children.

Again, I have no idea how to fix this, especially before students get to college. Like most professors—I hope—I hold my students to clear standards. I expect them to learn how to formulate their views and to argue them, calmly and logically. I grade them on their responses to the questions I ask on their exams and on the quality of their written work, not on their political views. I demand that they treat other students with respect and that they engage the ideas and beliefs of others in the classroom without emotionalism or personal attacks.

But when students leave my classroom, I am haunted by the realization that I cannot moderate their arguments forever. I cannot prevent them from dismissing others, from rejecting facts, from denouncing well-intentioned advice, or from demanding that their feelings be accepted in place of the truth. If they've spent four years showing such disrespect for their professors and their institutions, they cannot be expected to respect their fellow citizens. And if college graduates can no longer be counted on to lead reasoned debate and discussion in American life, and to know the difference between knowledge and feeling, then we're indeed in the kind of deep trouble no expert can fix.

4

Let Me Google That for You

How Unlimited Information Is Making Us Dumber

My mind now expects to take in information the way the Net dis-
tributes it: in a swiftly moving stream of particles. Once I was a
scuba diver in the sea of words. Now I zip along the surface like a
guy on a Jet Ski.

Nicholas Carr

Although the Internet could be making all of us smarter, it makes
many of us stupider, because it's not just a magnet for the curious.
It's a sinkhole for the gullible. It renders everyone an instant expert.
You have a degree? Well, I did a Google search!

Frank Bruni

Do not believe everything you read on the Internet, especially
quotes from famous people.

Abraham Lincoln (probably)

THE RETURN OF STURGEON'S LAW

Ask any professional or expert about the death of expertise, and most
of them will immediately blame the same culprit: the Internet. People
who once had to ask the advice of specialists in any given field now

plug search terms into a browser and get answers in seconds. Why rely on people with more education and experience than you—or, worse, have to make appointments with them—when you can just get the information yourself?

Chest pain? Ask your computer. "Why does my chest hurt?" will generate more than eleven million results (at least on the search engine I just used) in exactly 0.52 seconds. A stream of information will fill your screen, with helpful advice from sources ranging from the National Institutes of Health to other outfits whose bona fides are a tad less reputable. Some of these sites will even walk the would-be patient through a diagnosis. Your doctor might have a different opinion, but who is he to argue with a glowing screen that will answer your question in less than a single second?

In fact, who is anyone to argue with anyone? In the Information Age, there's no such thing as an irresolvable argument. Each of us is now walking around with more accumulated information on a smartphone or tablet than ever existed in the entire Library of Alexandria. At the beginning of this book, I mentioned the character Cliff Clavin from the classic television show *Cheers*, the local know-it-all who routinely lectured the other regulars in a Boston pub on every subject under the sun. But Cliff couldn't exist today: at the first claim of "it's a known fact," everyone in the bar could pull out a phone and verify (or more likely disprove) any of Cliff's claims.

Put another way, technology has created a world in which we're *all* Cliff Clavin now. And that's a problem.

Despite what irritated professionals may think, however, the Internet is not the primary cause of challenges to their expertise. Rather, the Internet has accelerated the collapse of communication between experts and laypeople by offering an apparent shortcut to erudition. It allows people to mimic intellectual accomplishment by indulging in an illusion of expertise provided by a limitless supply of facts.

Facts, as experts know, are not the same as knowledge or ability. And on the Internet, "facts" are sometimes not even facts. In the various skirmishes in the campaigns against established knowledge, the Internet is like artillery support: a constant bombardment of random, disconnected information that rains down on experts and ordinary citizens alike, deafening all of us while blowing up attempts at reasonable discussion.

Internet users have created many humorous laws and corollaries to describe discussion in the electronic world. The tendency to bring up Nazi Germany in any argument inspired Godwin's Law and the related *reductio ad Hiterlum*. The deeply entrenched and usually immutable views of Internet users are the foundation of Pommer's Law, in which the Internet can only change a person's mind from having *no* opinion to having a *wrong* opinion. There are many others, including my personal favorite, Skitt's Law: "Any Internet message correcting an error in another post will contain at least one error itself."

When it comes to the death of expertise, however, the law to bear in mind is an observation coined long before the advent of the personal computer: Sturgeon's Law, named for the legendary science-fiction writer Theodore Sturgeon. In the early 1950s, highbrow critics derided the quality of popular literature, particularly American science fiction. They considered sci-fi and fantasy writing a literary ghetto, and almost all of it, they sniffed, was worthless. Sturgeon angrily responded by noting that the critics were setting too high a bar. Most products in most fields, he argued, are of low quality, including what was then considered serious writing. "Ninety percent of *everything*," Sturgeon decreed, "is crap."

Where the Internet is concerned, Sturgeon's Law of 90 percent might be lowballing. The sheer size and volume of the Internet, and the inability to separate meaningful knowledge from random noise, mean that good information will always be swamped by lousy data and weird detours. Worse, there's no way to keep up with it all, even if any group or institution wanted to try. In 1994, there were fewer than three thousand websites online. By 2014, there were more than *one billion* sites.[1] Most of them are searchable and will arrive before your eyes in mere seconds, regardless of their quality.

The good news is that even if Sturgeon's Law holds, that's still one hundred million pretty good websites. These include all the major news publications of the world (many of which are now read more in pixels than on paper), as well as the home pages of think tanks, universities, research organizations, and any number of important scientific, cultural, and political figures. The bad news, of course, is that finding all of this information means plowing through a blizzard of useless or misleading information posted by everyone from well-intentioned grandmothers to the killers of the Islamic State. Some of the smartest people on earth have a significant presence on the Internet. Some of the stupidest people on the same planet, however, reside just one click away on the next page or hyperlink.

The countless dumpsters of nonsense parked on the Internet are a Sturgeon's Law nightmare. People who already have to make hard choices about getting information from a few dozen news channels on their televisions now face millions upon millions of web pages produced by anyone willing to pay for an online presence. The Internet is without doubt a great achievement that continues to change our lives for the better by allowing more people more access to information—and to each other—than ever before in history. But it also has a dark side that is exerting important and deeply negative effects on the ways people gain knowledge and respond to expertise.

The most obvious problem is that the freedom to post anything online floods the public square with bad information and half-baked thinking. The Internet lets a billion flowers bloom, and most of them stink, including everything from the idle thoughts of random bloggers and the conspiracy theories of cranks all the way to the sophisticated campaigns of disinformation conducted by groups and governments. Some of the information on the Internet is wrong because of sloppiness, some of it is wrong because well-meaning people just don't know any better, and some of it is wrong because it was put there out of greed or even sheer malice. The medium itself, without comment or editorial intervention, displays it all with equal speed. The Internet is a vessel, not a referee.

This, of course, is no more and no less than an updated version of the basic paradox of the printing press. As the writer Nicholas Carr pointed out, the arrival of Gutenberg's invention in the fifteenth century set off a "round of teeth gnashing" among early humanists, who worried that "printed books and broadsheets would undermine religious authority, demean the work of scholars and scribes, and spread sedition and debauchery."[2]

Those medieval naysayers weren't entirely wrong. The printing press was used to mass-produce Bibles, to teach people to read, and eventually to empower the literacy that drives so much of human freedom. Of course, it also enabled the dissemination of insanity like the *Protocols of the Elders of Zion*, taught people to confuse words with facts, and supported the creation of totalitarian propaganda that undermined that same human freedom. The Internet is the printing press at the speed of fiber optics.

In addition to enabling torrents of misinformation, the Internet is weakening the ability of laypeople and scholars alike to do basic research, a skill that would help everyone to navigate this wilderness of bad data. This might seem an odd claim coming from a member of the scholarly community, because I gladly admit that Internet access makes my work as a writer a lot easier. In the 1980s, I had to put together a dissertation by lugging around armloads of books and articles. Today, I keep browser bookmarks and folders full of electronically readable articles at my fingertips. How can that not be better than the hours I spent going blind in front of a copier in the bowels of a library?

In some ways, the convenience of the Internet is a tremendous boon, but mostly for people already trained in research and who have some idea what they're looking for. It's much easier to subscribe to the electronic version of, say, *Foreign Affairs* or *International Security* than it is to decamp to the library or impatiently check an office mailbox. This is no help, unfortunately, for a student or an untrained layperson who has never been taught how to judge the provenance of information or the reputability of a writer.

Libraries, or at least their reference and academic sections, once served as a kind of first cut through the noise of the marketplace. Visiting a library was an education in itself, especially for a reader who took the time to ask for help from a librarian. The Internet, however, is nothing like a library. Rather, it's a giant repository where anyone can dump anything, from a first folio to a faked photograph, from a scientific treatise to pornography, from short bulletins of information to meaningless electronic graffiti. It's an environment almost entirely without regulation, which opens the door to content being driven by marketing, politics, and the uninformed decisions of other laypeople rather than the judgment of experts.

Can fifty million Elvis fans really be wrong? Of course they can.

In practice, this means that a search for information will cough up whatever algorithm is at work in a search engine, usually provided by for-profit companies using criteria that are largely opaque to the user. A youngster who takes to the Internet to satisfy a curiosity about tanks in World War II will more likely come up with the TV personality Bill O'Reilly's ridiculous—but best-selling—*Killing Patton* than with the chewier but more accurate work of the best military historians of the twentieth century. On the Internet as in life, money and popularity unfortunately count for a lot.

Plugging words into a browser window isn't research: it's asking questions of programmable machines that themselves cannot actually understand human beings. Actual research is hard, and for people raised in an environment of constant electronic stimulation, it's also boring. Research requires the ability to find authentic information, summarize it, analyze it, write it up, and present it to other people. It is not just the province of scientists and scholars, but a basic set of skills a high school education should teach every graduate because of its importance in any number of jobs and careers. But why bother with all that tedious hoop-jumping when the screen in front of us already has the answers, generated by the millions in just seconds, and beautifully laid out in colorful, authoritative-looking websites?

The deeper issue here is that the Internet is actually changing the way we read, the way we reason, even the way we *think*, and all for the worse. We expect information instantly. We want it broken down, presented in a way that is pleasing to our eye—no more of those small-type, fragile textbooks, thank you—and we want it to say what we want it to say. People do not do "research" so much as they "search for pretty pages online to provide answers they like with the least amount of effort and in the shortest time." The resulting flood of information, always of varying quality and sometimes of uncertain sanity, creates a veneer of knowledge that actually leaves people worse off than if they knew nothing at all. It's an old saying, but it's true: it ain't what you don't know that'll hurt you, it's what you do know that ain't so.

Finally, and perhaps most disturbingly, the Internet is making us meaner, shorter-fused, and incapable of conducting discussions where anyone learns anything. The major problem with instantaneous communication is that it's instantaneous. While the Internet enables more people to talk to each other than ever before—a distinctly new historical condition—everyone talking immediately to everyone else might not always be such a good idea. Sometimes, human beings need to pause and to reflect, to give themselves time to absorb information and to digest it. Instead, the Internet is an arena in which people can react without thinking, and thus in turn they become invested in defending their gut reactions rather than accepting new information or admitting a mistake—especially if it's a mistake pointed out by people with greater learning or experience.

WHAT'S FAKE ON THE INTERNET: EVERYTHING

There aren't enough pages in this or any other book to catalog the amount of bad information on the Internet. Miracle cures, conspiracy theories, faked documents, misattributed quotes—all of these and more are the crabgrass and weeds that have rapidly overgrown a global garden of knowledge. The healthier but less sturdy grasses and flowers don't stand a chance.

Durable old urban legends and conspiracy theories, for example, have been reconditioned and given new life online. We've all heard stories of alligators in the sewers, improbable celebrity deaths, and libraries that fell down because no one counted on the weight of the books in them, told and retold mostly by word of mouth. On the Internet, these stories are presented with beautiful layouts and graphics. They now spread so fast through email and social media that there are groups, like the admirable project at Snopes.com and other fact-checking organizations, who do nothing but stomp out these intellectual wastebasket fires all day long.

Unfortunately, they're shoveling against the tide. People do not come to the Internet so that their bad information can be corrected or their cherished theories disproven. Rather, they ask the electronic oracle to confirm them in their ignorance. In 2015 a *Washington Post* writer, Caitlin Dewey, worried that fact-checking could never defeat myths and hoaxes because "no one has the time or cognitive capacity to reason all the apparent nuances and discrepancies out."[3] In the end, she sighed, "debunking them doesn't do a darn thing."

Two months after she wrote those words, Dewey and the *Post* threw in the towel and ceased her weekly "what was fake on the Internet" column. There was no way to keep up with the madness, especially once hoaxers figured out how to make money out of spreading myths for precious clicks on websites. "Frankly," Dewey told her readers, "this column wasn't designed to address the current environment. This format doesn't make sense." More alarming were the conversations Dewey had with professional researchers who told her that "institutional distrust is so high right now, and cognitive bias so strong *always*, that the people who fall for hoax news stories are frequently only interested in consuming information that conforms with their views—even when it's demonstrably fake" (emphasis in the original).[4] Dewey and the *Post* fought the Internet, and the Internet won.

A lot of nonsense, particularly in politics, thrives on the reach and staying power of the Internet. A stubborn group of cranks might still believe the earth is flat or that Americans never walked on the moon, but eventually all the pictures from space are good enough for the rest of us. When it comes to urban legends like Barack Obama's African birth, George W. Bush's orchestration of the 9/11 terror attacks, or the US Treasury's secret plan to replace the dollar with a global currency, astronauts with cameras cannot help. Social media, websites, and chat rooms turn myths, stories heard from a "friend of a friend," and rumors into "facts."

As the British writer Damian Thompson has explained, instant communication is empowering people and groups dedicated to crackpot ideas, some of them quite dangerous. Thompson calls this "counterknowledge," in that it all flies in the face of science and is completely impervious to contrary evidence.

> Now, thanks to the internet . . . a rumor about the Antichrist can leap from Goths in Sweden to an extreme traditionalist Catholic

sect in Australia in a matter of seconds. Minority groups are becoming ever more tolerant of each other's eccentric doctrines. Contacts between black and white racists, which began tentatively decades ago, are now flourishing as the two groups swap conspiracy stories.[5]

In a slower, less-connected world, these kinds of groups could not reinforce their beliefs with instantaneous affirmation from other extremists online. The free movement of ideas is a powerful driver of democracy, but it always carries the risk that ignorant or evil people will bend the tools of mass communication to their own ends and propagate lies and myths that no expert can dispel.

Worse, bad information can stay online for years. Unlike yesterday's newspaper, online information is persistent and will pop up in subsequent searches after appearing just once. Even when falsehoods or mistakes are deleted at the source, they'll show up in an archive somewhere else. If the stories in them go "viral" and travel the electronic world in days, hours, or even minutes, they're effectively impossible to correct.

For example, in 2015 the conservative gadfly Allen West broke a make-believe scoop that President Obama was forcing members of the US military to pray like Muslims for Ramadan.[6] West's website juxtaposed a blaring headline—"Look what our troops are being FORCED to do"—against a picture of US soldiers kneeling with their heads to prayer mats. It was a startling visual and the story spread rapidly through social media.

No such thing had occurred. West had recycled a picture, taken several years earlier, of actual *Muslims* in the US military at prayer. Even after objections were raised to the misleading picture (by me, among others), West did not pull the story. It wouldn't have mattered, since it was already archived on blogs and other sites. People surfing the Internet who have neither the training nor the time to ascertain the provenance of the information will from now on come across not only the original story but also thousands of repetitions of it and never know that the whole thing is bunk.

Today, no one need be frustrated by fussy fact-checkers or resolute editors. Just as a nicely bound book could once mislead people into thinking its contents were authoritative, so, too, do slick websites provide the visual cues of reliability and authenticity that help uninformed readers spread bad information faster than any headline that William Randolph Hearst could have imagined. Experts and other professionals who insist on the dreary rigor of logic and factual accuracy cannot compete with a machine that will always give readers their preferred answer in sixteen million colors.

OF COURSE IT'S SAFE, I GOOGLED IT

Leaving aside slick, self-produced websites and the inevitable Facebook posts and memes that crowd the Internet, the search for quick answers has also facilitated the growth of entire industries based on selling bad ideas to the public and charging them for the privilege of being misinformed. I refer here not to online journalism—that's in the next chapter—but rather to the many outlets, often fronted by celebrities, that offer advice meant to supplant and replace established knowledge from experts.

Are you a woman concerned about your reproductive health? I have no experience in these matters, but I'm told by the women in my life that regular visits to the gynecologist are not something they particularly enjoy. Now that the Internet has arrived, however, women have an alternative source of information other than medical professionals: the actress Gwyneth Paltrow has her own "lifestyle magazine," GOOP.com, and she can discuss with you, in the privacy of your home or via your smartphone, the many things women can do to maintain their gynecological health, including steaming their vaginas.

If you're unfamiliar with this practice, Ms. Paltrow highly recommends it. "You sit on what is essentially a mini-throne," she said in 2014, "and a combination of infrared and mugwort steam cleanses your uterus, et al. It is an energetic release—not just a steam douche—that balances female hormone levels. If you're in [Los Angeles], you have to do it."

Actual gynecologists, however, do not recommend that women in Los Angeles or anywhere else steam any of their middle anatomy. A gynecologist named Jen Gunter took to her own (distinctly less glamorous) website with a clear alternative recommendation:

Steam isn't going to get into your uterus from your vagina unless you are using an attachment with some kind of pressure and MOST DEFINITELY NEVER EVER DO THAT. Mugwort or wormwood or whatever when steamed, either vaginally or on the vulva, can't possibly balance any reproductive hormones, regulate your menstrual cycle, treat depression, or cure infertility. Even steamed estrogen couldn't do that.

If you want to feel relaxed get a good massage.

If you want to relax your vagina, have an orgasm.[7]

Paltrow's site, however, is the epitome of hip, at least for a particular demographic. A satirist named Laura Hooper Beck captured the credulousness of Paltrow's fans perfectly: "Basically, if a doctor tells me to do it, I'm gonna take a hard pass. But if a skinny blonde in an ugly wig tells me that blowing hot air up my vagina is going to cure everything I've ever suffered from, including a bad relationship with my mother, well, then, I'm gonna listen to Gwyneth Paltrow, because girlfriend knows science."[8]

It's easy—too easy, I know—to make fun of vacuous celebrities, and since this is now more about steam and vaginas than I've ever written in my entire career, let's leave Paltrow and her health advice aside. There is nevertheless an important point here about the influence of the Internet on the death of expertise, because in an earlier time, a sensible American woman would have had to exert a great deal of initiative to find out how a Hollywood actress parboils her plumbing. Now, a woman searching for answers on everything from fashion to uterine cancer could accidentally spend more time reading GOOP than talking to her doctor.

Celebrities abusing their status as celebrities is nothing new, but the Internet amplifies their effect. While we might dismiss Jim Carrey's antivaccine rants as the extension of the comedian's already unconventional personality, people with more storied names get sucked into the electronic funhouse as well.

In 2015, the *New York Times* columnist Frank Bruni got a call from Robert F. Kennedy, Jr., son of the senator and presidential candidate assassinated in 1968. It was important, Kennedy told Bruni, that they meet. Kennedy was insistent about correcting Bruni on the issue of vaccination. Like too many other Americans, Kennedy was lugging around ill-informed paranoia about vaccines causing, in Kennedy's words, "a holocaust" among American children. (Indeed, Bruni noted that Carrey "has obviously done worship in the church of Robert Kennedy Jr.") Bruni later recalled of the meeting: "I had sided with the American Medical Association, the American Academy of Pediatrics, the National Institutes of Health and the Centers for Disease Control and Prevention. [But] Kennedy knew better."[9]

Kennedy, Carrey, and others did what many Americans do in such situations: they decided beforehand what they believed and then went looking for a source on the Internet to buttress that belief. As Bruni pointed out, "The anti-vaccine agitators can always find a

renegade researcher or random 'study' to back them up. This is erudition in the age of cyberspace: You surf until you reach the conclusion
you're after. You click your way to validation, confusing the presence
of a website with the plausibility of an argument."

This kind of Internet grazing—mistakenly called "research" by
laypeople—makes interactions between experts and professionals
arduous. Once again, confirmation bias is a major culprit: although
many stories on the Internet are false or inaccurate, the one-in-a-
billion story where Google gets it right and the experts get it wrong
goes viral. In a tragic case in 2015, for example, a British teenager was
misdiagnosed by doctors who told her to "stop Googling her symptoms."[10] The patient insisted she had a rare cancer, a possibility the
doctors dismissed. She was right, they were wrong, and she died.

The British teen's story made big news, and a rare mistake likely
convinced a great many people to be their own doctors. Of course,
people who have died because they used a computer to misdiagnose
their heart disease as indigestion never make the front page. But none
of that matters. These David-and-Goliath stories (a teenager against
her team of doctors) feed the public's insatiable confirmation bias
and fuel their cynicism in established knowledge while bolstering
their false hopes that the solutions to their problems are just a few
mouse clicks away.

Once upon a time, books were at least a marginal barrier to the
rapid dissemination of misinformation, because books took time to
produce and required some investment and judgment on the part
of a publisher. "I read it in a book" meant "this probably isn't crazy,
because a company spent the money to put it between two covers and
publish it." This was never entirely true about books, of course; some
of them are carefully fact-checked, peer reviewed, and edited, while
others are just slammed between covers and rushed to bookstores.

Nonetheless, books from reputable presses go through at least a
basic process of negotiation between authors, editors, reviewers, and

publishers, including the book you're reading right now. Books from self-published "vanity presses," by contrast, are looked down upon by reviewers and readers alike, and with good reason. Today, however, the Internet is the equivalent of hundreds of millions of vanity presses all cranking out whatever anyone with a keyboard wants to say, no matter how stupid—or how vile. (As *National Journal's* Ron Fournier has said, in the age of the Internet, "every bigot is a publisher.") There's a fair amount of wisdom and information hiding out there, but there's no escaping Sturgeon's Law.

Accessing the Internet can actually make people dumber than if they had never engaged a subject at all. The very act of searching for information makes people think they've learned something, when in fact they're more likely to be immersed in yet more data they do not understand. This happens because after enough time surfing, people no longer can distinguish between things that may have flashed before their eyes and things they actually *know*.

Seeing words on a screen is not the same as reading or understanding them. When a group of experimental psychologists at Yale investigated how people use the Internet, they found that "people who search for information on the Web emerge from the process with an inflated sense of how much they know—even regarding topics that are unrelated to the ones they Googled."[11] This is a kind of electronic version of the Dunning-Kruger Effect, in which the least competent people surfing the web are the least likely to realize that they're not learning anything.

People looking for information, say, about "fossil fuels" might end up scrolling past many pages on a related term, like "dinosaur fossils." After enough websites fly by, they eventually lose the ability to recognize that whatever they just read about either subject isn't something they actually knew before they looked at a screen. Instead, they just assume that they knew things about both dinosaurs and diesel fuel because they're just that smart. Unfortunately, people thinking they're smart because they searched the Internet is like thinking they're good swimmers because they got wet walking through a rainstorm.

The Yale team somewhat gently described this problem as "mistaking outsourced knowledge for internal knowledge." A blunter way of putting it would be to say that people can't remember most of what they see while blowing through dozens of mouse clicks. As the writer Tom Jacobs observed, searching "appears to trigger an utterly unjustified belief in one's own knowledge—which, given the increasingly popular habit of instinctively looking online to answer virtually any question, is a bit terrifying."[12]

It may well be terrifying, but it's definitely annoying. These mistaken assertions of gained knowledge can make the job of an expert nearly impossible. There is no way to enlighten people who believe they've gained a decade's worth of knowledge because they've spent a morning with a search engine. Few words in a discussion with a layperson can make an expert's heart sink like hearing "I've done some research."

How can exposure to so much information fail to produce at least some kind of increased baseline of knowledge, if only by electronic osmosis? How can people read so much yet retain so little? The answer is simple: few people are actually reading what they find.

As a University College of London (UCL) study found, people don't actually read the articles they encounter during a search on the Internet. Instead, they glance at the top line or the first few sentences and then move on. Internet users, the researchers noted, "are not reading online in the traditional sense; indeed, there are signs that new forms of 'reading' are emerging as users 'power browse' horizontally through titles, contents pages and abstracts going for quick wins. It almost seems that they go online to avoid reading in the traditional sense."[13] This is actually the *opposite* of reading, aimed not so much at learning but at winning arguments or confirming a preexisting belief.

Children and younger people are especially vulnerable to this tendency. The UCL study suggested that this is because they "have unsophisticated mental maps of what the internet is, often failing to appreciate that it is a collection of networked resources from different providers," and so they spend little time actually "evaluating information, either for relevance, accuracy or authority." These youngsters "do not find library-sponsored resources intuitive and therefore prefer to use Google or Yahoo! instead," because these services "offer a familiar, if simplistic solution, for their study needs." Teachers and other experts are not immune from the same temptations. "Power browsing and viewing," according to the study, "appear to be the norm for all. The popularity of abstracts among older researchers rather gives the game away."

"Society," the UCL study's authors conclude, "is dumbing down."

This already serious problem might even be a bit scarier than it looks. Internet users tend to gravitate toward, and to believe, whichever results of a search come up first in the rankings, mostly without regard to the origins of those results. After all, if the search engine trusted it enough to rank it highly, it must be worthwhile. This is why anyone pushing content on the Internet looks at ways to improve where their product shows up in a search: if you sell soup, you'll do what you can to rattle a search engine so that people looking for soup recipes are instead steered toward coupons for your brand of soup.

But what if you're selling something more important than soup, like a political candidate? There is at least some evidence that search-engine rankings can alter people's perceptions of political reality. In 2014, two psychologists completed a study of what they called the "search engine manipulation effect" and claimed that their tests showed an ability "to boost the proportion of people who favored any candidate by between 37 and 63 percent after just one search session," and that this potentially constitutes a "serious threat to the democratic system of government."[14] It's too early to say that search engines are undermining democracy—at least yet—but it's hard to argue with the reality that most laypeople can no longer tell the difference between real information and whatever a search engine burps up.

THE WISDOM OF MEGA-CROWDS

Obviously, nonexperts are not always wrong about everything, nor are experts always right. Once in a blue moon, a teenager can get it right and a team of doctors can get it wrong. Experts are important, but ordinary people do manage to live their lives every day without the advice of professors, intellectuals, and other know-it-alls. The Internet, used properly, can help laypeople reach out to each other for basic information that might be too costly or difficult to access from professionals. In fact, the Internet, like the stock market and other mechanisms that aggregate the public's guesses and hunches about complicated matters, can produce moments where laypeople outperform experts.

The way in which a lot of wrong guesses can be milled into one big right guess is a well-established phenomenon. Unfortunately, the way people think the Internet can serve as a way of crowd-sourcing knowledge conflates the perfectly reasonable idea of what the writer James Surowiecki has called "the wisdom of crowds" with the completely unreasonable idea that the crowds are wise because each member of the mob is also wise.

Sometimes, people without any specialized knowledge can make a better guess at something in a large group than any one member of the group. This tends to be true especially for decisions where the amalgamation of a lot of guesses might produce a better aggregate guess than any one expert's opinion. Surowiecki recounted the story, for example, of an English county fair in 1906, when the public was asked to guess the weight of an ox. The average of the guesses was better than any one person's guess and ended up almost exactly on the mark.[15] Likewise, the world's stock exchanges collectively are generally better than any one stock analyst at betting on stocks.

There are a lot of reasons crowds are better at estimation than individuals, including the way in which a large number of guesses among a lot of people can help to wash out a certain amount of confirmation bias, misperception, or any other number of errors. It also allows people with only partial information to bring those small amounts of knowledge to a problem and help solve it, much in the way a thousand people can complete a huge jigsaw puzzle even though each of them may only have a few pieces.

To take one example, the unbiased eye of the crowd actually cost one of the most prominent journalists in America his job. In 2004, at the height of a US presidential election, longtime CBS news anchor Dan Rather and his producers went on the air with a story about incumbent President George W. Bush's military record. CBS claimed to have documents from the early 1970s proving that Bush ditched his Air National Guard unit and never finished his required service. Bush, a commander-in-chief who at that point had led America into two major wars, was running against Senator John Kerry, a decorated war hero, and the charge was naturally electrifying in a race that focused heavily on military issues.

Bush supporters objected to what they claimed was dodgy sourcing and sloppy reporting, but in the end ordinary people on the Internet, not angry partisans, brought the story down. Laypeople with no experience in journalism but who spent plenty of time around computers noticed that the font in the documents closely matched those generated by Microsoft's Word software. Obviously, in 1971 the Air Force used typewriters. Microsoft and its programs didn't exist then. The documents had to be fakes.

Faced with this crowd-sourced challenge to the story, CBS ordered an investigation. The network ended up repudiating the documents and the story. The segment's producer was fired. Dan Rather, convinced to this day that he was right and everyone else was wrong, retired and sued his old employer. He lost.

So who needs experts? If we ask the same question enough times, or set enough people to work on the same subject, why not rely on their collective wisdom instead of seeking the flawed or biased opinion of only a handful of self-anointed Wise Ones? If one person is smart and a hundred smarter, then a billion communicating instantly must be even smarter still.

Enthusiasts of the online reference site Wikipedia, among others, have argued that the future rests with this kind of collective knowledge rather than with the expert vetting of references and information. In theory, with a public and open encyclopedia to which anyone can contribute, the sheer number of people watching over each entry should root out error and bias. The articles would be geared toward the inquisitive minds of ordinary human beings rather than the narrow interests of a panel of scholars or editors. Not only would the entries be in a constant and evolving state of accuracy, but the articles themselves by definition would constitute a collection about things that actually engage the readers instead of a systematic but useless compendium of esoteric knowledge.

Unfortunately, things have not always worked out that way, and Wikipedia is a good lesson in the limits of the Internet-driven displacement of expertise. As it turns out, writing articles about any number of complicated subjects is a lot more difficult than guessing the weight of a bull. Although many well-intentioned people have contributed their time as Wikipedia editors, for example, some of them were also employed by companies and celebrity public relations firms that had an obvious interest in how things appeared in an encyclopedia for the masses. (Nine out of ten Wikipedia contributors are also male, which would likely raise flags among readers—if readers knew it.)

Even with the best of intentions, crowd-sourced projects like Wikipedia suffer from an important but often unremarked distinction between laypeople and professionals: volunteers do what interests them at any given time, while professionals employ their expertise every day. A hobby is not the same thing as a career. As a saying attributed to the British writer Alastair Cooke goes, "Professionals are people who can do their best work when they don't feel like it." The enthusiasm of interested amateurs is not a consistent substitute for the judgment of experts.

Wikipedia's initial efforts fell prey to inconsistency and a lack of oversight, which is exactly what might have been expected from a group homework project. A researcher who studied these trends suggested that Wikipedia after 2007 should have changed its motto from "the encyclopedia that anyone can edit" to "the encyclopedia that anyone who understands the norms, socializes him or herself, dodges the impersonal wall of semi-automated rejection and still wants to voluntarily contribute his or her time and energy can edit."[16]

Eventually, Wikipedia imposed stricter editing controls, but those restrictions in turn discouraged new contributors. As a 2013 article in the *MIT Technology Review* noted, the size of the volunteer force that built Wikipedia and "must defend it against vandalism, hoaxes, and manipulation" has "shrunk by more than a third since 2007 and is still shrinking." Wikipedia still struggles to maintain the quality of its own articles, even measured by its own criteria:

> Among the significant problems that aren't getting resolved is the site's skewed coverage: its entries on Pokemon and female porn stars are comprehensive, but its pages on female novelists or places in sub-Saharan Africa are sketchy. Authoritative entries remain elusive. Of the 1,000 articles that the project's own volunteers have

tagged as forming the core of a good encyclopedia, most don't earn even Wikipedia's own middle-ranking quality scores.[17]

Wikipedia does have "featured articles," which must be "well-written," "comprehensive," and "well-researched," including "a thorough and representative survey of the relevant literature," with claims verified against "high-quality reliable sources."

In other words, what Wikipedia really wants is for its best pieces to be just like peer-reviewed scholarship—only without using actual peers. Peer review is a difficult beast to manage even in optimal conditions, with editors trying to assign oversight to the best in each field while avoiding professional rivalries and other conflicts of interest. Translating this process into a project for millions of people with minimal supervision was an unreasonable goal. For something like Wikipedia to work, practically every subject-matter expert in the world would have to be willing to babysit every entry.

Of course, if measured by readership, Wikipedia works just fine. And on some subjects, Wikipedia is a perfectly serviceable source of information. As the MIT article noted, articles are skewed "toward technical, Western, and male-dominated subject matter," so when it comes to tangible—and, more important, uncontroversial—information, Wikipedia has succeeded in bringing together a lot of data in a reliable and stable format. (Personally, I love that Wikipedia is a great source for the plot of almost any movie, no matter how small or obscure.) If you want to know who discovered strontium, who attended the Washington Naval Conference of 1925, or a quick explanation of last year's Nobel Prizes, Wikipedia is a lot better than a random search engine.

Once any kind of political agenda gets involved, things get a lot dicier. The Wikipedia entry on the chemical weapon Sarin, for example, became an arena for infighting among people who had conflicting agendas over whether the Syrian government used the substance on its own people. Even the basic science fell under attack. A London-based analyst, Dan Kaszeta—the Sarin expert I mentioned in the last chapter who learned a hard lesson about trying to help a college student—told me in late 2015 that

> if someone were to rely on the current Wikipedia page for accurate information about the chemical warfare agent Sarin, they would be misled by half-truths and numerous vague statements not supported by the supplied references. Some of the information on the Wiki page, while technically correct in some aspects, is worded in ways that are misleading. Some of the statements are false.

Kaszeta added that he "spent many hours after the 2013 use of Sarin in Syria correcting misconceptions about Sarin, many of which were doubtless attributable to errors and half-truths on relevant Wikipedia pages."

What people misunderstand about Wikipedia and other online resources, and about the wisdom of crowds in general, is that knowledge is about a lot more than assembling a box of factoids or making coin-toss predictions. Facts do not speak for themselves. Sources like Wikipedia are valuable for basic data as a kind of perpetually updating almanac, but they're not much help on more complex matters.

Crowds can be wise. Not everything, however, is amenable to the vote of a crowd. The Internet creates a false sense that the opinions of many people are tantamount to a "fact." How a virus is transmitted from one human being to another is not the same thing as guessing how many jelly beans are in a glass barrel. As the comedian John Oliver has complained, you don't need to gather opinions on a fact: "You might as well have a poll asking: 'Which number is bigger, 15 or 5?' or 'Do owls exist?' or 'Are there hats?'"

Likewise, public policy is not a parlor game of prediction; it is about long-term choices rooted in thoughtful consideration of costs and alternatives. Asking crowds to guess about specific events in short-term, mental dart–throwing matches just isn't much help when trying to navigate in difficult policy waters. "Will Bashar Assad of Syria use chemical weapons at some point in 2013" is an even bet, like putting a chip on one color in roulette. It's a yes-or-no question, and at some point, you've either won or lost the bet. It's not the same question as "*Why* would Bashar Assad use chemical weapons?" and it is light-years away from the dilemma of "What should America *do* if Bashar Assad uses chemical weapons?" The Internet, however, conflates all three of these questions, and it turns every complicated issue into a poll with a one-click radio button offering a quick solution.

The ease with which people can weigh in on these issues, and even sometimes get a prediction about them right when experts might have been wrong, bolts another layer of anti-intellectual armor to the resistance among laypeople to views more informed than their own.

I UNFRIEND YOU

Learning new things requires patience and the ability to listen to other people. The Internet and social media, however, are making us less social and more confrontational. Online, as in life, people are clustering into small echo chambers, preferring only to talk to those with whom they already agree. The writer Bill Bishop called this "the big sort" in a 2008 book, noting that Americans now choose to live, work, and socialize more with people like themselves in every way. The same thing happens on the Internet.

We're not just associating with people more like ourselves, we're actively breaking ties with everyone else, especially on social media. A 2014 Pew research study found that liberals are more likely than conservatives to block or unfriend people with whom they disagreed, but mostly because conservatives already tended to have fewer people with whom they disagreed in their online social circles in the first place. (Or as a *Washington Post* review of the study put it, conservatives have "lower levels of ideological diversity in their online ecosystem.")[18] Liberals were also somewhat more likely to end a friendship over politics in real life, but the overall trend is one of ideological segregation enabled by the ability to end a friendship with a click instead of a face-to-face discussion.

This unwillingness to hear out others not only makes us all more unpleasant with each other in general, but also makes us less able to think, to argue persuasively, and to accept correction when we're wrong. When we are incapable of sustaining a chain of reasoning past a few mouse clicks, we cannot tolerate even the smallest challenge to our beliefs or ideas. This is dangerous because it both undermines the role of knowledge and expertise in a modern society and corrodes the basic ability of people to get along with each other in a democracy.

Underlying much of this ill temper is a false sense of equality and the illusion of egalitarianism created by the immediacy of social media. I have a Twitter account and a Facebook page, and so do you, so we're peers, aren't we? After all, if a top reporter at a major newspaper, a diplomat at the Kennedy School, a scientist at a research hospital, and your Aunt Rose from Reno all have an online presence, then all of their views are just so many messages speeding past your eyes. Every opinion is only as good as the last posting on a home page.

In the age of social media, people using the Internet assume that everyone is equally intelligent or informed merely by virtue of being online. As the *New York Times* movie critic A. O. Scott has put it,

On the Internet, everyone is a critic—a Yelp-fueled takedown artist, an Amazon scholar, a cheerleader empowered by social media to Like and to Share. The inflated, always suspect authority of ink-stained wretches like me has been leveled by digital anarchy. Who needs a cranky nag when you have a friendly algorithm telling you, based on your previous purchases, that there is something You May Also Like, and legions of Facebook friends affirming the wisdom of your choice?[19]

The anonymity of social media tempts users into arguing as though every participant is the same, a group of peers starting from the same level of background and education. This is a rule very few people would use in real life, but on the Internet, the intellectual narcissism of the random commenter displaces the norms that usually govern face-to-face interactions.

This strange combination of distance and intimacy poisons conversation. Reasonable arguments require participants to be honest and well intentioned. Actual proximity builds trust and understanding. We are not just brains in a tank processing disparate pieces of data; we hear out another person in part by relying on multiple visual and auditory cues, not just by watching their words stream past our eyes. Teachers, especially, know that the same material delivered at a distance or on a screen has a different impact than personal interaction with a student who can ask questions, furrow a brow, or show an expression of sudden understanding.

Distance and anonymity remove patience and presumptions of goodwill. Rapid access to information and the ability to speak without having to listen, combined with the "keyboard courage" that allows people to say things to each other electronically they would never say in person, kill conversation. As the writer Andrew Sullivan has noted, this is in part because nothing on the Internet is dispositive, and so every participant in a debate demands to be taken as seriously as every other.

And what mainly fuels this is precisely what the Founders feared about democratic culture: feeling, emotion, and narcissism, rather than reason, empiricism, and public-spiritedness. Online debates become personal, emotional, and irresolvable almost as soon as they begin. Yes, occasional rational points still fly back and forth, but there are dramatically fewer elite arbiters to establish which of those points is actually true or valid or relevant.[20]

Twitter, Facebook, Reddit, and other online sites can be outlets for intelligent discussion, but too often these and other venues become nothing more than a fusillade of assertions, certainties, poor information, and insults rather than actual exchanges.

To be sure, the Internet is also facilitating conversations among people who might never otherwise have encountered each other. Introverts might argue that an arena like Reddit or the comments section of an online journal opens the door for more interaction from people who in an earlier time might have been reluctant to engage in a public discussion. Unfortunately, allowing anyone to express a view means that almost anyone *will* express a view, which is why so many publications, from the *Toronto Sun* to the *Daily Beast*, have been shutting down their online comments sections.

All of this interaction is doing little to loosen the attachment of laypeople to misinformation. In fact, the problem may be worse than we think. When confronted by hard evidence that they're wrong, some people will simply double-down on their original assertion rather than accept their error. This is the "backfire effect," in which people redouble their efforts to keep their own internal narrative consistent, no matter how clear the indications that they're wrong.[21]

The Internet, as David Dunning points out, sharpens this problem in multiple ways, not least that refuting a dumb idea requires repeating it at least once in the course of the discussion. This creates a minefield for teachers and other experts who risk confirming a mistake merely by acknowledging its existence:

Then, of course, there is the problem of rampant misinformation in places that, unlike classrooms, are hard to control—like the Internet and news media. In these Wild West settings, it's best *not* to repeat common misbeliefs at all. Telling people that Barack Obama is not a Muslim fails to change many people's minds, because they frequently remember everything that was said—except for the crucial qualifier "not."[22]

Experts trying to confront this kind of stubborn ignorance may think they're helping, when in fact they're basically trying to throw water on a grease fire. It doesn't work and only spreads the damage around.

The Internet is the largest anonymous medium in human history. The ability to argue from a distance, and the cheapened sense of equality it provides, is corroding trust and respect among all of us, experts and laypeople alike. Alone in front of the keyboard but awash in websites, newsletters, and online groups dedicated to confirming any and every idea, the Internet has politically and intellectually mired millions of Americans in their own biases. Social media outlets such as Facebook amplify this echo chamber; as Megan McArdle wrote in 2016, "Even if we are not deliberately blocking people who disagree with us, Facebook curates our feeds so that we get more of the stuff we 'like.' What do we 'like'? People and posts that agree with us."[23]

This is especially dangerous now that social media like Facebook and Twitter have become the primary sources of news and information for many Americans, and experts trying to break through this shell of political insularity and self-assured ignorance do so at their peril. It's difficult enough to argue with one person who has gotten something wrong; it's quite another to try to reason with someone as they gather pretty websites as "evidence" and marshal legions of anonymous, like-minded social media friends with equally uninformed views for support. Meanwhile, scholars and professionals who insist on logic, foundational knowledge, and basic rules about sources risk condemnation by twenty-first-century online users as nothing more than elitists who do not understand the miracles of the Information Age.

Websites and Internet polls might be unreliable, but reporters can dig out the truth instead of getting pulled down in the whirlpool. Journalists can still serve as the arbiters of all this chaos, using the careful tools of investigation, sourcing, and fact-checking.

Or, as we'll see in the next chapter, perhaps not.

The "New" New Journalism, and Lots of It

Charlie: Mom, I find it interesting that you refer to the *Weekly World News* as "The Paper." The paper contains *facts.*

May: This paper contains facts. And this paper has the eighth highest circulation in the whole wide world. Right? Plenty of facts. "Pregnant man gives birth." That's a fact.

So I Married an Axe Murderer

I READ IT IN THE PAPER

Did you know that chocolate can help you lose weight? Sure you do. You read it in the paper. In fact, you might have read it in several papers, and woe to any expert, including a doctor, who might have told you otherwise. After all, hiding the miraculous weight-decreasing qualities of the tastiest thing in the world is just the kind of thing experts would do. Thankfully, a German scientist, Johannes Bohannon of the Institute of Diet and Health, wrote a paper that was published in a journal and then joyfully covered in press throughout the world, and he verified what we have all suspected all along: chocolate is really good for you.

Except Johannes Bohannon doesn't exist. Neither does the Institute of Diet and Health. The journal that published the paper is real, but apparently it is less than scrupulous about things like peer review and editing. "Johannes" Bohannon was in fact a journalist named John Bohannon, who was (in Bohannon's words) "part of a team of gonzo journalists and one doctor" who wanted to "demonstrate just how easy it is to turn bad science into the big headlines behind diet fads."[1]

So chocolate won't make you thinner. But did you know that the West Bank and Gaza, the occupied Palestinian areas on two sides of Israel, are connected by a bridge, one on which the Israelis sometimes maliciously limit Palestinian traffic? You might well have read that one in the "news," too. In 2014, the online journal *Vox*—which bills itself as a source that explains complicated issues to everyone else—listed "11 crucial facts to understand the Israel-Gaza crisis." Fact number one included the Gaza–West Bank bridge.

It doesn't exist.

Vox corrected its error—the writer claimed he'd seen an article about a proposed bridge but didn't realize it was never built—but not before critics had a good laugh at *Vox*'s expense. As the writer Mollie Hemingway noted, no journalist can avoid the occasional mistake, and few can be experts in any one subject, but the "bridge to Gaza" was not "about getting a name wrong or not knowing about some arcane detail," it required being "completely unfamiliar with the area."[2] As is the case with all corrections, one can only wonder how many people remember the story but not the correction.

Vox is a regular target for such criticism, and for good reason. In early 2016 *Vox* ran a headline that said, "The most radical thing the Black Panthers did was give kids free breakfast." The Panthers, a radical group formed in the late 1960s that fused black nationalism and Marxism-Leninism, were involved in multiple cases of violence and murder, including shoot-outs with the police. They were not exactly the friendly staff of a day-care center. The *Vox* piece prompted the *Daily Beast* columnist Michael Moynihan to tweet, "Remember when 'explainer' writers had to know something about what they were explaining? Nor do I."

So, chocolate isn't a weight-loss miracle, and there's no bridge between Gaza and the West Bank. Maybe the Panthers were a bit rougher than we remember. But perhaps you weren't aware of the real meaning of Easter to Christians, which celebrates the resurrection of Jesus Christ directly up to Heaven. The *New York Times* said so in 2013. Now, the Gospels make some sort of reference to Jesus walking around for a bit first, which is probably the version that local parish priests and ministers relate every spring. Those members of the clergy might be smart, and there might even be some theology degrees scattered in among them, but who are they to argue with the *New York Times*?

There are well over a billion Christians in the world, and amazingly enough, a few of them caught the error. The *Times* quietly ran what might be one of the most understated corrections in newspaper history: "An earlier version of this article mischaracterized the Christian holiday of Easter. It is the celebration of Jesus's resurrection from the dead, not his resurrection into heaven."[3] That is a more accurate statement of the official version, but to get it wrong in the first place means that someone at the *Times* had no idea about the story of the "Doubting Thomas" or of other common cultural references derived from moments in the New Testament where Jesus appeared in person, rather than taking the direct elevator to the top floor on Easter Sunday.

If keeping up with all this misinformation tires you out, you can always retreat back to some fine literature and perhaps read one of the great novels by Evelyn Waugh. After all, Waugh was listed in 2016 by *TIME* magazine as one of the "100 greatest female writers of all time," so her work might well be worth a look.

Except, of course, that Evelyn Waugh (who lived until 1966) was a man.

These kinds of howlers aren't just a product of the Internet era. A front-page story in the *Washington Post* from more than thirty years ago, for example, referred to Ireland as a member of NATO, which would have been a shock not only to the famously neutral people of Ireland, but to both the Soviet Union and the United States. Everyone makes mistakes, including experts, journalists, editors, and fact-checkers. These things happen.

Unfortunately, however, these kinds of mistakes happen a lot more frequently in the new world of twenty-first-century journalism. Worse, because of the Internet, misinformation spreads a lot faster and sticks around a lot longer. In a world of constant information, delivered at high speed and available twenty-four hours a day, journalism is now sometimes as much a contributor to the death of expertise as it is a defense against it.

I realize it seems churlish to complain about the feast of news and information brought to us by the Information Age, but I'm going to complain anyway. Changes in journalism, like the increased access to the Internet and to college education, have had unexpectedly corrosive effects on the relationship between laypeople and experts. Instead of making people better informed, much of what passes for news in the twenty-first century often leaves laypeople—and sometimes experts—even more confused and ornery.

Experts face a vexing challenge: there's more news available, and yet people seem less informed, a trend that goes back at least a quarter century. Paradoxically, it is a problem that is worsening rather than dissipating. Not only do people know less about the world around them, they are less interested in it, despite the availability of more information than ever before.

As long ago as 1990, for example, a study conducted by the Pew Trust warned that disengagement from important public questions was actually worse among people under thirty, the group that should have been most receptive to then-emerging sources of information like cable television and electronic media. This was a distinct change in American civic culture, as the Pew study noted:

> Over most of the past five decades younger members of the public have been at least as well informed as older people. In 1990, that is no longer the case.... Those under 30 know less than younger people once did. And, they are less interested in what's happening in the larger world around them. Social scientists and pollsters have long recognized that younger people have usually been somewhat less attuned to politics and serious issues. But the difference has been greatly sharpened.[4]

Those respondents are now themselves middle-aged, and their children are faring no better. A 2011 University of Chicago study found that America's college graduates "failed to make significant gains in critical thinking and complex reasoning during their four years of college," but more worrisome, they "also failed to develop dispositions associated with civic engagement."[5] Like their parents, these young people were not only less informed than we might have expected, but they were also less interested in applying what little they might have learned to their responsibilities as citizens.

Thus, when a layperson's riposte to an expert consists of "I read it in the paper" or "I saw it on the news," it may not mean very much. Indeed, the information may not have come from "the news" or "the paper" at all, but from something that only looks like a news source. More likely, such an answer means "I saw something from a source I happen to like and it told me something I wanted to hear." At that point, the discussion has nowhere to go; the original issue is submerged or lost in the effort to untangle which piece of misinformation is driving the conversation in the first place.

How did this happen? How can people be more resistant to facts and knowledge in a world where they are constantly barraged with facts and knowledge? The short answer where journalism is concerned—in an explanation that could be applied to many modern innovations—is that technology collided with capitalism and gave people what they wanted, even when it wasn't good for them.

I realize that criticizing journalism and the modern news media puts me at risk of violating the Prime Directive for experts: never tell other experts how to do their jobs. While I'm not an expert in journalism, however, I am a consumer of its products. I rely on the news as part of my own profession, both as a teacher and as a policy analyst. I have to navigate the hurdles every expert faces in communicating complex events and ideas to laypeople every day. In some ways, the modern media have made my job—helping people make sense of a complicated world—harder than it was even twenty years ago.

TOO MUCH OF A GOOD THING IS TOO MUCH

The challenges to expertise and established knowledge created by modern journalism all flow from the same problem that afflicts so much of modern American life: there is too much of everything.

There are more sources of news in the twenty-first century than ever before. Thanks to radio, television, and the Internet, people can access those sources easily and share them electronically; thanks to universal education, they can read them and discuss them more widely than in the past. It's a banquet of information, served up with various kinds of garnish on any number of platters. So why do people remain resolutely ignorant and uninformed, and reject news, along with expert opinion and advice, even when it's all delivered to them almost without effort? Because there's too much of it, and it is too closely fused with entertainment.

Today, anyone with electricity is up to their neck in news from every direction whenever they want it. Most newspapers and local television stations in America are instantaneously available in electronic format and are updated regularly. Consumers with access to satellite or cable television—which is to say, almost anyone in most of the developed world—can take their pick of dozens of newscasts from around the planet. Today, there is a news source for every taste and political view, with the line between journalism and entertainment intentionally obscured to drive ratings and clicks.

To put this in perspective, the average American home in 1960 had three television stations available to it along with eight radio stations, one newspaper, and three or four magazines.[6] By 2014, the Nielsen rating organization estimated that the average US home had 189 television channels (60 more than it had in 2008) with consumers tuning in consistently to about 17 of those channels. Add to this the amount of media delivered to consumers through their mobile devices and home computers, estimated by a researcher at the San Diego Supercomputer Center in 2015 to be the equivalent of nine DVDs worth of data per person per day. This much information would take the average person more than fifteen hours a day to see or hear.[7]

But *more* of everything does not mean *more quality* in everything. (Sturgeon's Law is inescapable everywhere.) To say that the citizens of the United States now have many more sources of news than ever before is like saying that they also have more dining choices than ever before: it's true, but it doesn't mean that anyone's getting healthier by eating in America's nearly three hundred thousand cheap chain restaurants and fast-food outlets.

Affluence and technology lowered the barriers to journalism and to the creation of journalistic enterprises in the late twentieth and early twenty-first centuries, with predictable consequences. More media meant more competition; more competition meant dividing the audience into identifiable political and demographic niches; more opportunity at more outlets meant more working journalists, regardless of whether they were competent to cover important issues. All of this competition was at the behest of the American consumer, who wanted everything simpler, faster, prettier, and more entertaining.

Forty years ago the media were more conscientious about separating "news" from everything else. This also meant, however, that the "news" was in fact not a fully realized picture of the world. Instead, it was a carefully curated and edited stream of information. The small number of networks and news outlets, and the relatively tiny amount of time devoted to news on television, meant that the public saw the world as it was viewed by the corporations who ran the networks. News organizations had to try to cover the broadest and most demographically marketable audience, and so newscasts in the United States through the 1960s and 1970s were remarkably alike, with calming, authoritative figures like Walter Cronkite and Harry Reasoner reporting even the most awful events with aplomb and detachment.

However, this also meant that not everything counted as news. There was more corporate and elite control over the news before the 1990s—and that wasn't entirely a bad thing. When each network only had thirty minutes in which to capture the day's events, an arms control treaty with the Soviet Union was likely to get more play than which celebrities were getting divorces. Networks rarely broke into their programming with news except for the dread-inducing "special reports," which were usually about a major disaster of some kind. If something important happened in the world, everyone in America had to wait for the paperboy—a solemn childhood office I occupied in the early 1970s—or for their evening newscast.

Not only is there more news, but there is more interactivity with the news. Americans no longer read whatever fits into a set number of newspaper columns, nor do they sit passively in front of a television and receive a digest of events. Instead, they're asked, constantly, what they think of the information they're being given, often in real time. Twitter and Facebook are the new news tickers, crowd-sourced streams of information that break news and spread rumors with equal force. Talk shows and news broadcasts—increasingly difficult to distinguish from each other—often ask viewers to weigh in via social media or on a website instant poll, with the clear assumption that the audience is watching the news with a smartphone, tablet, or laptop nearby.

Interactivity is also driving the selection of stories, which can make one yearn for the days of corporate editorial control. When the *Dallas Morning News* hired a new editor in 2015, it reached out to Mike Wilson, a journalist from the Internet news site FiveThirtyEight, which specializes in "data-driven" stories rather than breaking news. "I think what we need to throw out are some old notions of what our readers need," Wilson said in an interview after he was hired.

> We just have to be more responsive to what the audience wants.
> I think the tradition in newspapers has been that we have set the
> agenda and we've told readers what we think they want to know.
> I think we need to come down off of that mountain a little bit and
> ask people, involve people in the conversation a little bit more.[8]

Larger papers agree. "How can you say you don't care what your customers think?" Alan Murray, who oversees online news at the *Wall Street Journal*, said in 2015. "We care a lot about what our readers think. But our readers also care a lot about our editorial judgment. So we're always trying to balance the two."[9]

Journalists and their editors swear up and down that they are not allowing the public to drive their selection and coverage of stories, but that is hard to believe. A 2010 *New York Times* report tried to put the best face on it after describing how closely the *Washington Post* and other papers monitor their web traffic: "Rather than corrupt news judgment by causing editors to pander to the basest reader interests, the availability of this technology so far seems to be leading to more surgical decisions about how to cover a topic so it becomes more appealing to an online audience."[10] The *Post's* readers, the story proudly notes, were less interested in the 2010 British elections than in Crocs (an ugly shoe fad), but that didn't make the *Post* alter its coverage. That might be a relief to hear, but it is unsettling that this assurance had to be given at all.

To judge from the public's awareness of major issues, what readers need is not more input into the stories, but basic information, including the occasional map with a "You Are Here" pointer on it. It is difficult to imagine a media outlet in a less competitive, less crowded market asking its readers what they want in the same way, but in a market glutted by information, it was only a matter of time before the tables were turned and journalists were asking readers what they would like to read instead of informing them about things they must know.

This fusing of entertainment, news, punditry, and citizen participation is a chaotic mess that does not inform people so much as it creates the illusion of being informed. Just as clicking through endless Internet pages makes people think they're learning new things, watching countless hours of television and scrolling through hundreds of headlines is producing laypeople who believe—erroneously—that they understand the news. Worse, their daily interaction with so much media makes them resistant to learning anything more that takes too long or isn't entertaining enough.

This information overload isn't just overwhelming laypeople either. The fact is that everyone is drowning in data, including professionals who pay a lot of attention to news and who try to be discriminating consumers. In 2015 the *National Journal* surveyed people it called "Washington Insiders," mostly composed of congressional staff, federal government executives, and private-sector public affairs professionals, and asked them how they get their news. According to the study, it was now easier than ever for these "insiders" to obtain information, "but harder than ever for them to make sense of it all." Professionals in Washington, like everyone else, were "somewhat paralyzed" by a "glut" of news that left them "lacking confidence in individual sources and information."[11]

If professional policymakers and staff in Washington can't make sense of the news, how can anyone else? Who has enough time to sort through it all? The *National Journal* study even nodded to this time pressure by including a note that the study itself should take forty-five minutes to read in full, but only twenty to skim. The irony is both obvious and disturbing.

This endless stream of news and tailored interactive broadcasting actually predates the Internet and cable. It even predates television. Radio is where it all began; more accurately, radio is where people first immersed themselves in endless news and talk, in a medium that was supposedly killed off by television in the 1960s but found new life at the end of the twentieth century.

RADIO KILLED THE VIDEO STAR

While many professionals and experts tend to blame the Internet for the profusion of would-be know-it-alls lecturing them in their offices, others invoke the twenty-four-hour news cycle as another culprit, drowning people in stories and facts faster than they can absorb them. As with the accusations against the Internet, there's good reason for those complaints. Americans now watch the news as if they're in the situation room of the White House, hanging on every new scrap of information as if they were personally going to make the call on launching a war. (CNN even appeals to this viewer vanity by calling its afternoon broadcast "The Situation Room.")

This doesn't explain, however, why Americans erroneously end up thinking they're better informed than the experts on the myriad issues flooding across their screens. For this, we have to look a little more closely at how the public's relationship with the media developed after the 1970s. The decade of Watergate, "stagflation," and defeat in Vietnam is the benchmark not only because it was on the cusp of the addition of new technologies like cable, but also because those developments coincided with an accelerating collapse of trust in government and other institutions in American life. The growth of new kinds of media and the decline of trust are both intimately related to the death of expertise.

Television in the 1950s was supposed to displace radio for most kinds of programming. AM radio nonetheless dominated music and sports, with a wide audience reach but a tinny, monaural sound. This inferior sound quality couldn't compete with the obvious problem that human beings, equipped with two ears, prefer listening to everything in stereo. FM offered better sound—as the band Steely Dan promised in a hit song called "FM," there was "no static at all"—but it took until 1978 for FM radio broadcasts to reach more listeners than AM. Television, meanwhile, with its ability to add visual elements to its reports, grabbed the news and other staples of American life once primarily found on radio.

Radio wasn't dead, however. Especially on the AM band, radio offered something television could not: an interactive format. Relatively unhindered by the limits of airtime and cheap to produce, the idea behind talk radio was simple: give the host a microphone, hit the switch, and take calls from people who wanted to talk about the news and express their own views. With other forms of entertainment gravitating to television or to the richer sound of FM, it was an obvious choice for stations looking for affordable programming.

Talk radio had immense political consequences, and it provided the foundations for attacks on established knowledge that flowered later on social media. No one did more to drive the ascendance of talk radio than the broadcaster Rush Limbaugh, who in the late 1980s created an alternative to a still-stodgy world of Sunday-morning television punditry. Limbaugh wasn't the first: radio talk shows were scattered throughout the United States since at least the 1950s, often relegated to evenings and late nights. Limbaugh, however, did something unique, by setting himself up as a source of truth in opposition to the rest of the America media.

Within a few years of his first broadcasts, Limbaugh was heard on more than six hundred stations nationwide. He told his listeners that the press and the national television networks were conspiring in a liberal echo chamber, and especially that they were in the tank for the new administration of President Bill Clinton. Not all of these charges were entirely fair, but not all of them were wrong either, and Limbaugh was able to mine the established media daily for examples of bias—of which there were plenty—and run with them. With three solid hours of uninterrupted airtime, Limbaugh had an advantage television wouldn't have until cable.

Limbaugh and other talkers also built a loyal national base of followers by allowing them to call in and express their support. The calls were screened and vetted; according to a manager at one of Limbaugh's early affiliates, this was because Limbaugh felt that he was not very good at debate. Debate, however, was not the point: the object was to create a sense of community among people who already were inclined to agree with each other. Later, the Internet would overtake this kind of network building among people who rejected the mainstream media, but the phenomenon began on radio.

The television networks and print media were taken by surprise to find not only that millions of people were listening but that these listeners were turning against traditional sources of news. In 1970, Vice President Spiro Agnew charged the press with liberal bias, hauling off the immortal zinger (penned by the speechwriter William Safire) that the media was full of "nattering nabobs of negativism." Twenty years later, talk radio made the same case and this time made it stick.

The irony, of course, is that Limbaugh himself, along with other conservative talkers, soon *became* the mainstream. By the early twenty-first century, broadcast radio was again slumping as a market, but Limbaugh held on to twenty million listeners, and in 2008 he scored a $400 million contract whose size was second only to shock-jock Howard Stern's half-billion dollar deal with Sirius satellite radio. In the early age of television, video nearly put radio out of business; soon enough, however, television and talk radio would become complementary rather than competing media as radio's top stars moved to cable, and vice versa.

Liberal talk radio could not compete in this realm and had far less of an impact. Liberals might say this is because they refused to stoop to the level of their competitors. (The progressive radio host Randi Rhodes, on the now-defunct progressive network Air America, *did* call Hillary Clinton "a big [expletive] whore" on the air in 2008, which suggests that at least some liberals were willing to go the distance.) Conservatives, for their part, have argued that liberal talk radio, in a country dominated by liberal media outlets, was a solution to a nonexistent problem, because liberals already had plenty of places to be heard. For whatever reason, left-leaning talkers never gained traction. The popular progressive talker Alan Colmes, for example, has a fraction of the audience commanded by Limbaugh or by Colmes's own former talk-show partner Sean Hannity (who divides his time between radio and a show on Fox News).

The rise of talk radio challenged the role of experts by reinforcing the popular belief that the established media were dishonest and unreliable. Radio talkers didn't just attack established political beliefs: they attacked everything, plunging their listeners into an alternate universe where facts of any kind were unreliable unless verified by the host. In 2011, Limbaugh referred to "government, academia, science, and the media" as the "four corners of deceit," which pretty much covered everyone except Limbaugh.

There are many other examples. Glenn Beck once told his listeners that the Obama White House science adviser John Holdren was an advocate of compulsory abortion. (He wasn't, but the story still makes the rounds.) Hannity and others latched on to a rumor that the Egyptian government was going to legalize necrophilia. (Limbaugh asked who might provide the condoms for such an encounter.) The story, according to the *Christian Science Monitor* foreign correspondent Dan Murphy, was "utter hooey," but that didn't matter.

There is a reasonable argument that talk radio in the 1980s and 1990s was a necessary antidote to television and print outlets that had become politically complacent, ideologically monotonous, and too self-regarding. Limbaugh and his talk-radio imitators did not create middle America's resentment and distrust of the media, as Agnew's famous attack on the press showed. Radio talkers, however, fueled that distrust with renewed energy. Eventually, talk radio became as dogmatic and one-sided as the culture it claimed to be supplanting, and while conservative talkers may have been able to bring forward debates that major television networks would prefer to have ignored, they also intensified the voices of people who think everything is a lie and that experts are no smarter, and far more mendacious, than anyone else.

AMERICA HELD HOSTAGE: DAY 15,000

The radio insurgency against the print and electronic media might not have spread farther than the AM band were it not for cable television and the Internet. Cable and the Internet, as alternative sources of news—and as platforms for attacks on established knowledge—actually reinforced each other throughout the 1990s. Even Limbaugh, after conquering the best-seller lists with a foray into book writing, took a stab at syndicated television for a few years. A previously narrow media gate was now large enough to accommodate a stampede. Stories originating in one medium quickly bounced to another and then returned more loudly, like the ear-splitting feedback of a microphone held in front of a speaker.

The irony, however, is that neither cable nor the Internet pioneered the twenty-four-hour news cycle. For that, we can thank the late Ayatollah Khomeini of Iran.

In November 1979, Iranian revolutionaries overran the US embassy in Tehran, taking dozens of American personnel as hostages. The spectacle shocked Americans who saw it all happen nearly in real time. The Iranian hostage drama was something new, a story in between a war and a crisis: Vietnam was a slow-motion debacle that dragged on for a decade, while the Cuban missile crisis took place in two weeks, faster than television and newspapers could fully report it. The hostage taking was fast, and then slow, with a few days of violence followed by a long grind of waiting and worrying.

The news media were in a jam. On the one hand, Americans were in grave danger in a foreign country; on the other, nothing was actually *happening*. Like the comedian Chevy Chase announcing each week on *Saturday Night Live* that Spain's Francisco Franco was *still* dead, so, too, were network anchors left with little more to say than that the hostages were still hostages.

The ABC television network at the time decided to try something different by moving the daily Iran briefing to the late evening. This was also a marketing decision: ABC had no late-night programming against Johnny Carson's venerable talk show on its rival NBC, and news programming was, by comparison, cheap. ABC filled the evening slot with a new program called *Nightline* devoted solely to coverage of the crisis. Each night, ABC would splash the screen with "America Held Hostage," followed by the number of days of captivity.

The anchor (usually the veteran ABC newsman Ted Koppel) would then fill the time by interviewing experts, journalists, and other figures associated with the crisis.

Over a year later, the hostages came home, but Koppel and *Nightline* stayed on and ran for many more years. Cable provided the technology for later imitators, but *Nightline* provided the model. The "breaking" alerts and the chyrons—those little ribbons of news factoids that now scroll across the bottom of the screen on news networks—all originated with a program that was, in effect, created on the fly in response to a crisis.

Another legacy of the *Nightline* era and the advent of the twenty-four-hour news cycle is the devaluation of expert advice in the media. As the Army War College professor Steven Metz rightly noted in 2015, in an earlier time, "the public tended to defer to national security authorities who had earned their influence through experience and expertise as elected officials, military leaders, political appointees, academics, members of the media or think tank analysts." And then things changed:

> Hard-earned expertise was unnecessary when there were hours of radio and television air time or online discussion boards to fill. . . . For decades now, deference to authority has eroded across the political landscape. The profusion of information and communication technology gave voice, and self-confidence, to people who previously would defer to authority.[12]

"Armed with a bit of information," Metz concludes, such people "opined on an ever-expanding array of issues." Producers and reporters enabled those would-be experts by asking them to speak on anything and everything, a temptation few people can resist. (I am among those who are not without sin on this.)

Nightline was a success, but broadcast networks still saw no reason to run news day and night. After all, what viewer wanted to watch nothing but news? In 1980, the entrepreneur Ted Turner took a chance that people would, in fact, watch endless amounts of news when his invention, the Cable News Network, went on the air. CNN was denigrated by broadcast news executives as "the Chicken Noodle Network," an add-water-and-stir porridge of headlines and features. Turner got the last laugh, as CNN not only became a cable juggernaut but also later spawned its own competitors, including one—Fox News—that would eventually overtake it in the ratings.

Instead of older white males reading the news in stentorian voices, Turner gave CNN a far glossier look. On June 1, 1980, thirty-nine-year-old David Walker and his thirty-one-year-old wife, Lois Hart, anchored the first moments of the new CNN, delivering a story about President Jimmy Carter visiting the civil rights leader Vernon Jordan in the hospital. The news was no longer a half hour of listening to America's soothing middle-aged uncles like John Chancellor and Frank Reynolds, but an ongoing engagement with a roster of younger, more attractive anchors scattered throughout the day and night.

The twenty-four-hour news cycle had arrived, but it took a succession of crises and disasters throughout the 1980s and into the 1990s to capture an audience. The attempted assassination of President Ronald Reagan, the crash of a jet into the Potomac River in Washington, and the terrorist hijacking of a TWA flight, among others, all proved that Americans would leave their television sets tuned to a news channel for hours on end. Instead of a ritual where Americans gathered at a preset time, or rushed to their sets at the heart-stopping words "we interrupt this broadcast," news became a kind of open buffet where viewers could visit and graze all day long.

The testimony of the law professor Anita Hill and her allegations of sexual harassment against Supreme Court nominee Clarence

Thomas in 1991 proved that Americans would not only watch crises and disasters, but also stay riveted to their sets for political and court-room dramas as well—especially if they involved sex or murder or, in the best case, both. In 1991, after judicial rulings allowed more cameras into courtrooms, Court TV arrived on cable. Americans became armchair legal experts by watching endless cases about rape, murder, and other assorted skulduggery.

CNN was already more news than the average viewer could reasonably handle in a day, but the proliferation of cable outlets like Court TV was an expert's nightmare. In a 1991 review of the new network, *Entertainment Weekly* called Court TV "part C-SPAN, part *Monday Night Football*," although that might have been uncharitable to both. And by the time the spectacular 1995 murder trial of O. J. Simpson concluded, millions of laypeople had developed deep views on things they actually could not understand, from the statistics of DNA testing to the veracity of shoeprints. It was a ratings treasure trove, and it proved that what people really wanted from their news networks was not hours of boring news, but high-tension drama.

CNN launched a headlines-only channel in 1982. Devoted solely to news, it was supposed to be a rotating cycle of top stories every thirty minutes. Of course, that was too dry for the average viewer, and sure enough, the celebrity judge Nancy Grace soon camped out at what came to be renamed HLN. (Like Kentucky Fried Chicken renaming itself KFC to sidestep what it was doing to chickens—that is, frying them—HLN apparently needed to get "news" out of the title.)

HLN specialized in lurid stories interspersed with Grace's hyperbolic raging about justice. In a ghastly 2008 story, a mother in Florida named Casey Anthony was accused of murdering her toddler daughter. It was a disturbing story, a kind of rerun of the Simpson trial in which millions of people took sides quickly. HLN, however, didn't just cover Anthony's trial; Grace and others made it a staple of HLN's "news," running some *five hundred* stories about it.[13] By the time Anthony was acquitted in 2011, HLN's viewers were likely more versed in Florida murder statutes than in their own rights under the US Constitution.

There is no way to discuss the nexus between journalism and the death of expertise without considering the revolutionary change represented by the arrival of Fox News in 1996. The creation of the conservative media consultant Roger Ailes, Fox made the news faster, slicker, and, with the addition of news readers who were actual beauty queens, prettier. It's an American success story, in every good and bad way that such triumphs of marketing often are. (Ailes, in what seems almost like a made-for-television coda to his career, was forced out of Fox in 2016 after multiple allegations of sexual harassment were covered in great detail on the medium he helped create.)

Fox's history intersects with the death of expertise, however, in an important way: the arrival of Fox was, in its way, the ultimate expression of the partisan division in how people seek out sources of news in a new electronic marketplace. What Limbaugh tried to do with radio and a syndicated television show, Ailes made a reality with a network. Had Ailes not created Fox, someone would have, because the market, as talk radio proved, was already there. As the conservative author and Fox commentator Charles Krauthammer likes to quip, Ailes "discovered a niche audience: half the American people."

Fox put the last nail in the coffin of the news broadcast as a nominally apolitical review of the day's events. The editor of the conservative journal *First Things*, R. R. Reno, wrote in 2016 that Roger Ailes was "perhaps the single most influential person behind the transformation of politics into entertainment over the last generation," but that he's since had plenty of help:

> It's not just Fox. MSNBC and other networks have developed
> their own political shout shows—verbal versions of World Wide

Wrestling matches. Talking heads bluster, interrupt, and otherwise disport themselves in rude ways. Viewers rejoice in the spectacle. Advertising is sold. Money is made.[14]

Fox's "fair and balanced" motto was a zinger aimed at the hypocrisy of the traditional media, including by this point CNN, who all promoted themselves as above any agenda. Fox, like the radio talkers, positioned itself to be the alternative to the mainstream, a watchdog over a club to which it claimed it did not belong and to whom it owed nothing.

Of course, the idea that Fox was unique, or that the major networks were somehow apolitical, was always a fiction. Media bias, of various kinds and in every venue, is real. Fox, like other networks, tries to draw a line between its hard-news operations and its opinion programming; like other networks, it often fails. CNN, Fox, MSNBC, and the major networks all have excellent news organizations, and yet all of them engage in bias to some extent, if only to tailor their broadcasts to the demographic they're seeking. In the competition for viewers, simply putting "news" on television isn't enough.

Fox's influence is larger because of the sheer size of its audience, but all of the networks now feature partisan "infotainment" in their schedules. The bigger problem, on all of the major networks, is that the transition from news to entertainment is almost seamless and largely invisible: daytime fluff moves to afternoon updates and talk, which then gives way to the evening's hard news, which in turn then flows into celebrity programming, all within the space of hours.

As talk radio flourished and then cable stepped in, the Internet grew in size and speed, opening another arena not only for established news organizations, but for any would-be journalists who wanted to break into the game. The Internet and the proliferation of news media were already problems for experts, but the synergy created by the combination of news and the Internet is a problem of Gibraltarian proportions for experts trying to communicate with laypeople who already believe that staring at their phone while sitting on the subway is the equivalent of keeping up with the world's events.

TRUST NO ONE

For nearly thirty years, I've opened almost every class I teach at the college and graduate level by telling my students that no matter what else they do, they should consume a balanced daily diet of news. I tell them to follow the major newspapers; to watch at least two networks; to subscribe (online or otherwise) to at least one journal with which they consistently disagree.

I doubt I've had much success on that score. If my students are anything like other Americans, they tend to follow sources with which they already agree. In 2014, for example, a Pew survey asked Americans which television news sources they "trust the most to provide accurate information about politics and current events." The results are exactly what we would expect in a fractured media market: people gravitate toward sources whose views they already share.

Among all Americans, avowedly conservative outlet Fox News edged traditional broadcast news (that is, the long-standing evening news broadcasts by ABC, CBS, and NBC) as the "most trusted" overall, but by only a few points. CNN came in a close third. Together, Fox and CNN were "most trusted" by over four in ten respondents, but among self-identified political conservatives, Fox unsurprisingly was the "most trusted" source at 48 percent. Self-identified moderates split their choice for "most trusted" evenly between broadcast news and CNN (25 and 23 percent, respectively), with Fox and public television taking second and third place. Among self-identified liberals, network broadcast news led as "most trusted" at 24 percent, with CNN and public television essentially tied at 16 and 17 percent, respectively.

What was most startling in this study, however, was the presence of *The Daily Show*, a satire about the news hosted for many years by the comedian Jon Stewart, among the "most trusted" sources of news. Seventeen percent of liberal respondents named *The Daily Show* as their "most trusted source," putting Stewart in a tie with CNN and public television and surpassing progressive MSNBC by seven points. MSNBC (whose motto for a time was "lean forward," whatever that means) was the least-trusted source in 2014: every group surveyed placed it dead last, with even conservatives choosing Stewart over the progressive network by one percentage point.

There is a generational difference at work here, as younger viewers are more likely than their elders to tune to a nontraditional source of information. But this morphing of news into entertainment stretches across every demographic. The whole exercise of staying informed has become a kind of postmodern exercise in irony and cynicism, with words like "truth" and "information" meaning whatever people want them to mean. As a Johns Hopkins professor, Eliot Cohen, wrote in 2016, the difference between a generation that got its news from Walter Cronkite and David Brinkley and one that gets its information from Jon Stewart and fellow comic Stephen Colbert "is the difference between giggling with young, sneering hipsters and listening to serious adults."[15]

That kind of complaint, of course, sounds like just the sort of thing a middle-aged curmudgeon would say. Other critics, however, counter that the generic nature of television news is exactly why younger viewers turned to alternatives. As James Poulos, a writer (and a much younger member of Generation X) based in Los Angeles, said in 2016, "It is mind bending how the Baby Boomers went from trusting no one under 30 to trusting any idiot with a symmetrical face dressed in business casual." Stewart may be a comedian, but his younger viewers were likely better informed than those among their peers who watch no news at all.

The problem is not that all these networks and celebrities exist, but that viewers pick and choose among them and then believe they're informed. The modern media, with so many options tailored to particular views, is a huge exercise in confirmation bias. This means that Americans are not just *poorly* informed, they're *misinformed*.

There is a huge difference between these two maladies. A 2000 study on public knowledge conducted by the University of Illinois, as the political scientist Anne Pluta later noted, found that "uninformed citizens don't have any information at all, while those who are misinformed have information that conflicts with the best evidence and expert opinion." Not only do these people "fill the gaps in their knowledge base by using their existing belief systems," but over time those beliefs become "indistinguishable from hard data." And, of course, the most misinformed citizens "tend to be the most confident in their views and are also the strongest partisans."[16]

This is one reason why few Americans trust what little news, or newslike programming, they watch. Too many people approach the news with an underlying assumption that they are already well versed in the issues. They do not seek information so much as confirmation, and when they receive information they do not like, they will gravitate to sources they prefer because they believe others are mistaken or even lying. In an earlier time, those other sources were harder to find; when people had to make do with fewer outlets, they had to contend with news that was not specifically tailored to their prejudices. Today, hundreds of media outlets cater to even the narrowest agendas and biases.

This mindset, and the market that services it, creates in laypeople a combination of groundless confidence and deep cynicism, habits of thought that defeat the best attempts of experts to educate their fellow citizens. Experts can't respond to questions if most people already think they know the answers, nor does it help them to bring forward messages when so many people are already prone to shoot— or, at best, to ignore—the messengers. It's bad enough that people aren't keeping up with the news; it's worse when they don't trust what little news they do read and shop around until they find what they are looking for.

In part, American distrust of the media is just one symptom of the larger malady: Americans increasingly don't trust anyone any- more. They view all institutions, including the media, with disdain. Everybody hates the media—or, at least, everybody *claims* to hate the media. According to pollsters, news organizations are among the least trusted institutions in the United States; a Gallup poll in 2014 found that only four in ten Americans trust the media to report news "fully, accurately, and fairly," an all-time low.[17]

Of course, people don't really hate the media. They just hate the media that deliver news they don't like or transmit views with which they don't agree. A Pew study in 2012 noted that two-thirds of Americans think news organizations in general are "often inaccu- rate," but that same number drops to less than a third when people are asked the same question about the news organization "you use most."[18] This, as many observers have pointed out over the years, is much the same way everyone claims to hate Congress, when what they really mean is that they hate all the members of Congress *but their own*. Likewise, people who hate "the media" still watch the "the news" or read "the paper," as long as it's one they already trust.

In a democracy, this level of cynicism about the media is poi- sonous. All citizens, including experts, need news. Journalists relay events and developments in the world around us, providing a reser- voir of facts we use as the raw material for many of our own opin- ions, views, and beliefs. We have to rely on their judgment and their objectivity, because their reports are usually the first encounter the rest of us have with previously unknown events or facts. Around the world, journalists do their job amazingly well, often at risk to their own lives. And yet the majority of Americans distrust the information they provide.

ARE THE VIEWERS SMARTER THAN THE EXPERTS?

Are the viewers and readers right to be so mistrustful? As a professional in my own field, my instinct is to believe that journalists, as professionals in theirs, know what they're doing. In general, I trust the reporting and writing of most journalists. I also believe that the editors and producers who hired them know what they're doing. Like everyone else, however, I have no training in journalism, nor do I have expertise in most of the subjects about which I'm reading.

The question of competence arises if the journalist lacks that expertise as well. Journalists, without doubt, can be experts. Some foreign correspondents are fluent in the language of their area and have a deep knowledge of other cultures. Some science reporters are themselves scientists or have a fair amount of scientific training. There are Capitol Hill reporters who can explain the legislative process better than some members of Congress.

And yet there are journalists who think there's a bridge in Gaza or that Evelyn Waugh was a woman. This shallowness is not because journalism attracts unintelligent people, but because in an age when everything is journalism, and everyone is a journalist, standards inevitably fall. A profession that once had at least some barriers to entry is now wide open, with the same results we might expect if medicine, law enforcement, aviation, or archaeology were suddenly do-it-yourself projects.

This is partly the fault, as so much is these days, of "academizing" what used to be a trade. Rather than apprenticeships as part of a career track that includes writing obituaries and covering boring town meetings, journalism and communications are now undergraduate majors. These departments and programs crank out young people with little knowledge about the subjects of their correspondence. They are schooled in the structure of a story but not in the habits or norms of the profession. Many of them, accustomed to posting their deep thoughts online since high school, do not understand the difference between "journalism" and "blogging."

Veteran journalists, meanwhile, are being pushed out of newsrooms to make room for the youngsters who know how to generate clicks, as *The Nation* writer Dale Maharidge described in 2016.

> Old-school journalism was a trade, and legacy journalists find today's brand of personality journalism, with its emphasis on churning out blog posts, aggregating the labor of others, and curating a constant social-media presence, to be simply foreign. And the higher-ups share the new bias. One editor of a major national publication, who himself is well over 40, confided to me that he's reluctant to hire older journalists, that "they're stuck in the mentality of doing one story a week" and not willing to use social media.[19]

The market's focus on form rather than content, the need for speed, and the fashionable biases of the modern university combine to create a trifecta of misinformation. Little wonder that experienced writers like Joel Engel, an author and former *New York Times* and *Los Angeles Times* journalist, have lamented that America was better served "when 'journalists' were reporters who'd often barely graduated high school."

These inexperienced writers can have a significant impact on the information available to the sizable number of people who primarily get their news through social media. Facebook, for example, uses news curators to decide what shows up in a reader's Facebook news feed. According to a 2016 exposé by Gizmodo.com, Facebook treated these reporters as low-level contractors while giving them immense power over the news:

> The trending news section [at Facebook] is run by people in their 20s and early 30s, most of whom graduated from Ivy League and private East Coast schools like Columbia University and NYU. They've previously worked at outlets like the *New York Daily News*, Bloomberg, MSNBC, and the *Guardian*. Some former curators have left Facebook for jobs at organizations including the *New Yorker*, Mashable, and Sky Sports.
>
> According to former team members interviewed by Gizmodo, this small group has the power to choose what stories make it onto the trending bar and, more importantly, what news sites each topic links out to. "We choose what's trending," said one. "There was no real standard for measuring what qualified as news and what didn't. It was up to the news curator to decide."[20]

The obvious answer here is not to rely on Facebook for news. But many millions of people do, just as many also rely on Twitter—which itself is experimenting with algorithms meant to alter what appears, and with what priority, in a user's Twitter stream.

In fairness to these younger reporters, they're often put in an impossible situation by the nature of the market. As the Slate.com writer Will Saletan told me, complicated stories require a lot more time than just blurting out whatever produces a click. Saletan spent a year researching the food safety of genetically modified organisms (GMOs), a story that might exceed even the vaccine debate for the triumph of ignorance over science.[21] "You can't ask a young person to sort out this issue on the kind of time frame that's generally tolerated these days," Saletan said after his story—which blew apart the fake science behind the objections to GMOs—appeared in Slate. These kinds of stories require not only time but a willingness to do research and stay focused on dull details. As Saletan put it, "You really have to be a willful bastard to persist in researching a topic like [GMOs], which feels incredibly technical and boring when you're deep inside it, even if it excites passions when it becomes political."

Sometimes the errors are trivial and amusing. In the great "chocolate helps you lose weight" hoax, for example, the hoaxers never thought they'd get as far as they did; they assumed that "reporters who don't have science chops" would discover the whole faked study was "laughably flimsy" once they reached out to a real scientist. They were wrong: nobody actually tried to vet the story with actual scientists. "The key," as the hoaxers later said, "is to exploit journalists' incredible laziness. If you lay out the information just right, you can shape the story that emerges in the media almost like you were writing those stories yourself. In fact, that's literally what you're doing, since many reporters just copied and pasted our text."[22]

A dumb story about chocolate as a weight-loss gimmick isn't going to hurt too many people. (Chocolate junkies don't need scientific reasons to indulge.) But when the coverage turns to more serious issues, journalists who are lost in the subject matter and weighted down by their ideological biases can cause more confusion than illumination. The writer Joshua Foust some years ago zeroed in on the practice of "embedding" journalists overseas with military forces, creating the illusion of experience among reporters who in fact had little idea where they were:

> Far too many correspondents know nothing about the places they go to cover: whether Georgia or Afghanistan, basic knowledge is critically lacking from media accounts (one freelance reporter in Georgia told me that staff reporters were asking officials, "Where is Abkhazia?"). Personal experience suggests that the situation is largely the same in Afghanistan: "It's only a

one-week embed," the thinking seems to go, "so I don't have to do too much work—I can learn as I go."[23]

Without any foundational knowledge, young writers have nothing to fall back on but a college education in journalism, which, in the words of Joel Engel, is a "homogenizing process" that "ensures conformity" and produces young journalists who come out of college "seeing what they believe."

This kind of outright ignorance or even professional malpractice can do grievous damage to real people and their communities. In 2014, for example, *Rolling Stone* suffered a massive journalistic failure in its reporting of a now-infamous story about a gang rape at the University of Virginia. A reporter, determined to find a story of sexual assault on an elite American campus, found one. Her editors published it, in grotesque detail. The whole story quickly unraveled, however, and turned out to be a hoax. The result was a smoking wreck of lawsuits and destroyed reputations.

Rolling Stone ended up retracting the story and asking the Columbia School of Journalism to conduct an investigation. The Columbia investigators concluded that the reporter Sabrina Erdeley and her editors had violated even basic rules of journalism, all in the name of a story that was, apparently, just too good to check.[24] The case continued to drag on years later, with one of the university's administrative deans named in the story—a woman who supposedly failed to act on the initial rape claim—winning a suit against *Rolling Stone* for defamation.

The story was in part based on studies that claim that one in four (sometimes reported as one in five) women in America's colleges and universities will be sexually assaulted. Claims like these helped to enable the *Rolling Stone* hoax, when the statistics themselves and the studies on which they were based should have raised concerns. As Slate's Emily Yoffe wrote in 2014, "the one-in-four assertion would mean that young American college women are raped at a rate similar to women in Congo, where rape has been used as a weapon of war."[25] Another study central to this dire narrative later turned out to have included "college aged men" who were as old as *seventy-one,* whose average age was over twenty-six, and none of whom actually lived on a college campus. But no matter: the statistic is out there now more as a slogan than as a fact, and anyone arguing about it will say, understandably, that "they saw it in the news."

Similar to the "one in four" statistic is the now-common claim, repeated regularly in the American media, that US military veterans are killing themselves at an alarming rate because of the stress of fighting two major wars. "Twenty-two a day"—meaning twenty-two veteran suicides every twenty-four hours—has become the mantra both of veterans' service organizations as well as antiwar groups. Multiple stories have appeared in electronic and print media about the "epidemic" of veteran suicide in 2013 and after, with dramatic headlines and pictures of young men and women in uniform who'd ended their lives. The implications of the stories were clear: extended combat service is driving America's warriors to suicide, and a heartless government does not care.

When I first saw this statistic, I had a personal interest in pursuing the underlying studies. I work every day with military officers, many of whom have seen combat. I am also a former certified suicide-prevention counselor because of volunteer work I did briefly in my younger days. As someone with at least some experience in suicide prevention, I was concerned about people killing themselves; as someone who works with military personnel, I was worried about my students and friends; as a social scientist, I was bothered by a statistical argument that didn't seem plausible.

Unfortunately, the media were no help. Indeed, they were a fundamental part of the problem. It is true, in fact, that veterans are killing themselves at higher rates in the twenty-first century than in earlier years. But in part, that's because *everybody* has been killing themselves at higher rates—for reasons epidemiologists are still debating—and veterans are part of "everybody." Adding to the confusion, the studies that looked at "veteran" suicides also included everyone of any age who'd ever served in the military in any capacity, from reserve duty to sustained combat. In other words, a young person just home from a combat zone and a middle-aged man who'd done a few years in his local National Guard unit thirty years earlier were both counted as part of this new "epidemic" if they killed themselves at any point.

A beleaguered Veterans Administration—not exactly the most popular bureaucracy in America—tried in vain to note that according to a sizable 2012 study, suicides among veterans really hadn't changed all that much since 1999. The *New York Times* duly reported on this study with a headline that read "As Suicides Rise in U.S., Veterans Are Less of Total." The *Washington Post* headline implied an opposite conclusion: "VA Study Finds More Veterans Committing Suicide." Both of these headlines, amazingly, were about the same study, and both, in a strictly factual sense, were true.

The media, or at least some outlets, interviewed the scientist who wrote the study, but his answers made no difference to the narrative. "There is a perception that we have a veterans' suicide epidemic on our hands. I don't think that is true," said Robert Bossarte, the epidemiologist who conducted the study. "The rate is going up in the country, and veterans are a part of it."[26] Most of the stories didn't bother with this quote, nor did they include important benchmarks like the overall suicide rate in America or the suicide rate among men in the same age cohort as the young combat veterans. Nor were other occupations compared to the military, perhaps because relatively high rates among other groups—such as medical doctors, among others—would have taken some of the urgency out of the story.

The bad reporting continued with a slew of companion stories about how suicides among military personnel in 2012 actually outnumbered combat deaths. The message, of course, was that American soldiers were now more of a danger to themselves than the enemy. That's a grim picture, except for a small problem: it is statistically meaningless. The assertion that there were "more suicides than combat deaths" will always be true *by definition* in any year where US forces aren't involved in a lot of actual fighting.

You can do this statistical trick with any year in which there isn't a lot of combat: compare military suicides in, say, the late 1950s to combat deaths. To its credit, *TIME* ran a piece that got it right, even titling it "Military Suicides Top Combat Deaths—But Only Because the Wars Are Ending."[27] But, again, this should have been obvious to anyone who took even a moment to think about it, and it is remarkable that *TIME* or anyone else had to run such a story in the first place.

The point in all of this is that people genuinely concerned about veterans and suicide don't really know any more about what's going on with veterans today than they did before they read these stories. But they *think* they do, and heaven help the expert in any field who casts doubt on this public outrage or who even tries to explain the subject with a bit more nuance. Veterans are going crazy and killing themselves, and that's that. After all, *I read it in the paper.*

WHAT IS TO BE DONE

In the end, the question is whether journalists can ever be experts on the subject of their reporting; if not, how can experts do a better job helping them? I cannot, and will not, make recommendations here beyond hoping that younger journalists somehow acquire a background in the subject on which they write. That's generic advice and as far as I am willing to go in telling other professionals how to do their jobs. I say this while realizing fully that nothing can stop people from cherry-picking their sources, no matter how high quality the information available to them.

But I have one admonition for experts, and several for the consumers of journalism.

To experts, I will say, know when to say no. Some of the worst mistakes I ever made were when I was young and I could not resist giving an opinion. Most of the time, I was right to think I knew more than the reporter or the readers, but that's not the point: I also found myself out on a few limbs I should have avoided. In fairness to journalists, I have found that they will respect and report your views accurately—only on a few occasions did I ever feel ambushed or misquoted—but they will also respect your principled refusal to go too far out of your lane. It is your obligation, not theirs, to identify that moment.

The consumers of news have some important obligations here as well. I have four recommendations for you, the readers, when approaching the news: be humbler, be ecumenical, be less cynical, and be a lot more discriminating.

Be humble. That is, at least begin by assuming that the people writing the story, whatever their shortcomings, know more about the subject than you do. At the least, try to remember that in most cases, the person writing the story has spent more time with the issue than you have. If you approach any story in the media, or any source of information already assuming you know as much as anyone else on the subject, the entire exercise of following the news is going to be a waste of your time.

Be ecumenical. Vary your diet. You wouldn't eat the same thing all day, so don't consume the same sources of media all day. When I worked in national politics, I subscribed to a half-dozen journals at any given time, across the political spectrum. Don't be provincial: try media from other countries, as they often report stories or have a view of which Americans are completely unaware. And don't say you "don't have the time." You do.

Be less cynical—or don't be *so* cynical. It's extremely rare that anyone is setting out intentionally to lie to you. Yes, the people writing the stories often have an agenda, and there will always be another Sabrina Erdeley out there. And yes, the journalists you're reading or watching will get some things wrong, often with an astonishing lack of self-awareness. None of them have a monopoly on the truth, but they're not all liars. They're doing the best they can, by their lights, and most of them would be glad to know you're keeping tabs by reading other sources of news and information.

Be more discriminating. If you see something in a major media outlet that doesn't seem right to you, finding some half-baked website isn't the answer. Websites that are outlets for political movements, or other, even worse enterprises that cater specifically to zealots or fools, will do more harm than good in the search for accurate information. Instead, ask yourself questions when consuming media. Who are these writers? Do they have editors? Is this a journal or newspaper that stands by its reporting, or is it part of a political operation? Are their claims checkable, or have other media tried to verify or disprove their stories?

Conspiracy theorists and adherents of quack medicine will never believe anything that challenges their views, but most of us can do better. And remember: reading and following the news is a skill like any other at which we get better by repetition. The best way to become a good consumer of news is to be a *regular* consumer of news.

I've been unsparing in my criticism of the low level of foundational knowledge among Americans, about the narcissism and bias that prevents them from learning, about a college industry that affirms ignorance rather than cures it, about media who think their job is to entertain, and about journalists who are too lazy or too inexperienced to get their stories right. I've shaken my fist at most of

the groups I think bear a great responsibility for the death of expertise and for undermining established knowledge just when we need
it most.

I've let only one group off the hook so far: experts.

What happens when experts are wrong, and who should be
responsible for deciding when to listen to them and when to ignore
them? We'll confront this question in the next chapter.

When the Experts Are Wrong

Even when the experts all agree, they may well be mistaken.

Bertrand Russell

NO EXPERTS NEED APPLY

In 2002, a distinguished historian wrote that the widely told tales of "No Irish Need Apply" signs in late nineteenth-century America were myths. The University of Illinois professor Richard Jensen said that such signs were inventions, "myths of victimization," passed down from Irish immigrants to their children until they reached the unassailable status of urban legends. For over a decade, most historians accepted Jensen's scholarship on the matter. Opponents of Jensen's thesis were dismissed—sometimes by Jensen himself—as Irish-American loyalists.

In a 2015 story that seemed to encapsulate the death of expertise, an eighth grader named Rebecca Fried claimed that Jensen was wrong, not least because of research she did on Google. She was respectful, but determined. "He has been doing scholarly work for decades before I was born, and the last thing I want to do was show disrespect for him and his work," she said later. It all seemed to be just another case of a precocious child telling an experienced teacher—an emeritus professor of history, no less—that he had not done his homework.

As it turns out, she was right and he was wrong. Such signs existed, and they weren't that hard to find.

For years, other scholars had wrestled with Jensen's claims, but they fought with his work inside the thicket of professional historiography. Meanwhile, outside the academy, Jensen's assertion was quickly accepted and trumpeted as a case of an imagined grievance among Irish-Americans. (*Vox*, of course, loved the original Jensen piece.)

Young Rebecca, however, did what a sensible person would: she started looking through databases of old newspapers. She found the signs, as the *Daily Beast* later reported, "collecting a handful of examples, then dozens, then more. She went to as many newspaper databases as she could. Then she thought, *somebody had to have done this before, right?*" As it turned out, neither Jensen nor anyone else had apparently bothered to do this basic fact-checking.

Jensen later fired back, trying to rebut the work of a grade-schooler by claiming that he was right but that he could have been more accurate in his claims. Debate over his thesis, as the *Smithsonian* magazine later put it, "may still be raging in the comments section" of various Internet lists, but Fried's work proves "that anyone with a curious mind and a nose for research can challenge the historical status quo."[1] Miss Fried, for her part, has now entered high school with a published piece in the *Journal of Social History*.

In the 1970s, America's top nutritional scientists told the United States government that eggs, among many other foods, might be lethal. There could be no simpler application of Occam's Razor, with a trail leading from the barnyard to the morgue. Eggs contain a lot of cholesterol, cholesterol clogs arteries, clogged arteries cause heart attacks, and heart attacks kill people. The conclusion was obvious: Americans need to get all that cholesterol out of their diet.

And so they did. Then something unexpected happened: Americans gained a lot of weight and started dying of other things.

Eggs, it turned out, weren't so bad, or at least they weren't as bad as other things. In 2015 the government decided that eggs were acceptable, perhaps even healthy. As the columnist (and resident of egg-laden Vermont) Geoffrey Norman wrote at the time,

> A lot of [obese] people who got that way thought that they were following a government-approved diet. Egg consumption declined by over 30 percent when the government put them on its dietary blacklist. People have to eat, so they substituted other things for eggs. Things that helped to make them fat. The eggs they did not eat would not, it turns out, have clogged their arteries and killed them. The stuff they substituted for those eggs, however, might well have caused them to suffer from type 2 diabetes and worse.[2]

The egg scare was based on a cascade of flawed studies, some going back almost a half century. People who want to avoid eggs may still do so, of course. In fact, there are studies now that suggest that skipping breakfast entirely—which scientists also have long warned not to do—isn't as bad as anyone thought either.[3]

In 1982, one of the top experts on the Soviet Union, Seweryn Bialer, delivered a stern warning to readers of the prestigious journal *Foreign Affairs* that the USSR was a lot stronger than it looked at the time.

> The Soviet Union is not now nor will it be in the next decade in the throes of a true systemic crisis, for it boasts enormous unused reserves of political and social stability that suffice to endure the deepest difficulties. The Soviet economy, like any gigantic economy administered by intelligent and trained professionals, will not go bankrupt. It may become less effective, it may stagnate, it may even experience an absolute decline for a year or two; but, like the political system, it will not collapse.[4]

A year later, Bialer won a Macarthur Foundation "genius grant." Two years after that, the Soviet Communist Party—obviously facing the throes of a true systemic crisis—chose Mikhail Gorbachev as its new leader. Less than eight years after Bialer's finger-wagging lecture, the Union of Soviet Socialist Republics ceased to exist.

In the final months of the Soviet collapse, an MIT professor, Stephen Meyer, testified before the US Senate Foreign Relations Committee. American political leaders watching events in the USSR were concerned about the security of thousands of Soviet nuclear weapons pointed at the United States. Meyer, one of his generation's leading experts on Soviet military affairs, told everyone to calm down: Gorbachev was in control. "Hints of military coups" in the Soviet Union, he assured the assembled senators, were "pure flights of fancy."[5]

Meyer gave his testimony on June 6, 1991. Nine weeks later, Gorbachev was deposed in a coup led by a group that included the Soviet defense minister and the head of the feared security apparatus, the KGB. Chaos descended as tanks entered the streets of Moscow. But no matter: a year after the Soviet collapse, Meyer left the study of Russia and nuclear arms completely and worked instead on biodiversity issues, serving on various committees for the Massachusetts Department of Fisheries and Wildlife until his untimely death in 2006.

Bialer and Meyer were hardly a minority. As the historian Nick Gvosdev observed some years later, many Soviet experts substituted what they believed, or wanted to believe, about the USSR in place of "critical analysis of the facts on the ground." Two scholars of international relations noted that everyone else got it wrong, too. "Measured by its own standards, the [academic] profession's performance was embarrassing," Professors Richard Ned Lebow and Thomas Risse Kappen wrote in 1995. "None of the existing theories of international relations recognized the possibility that the kind of change that did occur could occur."[6]

Experts get things wrong all the time. The effects of such errors range from mild embarrassment to wasted time and money; in rarer cases, they can result in death and even lead to international catastrophe. And yet experts regularly ask citizens to trust their judgment and to have confidence not only that mistakes will be rare, but that the experts will identify those mistakes and learn from them.

Day to day, laypeople have no choice but to trust experts. We live our lives embedded in a web of social and governmental institutions meant to ensure that professionals are in fact who they say they are, and can in fact do what they say they do. Universities, accreditation organizations, licensing boards, certification authorities, state inspectors, and other institutions exist to maintain those standards. In general, these safeguards work well. We are shocked, for example, when we read a story about an incompetent doctor who kills a patient exactly because such stories, in a country where nearly a million physicians practice medicine safely every day, are so unusual.

This daily trust in professionals, however, is a prosaic matter of necessity. It is much the same way we trust everyone else in our daily lives, including the bus driver we assume isn't drunk or the restaurant worker we assume has washed her hands. This is not the same thing as trusting professionals when it comes to matters of public policy: to say that we trust our doctors to write us the correct prescription is not the same thing as saying we trust all medical professionals about whether America should have a system of national health care. To say that we trust a college professor to teach our sons and daughters the history of World War II is not the same thing as saying that we therefore trust all academic historians to advise the president of the United States on matters of war and peace.

For these larger decisions, there are no licenses or certificates. There are no fines or suspensions if things go wrong. Indeed, there is very little direct accountability at all, which is why laypeople understandably fear the influence of experts. In a democracy, elected officials who may have accepted—or rejected—expert advice provide accountability, a subject to which we'll return in the next and last chapter. But accountability is something that happens after the fact. It might be morally satisfying to hold someone responsible, but assigning blame doesn't heal the injured or restore the peace. In general, how do experts go wrong? "It is remarkable," as the journalist Salena Zito has said, "to witness experts not understanding the field in which they are experts," and for laypeople, it is more than a little unsettling. What can citizens do when they are confronted with expert failure, and how can they maintain their trust in expert communities? Likewise, what responsibilities do experts incur when they make mistakes, and how can they repair their relationship with their client, society?

THE MANY FACES OF FAILURE

There are several kinds of expert failure. The most innocent and most common are what we might think of as the ordinary failures of science. Individuals, or even entire professions, get important questions wrong because of error or because of the limitations of a field itself. They observe a phenomenon or examine a problem, come up with theories and solutions, and then test them. Sometimes they're right, and sometimes they're wrong. The process usually includes a lot of blind alleys and failed experiments along the way. Sometimes errors are undiscovered or even compounded by other experts.

This is how a generation of Americans got fat avoiding eggs. It's why the first US attempt to launch a satellite ended in a gigantic explosion on the launch pad. It's why top experts in foreign policy assumed for decades that the peaceful reunification of Germany was unlikely but then had to reconsider their views as celebratory fireworks filled the skies over a free Berlin.

Science is also learning by doing. The United States invented the nuclear bomb in 1945, but it took another decade of exploding test devices before scientists and researchers around the world gained a better understanding of the "electromagnetic pulse," or EMP, an invisible effect of nuclear detonations that plays havoc with electrical systems. The public, for their part, became more aware of EMP when a US test in the Pacific in 1962 blew out streetlights and shut down telephones hundreds of miles away in Hawaii, an effect the scientists had suspected but whose scale they had underestimated.

There isn't much anyone, including experts, can do about this kind of failure, because it is not so much a failure as it is an integral part of science and scholarship. Laypeople are uncomfortable with ambiguity, and they prefer answers rather than caveats. But science is a process, not a conclusion. Science subjects itself to constant testing by a set of careful rules under which theories can only be displaced by better theories. Laypeople cannot expect experts never to be wrong; if they were capable of such accuracy, they wouldn't need to do research and run experiments in the first place. If policy experts were clairvoyant or omniscient, governments would never run deficits and wars would only break out at the instigation of madmen.

Sometimes, too, expert error comes with *beneficial* effects, but these are rarely treated the same way as mistakes that cost lives or money. When scientists invented oral contraceptives, for example, they were trying to figure out how to help women prevent unwanted pregnancies. They were not directly trying to lower the risk of ovarian cancer—but apparently some kinds of birth control pills do exactly that, and by significant rates. For some women, oral contraceptives have risks; for others, the same pills might extend their lives. Of course, if birth control pills only *increased* cancer risks, we'd be lamenting yet another failure of science, but this positive side effect was just as unknown as many others a half century ago.

Likewise, experts who predicted an all-out international arms race in nuclear weapons at the end of the 1950s were wrong. But they were wrong at least in part because they underestimated the efficacy of their own efforts to limit the spread of nuclear weapons. President John F. Kennedy feared a world of as many as twenty-five nuclear armed powers by the 1970s. (As of 2017, only ten nations have crossed this threshold, including one—South Africa—that has renounced its arsenal.)[7] Kennedy's prediction, based on the best expert advice, was not impossible or even unreasonable; rather, the number of future nuclear powers was lowered with the assistance of policies advocated by those same experts.

In the end, experts cannot guarantee outcomes. They cannot promise that they will never make mistakes or that they will not fall prey to the same shortcomings that govern all human deliberations. They can only promise to institute rules and methods that reduce the chance of such mistakes and to make those errors far less often than a layperson might. If we are to accept the benefits of a profession's work, we have to accept something less than perfection, perhaps even a certain amount of risk.

Other forms of expert failure, however, are more worrisome. Experts can go wrong, for example, when they try to stretch their expertise from one area to another. This is not only a recipe for error, but is maddening to other experts as well. In some cases, the cross-expertise poaching is obvious, as when entertainers—experts in their own fields, to be sure—confuse art with life and start issuing explanations of complicated matters.

In other cases, the boundaries are less clear, and the issue is not expertise but *relative* expertise. A biologist is not a medical doctor, but in general terms, a biologist is likely to be relatively better able to understand medical issues than a layperson. Still, this does not mean that anyone in the life sciences is always better informed than anyone else on any issue in that area. A diligent person who has taken the time to read up on, say, diabetes could very well be more conversant in that subject than a botanist. A professional whose expertise is deep but narrow might not be any better informed than anyone else on matters outside his or her own field. Education and credentials in one area do not guarantee expertise in *all* areas.

In the natural sciences, prediction and explanation go hand in hand: once a physical phenomenon is understood, its behavior should be predictable, and can even sometimes be expressed as a law. Social scientists, historians, and other observers of human behavior, by contrast, tend to favor explanation over raw prediction. In many fields outside the hard sciences, conclusions are probabilistic rather than absolute. And yet, society as a client tends to demand far more prediction than explanation. Worse, laypeople tend to regard failures of prediction as indications of the worthlessness of expertise.

Experts face a difficult task in this respect, because no matter how many times scholars might emphasize that their goal is to explain the world rather than to predict discrete events, laypeople and policymakers prefer prediction. (And experts, even when they know better, often gladly oblige.) This is a natural but irresolvable tension between experts and their clients; most people would prefer to anticipate problems and avoid them, instead of explaining them in retrospect. The promises of a diagnosis, even if speculative, are always more welcome than the absolute certainties of an autopsy.

Finally, there is outright deception and malfeasance. This is the rarest but most dangerous category. Here, experts for their own reasons (usually careerist defenses of their own shoddy work) intentionally falsify their results. They hope on the one hand that laypeople will not be capable of catching them, and on the other that their colleagues will not notice or will attribute their fraud to honest error.

This most extreme category is the easiest to deal with, so we will start there.

WHEN EXPERTS GO BAD

The early twenty-first century has seen some rough years for scientists. Retractions from scientific journals have reached record proportions. Cases of fraud or misconduct now seem almost routine.

Expert deception is not hard to define, but it can be hard to identify. Obvious misconduct occurs when researchers or scholars falsify their results or when would-be experts lie about being credentialed or licensed to practice in their field. (Scientists describe this using the catch-all shorthand "FFP," meaning "fabrication, falsification, or plagiarism.") Such misconduct can be hard to detect specifically because it requires other experts to ferret it out; laypeople are not equipped to take apart scientific studies, no more than they are likely to look closely at a credential hanging on a wall to see if it is real.

Sometimes experts aren't experts. People lie, and lie brazenly, about their credentials. This is the kind of bravura fakery that the real-life "Great Pretender," Frank Abagnale, pulled off in the 1960s (later popularized in the movie *Catch Me If You Can*), including his impersonation of an airline pilot and a medical doctor. A more common but subtler kind of deception occurs when people who are actual experts augment their credentials with false honors or exaggerations. They might claim to be members of professional associations, or to have attended panels or symposia, or to be honorees or prizewinners, or other embellishments that are in fact fraudulent. Usually, such people are only caught when something happens that causes others to scrutinize their records.

When actual experts lie, they endanger not only their own profession but also the well-being of their client: society. Their threat to expertise comes in both the immediate outcome of their chicanery and the erosion of social trust such misconduct creates when it is discovered. This is why (aside from any legal sanctions that may exist for lying and fraud) professional organizations, scholarly foundations, think tanks, journals, and universities reserve some of their harshest punishments for willful misconduct.

Such punishments, contrary to the popular imagination, do exist. There is a myth among many Americans that it is impossible to fire researchers and university teachers. This is not entirely a baseless belief, because firing a tenured professor is in fact quite difficult. While many professors have "moral turpitude" clauses in their contracts, the social norms of the twenty-first century have lowered that bar to the point that almost nothing a professor does in his or her classroom or personal life can move a school to the point of revoking tenure. Obvious firing offenses like physically threatening a student or outright refusing to show up for work can still trigger a dismissal, but almost anything else in the category of personal conduct is usually overlooked.

Academic misconduct, however, is still a red line for many schools. Academic freedom guarantees the right to express unpopular or unconventional ideas, but it is not a license to produce sloppy or intentionally misleading research. When the University of Colorado, for example, fired Ward Churchill—an instructor who compared the victims of the 9/11 attacks in New York to Nazis—they fired him not for being an insensitive jerk, but because his comments generated new attention to his "scholarship," sections of which turned out to be plagiarized. Churchill, of course, claimed that he was a victim of political bias. He appealed his dismissal as a Colorado state employee all the way up to the Colorado Supreme Court and lost.

There can be no doubt that Churchill's record got a close look only because of his political views. Churchill appealed his dismissal on those very grounds, arguing that his plagiarism consisted of innocent mistakes that were only discovered when he took a controversial view. But this in itself is a disturbing position: does it take calling the people who died in the Twin Towers "little [Adolf] Eichmanns," as

Churchill did, before anyone takes a close look at a professor's scholarly work? To claim that plagiarism was discovered only because the professor managed to draw enough attention to himself with his odious comments is not much of a defense.

The Churchill case was in some ways unique, not least because of the publicity it attracted. Most cases of professional misconduct in academia go unnoticed by the public. The 2014 gay-marriage study, which represented wholesale falsification of data, was an exception, and gained significant attention largely because of the potential political impact of the conclusion. Most academic studies are not nearly as interesting as one that claims people can be talked out of homophobia, and so they do not generate the same level of interest.

Less publicized cases, however, are no less serious. In 2011, a postdoctoral researcher working on a US government grant at Columbia University was found to have falsified cell biology research related to Alzheimer's disease. The researcher agreed not to accept any federal grants for three years, but by the time the misconduct was discovered, his article had been cited by other scientists at least 150 times. In 2016, a Spanish researcher was dismissed from her institution as well for alleged fraud related to her work on cardiovascular disease.

In a more dramatic case, Andrew Wakefield, a doctor who published a controversial study linking vaccines and autism, had his medical license revoked in the United Kingdom in 2010. British medical authorities claimed that they pulled his license not because he argued for a controversial thesis, but because he broke a lot of basic rules of scientific conduct to do it. The UK General Medical Council found that Wakefield "had done invasive research on children without ethical approval, acted against the clinical interests of each child, failed to disclose financial conflicts of interest, and misappropriated funds."[8]

Like Ward Churchill, Wakefield's supporters argued that he was the victim of a witch-hunt. But discredited research is not the same as misconduct. For example, Peter Duesberg, one of the leading AIDS denialists, remains at Berkeley despite accusations from critics that he engaged in academic misconduct, charges against him that his university investigated and dismissed in 2010.

Still, there is no way around it: a non-negligible amount of published scientific research is shaky at best and falsified at worse. It might be a small consolation to laypeople, but the reason we know any of this misconduct is happening at all is because scientists across all fields admit it. When a 2005 study asked scientists if they personally had committed questionable research practices, about 2 percent of scientists self-reported fabrication, falsification, or "modifying" data at least once; 14 percent said they witnessed this behavior in colleagues. When asked about serious misconduct that falls short of hanging offenses like outright falsification, a third of the respondents admitted they had engaged in less obvious but still shady practices, such as ignoring findings that contradicted their own. More than 70 percent claimed to have witnessed these same behaviors in their colleagues.[9]

Most of this misconduct is invisible to laypeople because it is so dull. Unlike the dramatic stories of massive fraud people see in well-known movies like *Erin Brockovich* or *The Insider*, most of the retractions in scientific journals are over small-bore mistakes or misrepresentations in studies on narrow topics. The natural sciences seem to be more trouble-prone, but that is likely because their studies are easier to test.

Indeed, natural scientists could point out that retractions in themselves are signs of professional responsibility and oversight. The scientific and medical journals with the highest impact on their fields—the *New England Journal of Medicine*, for example—tend to have higher rates of retractions. No one, however, is quite sure why.[10] It could be due to more people checking the results, which would be a heartening trend. It could also happen because more people cut corners to get into top journals, which would be a depressing reality.

It could also be an effect of publishing in a prestigious journal: with more readers, someone is more likely to try to use the research in their own work and thus catch the misconduct further down the line.

The gold standard of any scientific study is whether it can be replicated or at least reconstructed. This is why scientists and scholars use footnotes: not as insurance against plagiarism—although there's that, too—but so that their peers can follow in their footsteps to see if they would reach the same conclusions. If scientists are cooking the books, then this would make their conclusions difficult to replicate, thus undermining or even falsifying their studies.

This kind of verification assumes, however, that anyone is bothering to replicate the work in the first place. Ordinary peer review does not include re-running experiments; rather, the referees read the paper with an assumption that basic standards of research and procedure were met. They decide mostly if the subject is important, whether the data are of sufficient quality, and whether the evidence presented supports the conclusions.

Of course, the replicability requirement seems to recommend greater confidence in the hard sciences like chemistry or physics. The social sciences, like sociology and psychology, rely on studies that often depend on human subjects and thus are therefore more difficult to reproduce. At the least, the natural scientists can claim to have clearer standards: if someone asserts that a certain plastic melts at 100 degrees, then everyone else with a sample of the same material and a Bunsen burner can check the finding. When one hundred student volunteers are asked to participate in a survey or exercise, things get a lot more difficult. The results might be a snapshot in time, or of a particular region, or skewed in some other way. The research design is supposed to account for these issues, but the only way to know is to try to replicate the experiments.

This is exactly what a team of researchers set out to do in the field of psychology. The results were surprising, to say the least. As the

New York Times reported in 2015, a "painstaking" effort to reproduce 100 studies published in three leading psychology journals found that more than half of the findings did not hold up when retested.

> The analysis was done by research psychologists, many of whom volunteered their time to double-check what they considered important work. . . . The vetted studies were considered part of the core knowledge by which scientists understand the dynamics of personality, relationships, learning and memory. Therapists and educators rely on such findings to help guide decisions, and the fact that so many of the studies were called into question could sow doubt in the scientific underpinnings of their work.[11]

This outcome is cause for concern, but is it fraud? Lousy research isn't the same thing as misconduct. In many of these cases, the problem is not that the replication of the study produced a different result but that the studies themselves were inherently "irreproducible," meaning that their conclusions may be useful but that other researchers cannot re-run those human investigations in the same way over and over.

Actually, the psychology studies might not even be poor research. Another group of scholars subsequently examined the investigation itself—this is how science works, after all—and concluded that it was, in the words of the Harvard scholar Gary King, "completely unfair—and even irresponsible." King noted that while reproducibility is an "incredibly important" question that should "obsess" scholars, "it isn't true that all social psychologists are making stuff up."[12] The whole business, including a rebuttal to the rebuttal, is now where it belongs: in the pages of the journal *Science*, where experts can continue to evaluate all of the arguments and subject them to further analysis.

Are the natural sciences, then, just catching more of their own shoddy or faked work than the social sciences? Perhaps not. When cancer researchers tried to replicate studies in their field, they ran into the same problems as the psychologists and others. Daniel Engber, a writer for Slate.com, reported in 2016 on a group of biomedical studies that suggested a "replication crisis" much like the one in psychology, and he noted that by some estimates "fully half of all results rest on shaky ground, and might not be replicable in other labs. These cancer studies don't merely fail to find a cure; they might not offer any useful data whatsoever."[13] The obstacles to replication were much the same as those that bedeviled the social scientists: sloppiness, the passage of time, the inability to reproduce exact conditions from the first trials, and so on.

Here, we move from work that is fraudulent to work that might merely be slipshod. This is too complicated a subject to engage here, but the "replication crisis" in the scholarly community is not based on pure fraudulence. In addition to the physical and temporal constraints on perfect replicability, other problems include poor oversight of grants, intense pressure from academic institutions to come up with publishable results (no matter how trivial), and the tendency among scholars to box up their previous work and throw it away once the paper or study is published.

Research in the social sciences and humanities is especially difficult to replicate because it is based not on experimental procedure but rather on expert interpretation of discrete works or events. A book of literary criticism is exactly what it sounds like: criticism. It is not science. It is, however, an expert judgment that requires a deep knowledge of the subject. Likewise, a study of the Cuban missile crisis is not the same as an experiment in the natural sciences. We cannot re-run October 1962 over and over again, and so an author examining the outcome of the crisis is presenting an expert analysis of one historical case. Such a study might be full of flawed conclusions, but it is the raw material for further discussion rather than a case of professional malfeasance.

Still, there have been some remarkable cases of outright fraud in the social sciences and humanities. In 2000, a historian at Emory University named Michael Bellesiles won Columbia University's prestigious Bancroft Prize in history for a book called *Arming America*, in which Bellesiles claimed to debunk the idea that American ideas about gun ownership were rooted not in the early colonial experience but in other influences nearly a century later. The study was instantly polarizing, because it argued that private gun ownership was uncommon in early America.

Once again, a study that might have gone unnoticed attracted closer scrutiny because of its subject matter, with gun control advocates and gun ownership groups immediately taking sides on the Bellesiles argument. As other scholars tried to find the sources on which Bellesiles relied, however, they concluded that he had either misused them or invented them. Columbia withdrew the Bancroft Prize. Emory conducted its own investigation and found that while some of Bellesiles's errors might be ascribed to incompetence, there were unavoidable questions about his scholarly integrity. Bellesiles resigned his post shortly thereafter. His book was dropped by its original publisher, although it was later reissued by a small commercial press.

In 2012, a writer named David Barton published a book on Thomas Jefferson. Barton had no background as a professional historian; his public prominence, was largely due to his stature in the evangelical movement. (In 2005, *TIME* called him one of the twenty-five most influential evangelicals in America.) His book attracted kudos and endorsements from leading conservatives, including 2012 presidential contenders Mike Huckabee and the historian-turned-politician Newt Gingrich.

Like the Bellesiles gun study, Barton's work attracted considerable attention because of its political implications as well as the prominence of its author. The book minced no words even in its title,

The Jefferson Lies: Exposing the Myths You've Always Believed about Thomas Jefferson. Barton's book argued that modern historians not only had smeared Jefferson's private life but also had ignored how many of his beliefs were actually supportive of modern conservative views. Considering Jefferson's admiration of revolutionary France and his later association with liberalism (in contrast to his conservative nemesis John Adams), this was a bold claim.

Most professional scholars ignored the book, coming as it did from an amateur historian and a non-academic religious publishing house. The book was not, in any case, aimed at scholars, but at an audience already eager to read it. Barton hit the mark: *The Jefferson Lies* quickly made the *New York Times* best-seller list.

The accuracy of the book was soon called into question not by godless liberals at a research university but by two scholars at Grove City College, a small Christian school in Pennsylvania. Under closer scrutiny, many of Barton's claims collapsed. The readers of the *History News Network* later voted it "the least credible book in print," but even more damning, the book's publishers agreed that the book was so flawed that they withdrew it from circulation. The *Atlantic* writer and law professor Garret Epps, in a scathing review of the matter, said, "Most of [Barton's] books are self-published and will never be withdrawn. But the rebuke from Christian scholars and a Christian publishing house is a mark of shame he will carry from now on."[14]

In all of these cases, the fraud and misconduct were found out. To a layperson, however, the eventual reckoning over such work is understandably irrelevant. The bedrock issue is whether studies, in any field, can be trusted.

In a way, this is the wrong question. Rarely does a single study make or break a subject. The average person is not going to have to rely on the outcome of any particular project, say, in cell research. When a group of studies is aggregated into a drug or a treatment of which that one study might be a part, this itself triggers successive studies looking at safety and efficacy. It is possible to fake one study. To fake hundreds and thus produce a completely fraudulent or dangerous result is another matter entirely.

Likewise, no one study in public policy establishes an expert's credentials. Even when a scholar comes to the attention of the policy community because of a book or an article, his or her influence does not rest on the scientific replicability of the work but on the ideas it puts forward. In the social sciences, as in the hard sciences, it is rare that any single study can influence the life of the average citizen without at least some reconsideration by other experts.

What fraud does in any field, however, is to waste time and to delay progress. Much in the same way an error buried early in a complex set of equations can bog down later calculations, fraud or misconduct can delay an entire project until someone figures out who screwed up—or intentionally fudged—the facts. When such cases are revealed to the public, of course, they have legitimate questions about the scope and impact of misconduct, especially if they're paying for it with public money.

I THOUGHT YOU WERE PRE-MED?

There are other sources of expert failure beyond willful fraud or staggering incompetence. One of the most common errors experts make is to assume that because they are smarter than most people about certain things, they are smarter than everyone about everything. They see their expert knowledge as a license to hold court about anything. (Again, I cannot cast the first stone here.) Their advanced education and experience serve as a kind of blanket assurance that they know what they're doing in almost any field.

These experts are like Eric Stratton in the classic comedy *Animal House*. When he rises to defend his unruly college fraternity in student court, his friends ask him if he knows what he's doing. "Take it easy, I'm pre-law," he assures his brothers. "I thought you were pre-med?" one of them asks. "What's the difference?" Stratton answers.

This overconfidence leads experts not only to get out of their own lane and make pronouncements on matters far afield of their expertise, but also to "over-claim" wider expertise even within their own general area of competence. Experts and professionals, just as people in other endeavors, assume that their previous successes and achievements are evidence of their superior knowledge, and they push their boundaries rather than say the three words every expert hates to say: "I don't know." No one wants to appear to be uninformed or to be caught out on some ellipsis in their personal knowledge. Laypeople and experts alike will issue confident statements on things about which they know nothing, but experts are supposed to know better.

Cross-expertise violations happen for a number of reasons, from innocent error to intellectual vanity. Sometimes, however, the motivation is as simple as the opportunity provided by fame. Entertainers are the worst offenders here. (And, yes, in their field, they are experts. Acting schools are not run by chemical engineers.) Their celebrity affords them easy access to issues and controversies, and to actual experts or policymakers who will work with them because of the natural proclivity to answer the phone when someone famous calls.

Talking with celebrities, however, is not the same thing as educating them. This creates bizarre situations in which experts in one field—entertainment—end up giving disquisitions on important questions in other fields. This bizarre phenomenon has a relatively recent history in the United States, but it began well before celebrities could bloviate at will on Twitter or on their own websites.

In 1985, for example, a California congressman, Tony Coelho, invited the actresses Jane Fonda, Sissy Spacek, and Jessica Lange to testify before the House Agriculture Committee on farm problems. Their qualification? They had played farmers' wives in three popular movies of the decade. The whole business was a stunt, of course, and when asked why he did it, Democrat Coelho took a shot at Republican President Ronald Reagan: "They probably have a better understanding of the problems of agriculture than the actor in the White House," he said at the time.[15]

This was not, however, an isolated incident. Over the years, celebrities have steeped themselves in disputes about which they have very little knowledge. They push fads, create false alarms, and change the daily habits of millions of gullible fans.

Timothy Caulfield, a Canadian health policy expert, is one of many experts who has had enough. He wrote a book criticizing assaults on established knowledge from celebrities, and by one celebrity in particular: *Is Gwyneth Paltrow Wrong about Everything? When Celebrity Culture and Science Clash.* (I discussed some of Paltrow's feminine-care recommendations—reluctantly—in chapter 4.) As Caulfield put it in a 2016 interview,

> If you ask someone, is Gwyneth Paltrow a credible source of information about breast cancer risk? Most people are going to say no. The science of nutrition? Most people will be skeptical. But because she has such a huge cultural footprint, and because she has made this brand for herself, people will identify with it.
>
> There's the availability bias, too: Celebrities are just everywhere. And the mere fact that they're everywhere, that influences in the impact they have. It's easy to call up a picture of [Paltrow] on *People* magazine talking about gluten-free as opposed to what the data actually says. And that allows celebrities to have a huge impact on our lives.[16]

This is not harmless. People are actually reluctant to vaccinate their children because of advice given by the actress Jenny McCarthy, a Playboy pinup who says she studied it all deeply at the "University of

Google." More people will see Paltrow and McCarthy and be exposed to their inane ideas than will ever see—or have the patience to listen to—a far less attractive oncologist or epidemiologist.

Activism is the right of every person in an open and democratic society. There is a fundamental difference, however, between activism and a celebrity abusing his or her fame. Activism among laypeople requires taking sides among experts, and advocating for preferred policies. When celebrities substitute their own judgment for that of experts, however—in effect demanding to be trusted merely by the fact of their own fame—they are no better than a microbiologist weighing in on modern art, or an economist arguing about pharmacology.

In some cases, experts overextend themselves because their trespass is into an area of expertise close enough to their own that a stretch of professional judgment seems reasonable. This is especially likely among experts who have already been lauded for the achievements in their own field. As society has become more complex, however, the idea of geniuses who can hit to any and all fields makes less sense: "Benjamin Franklin," the humorist Alexandra Petri once wrote, "was one of the last men up to whom you could go and say, 'You invented a stove. What do you think we should do about these taxes?' and get a coherent answer."[17]

The Nobel Prize–winning chemist Linus Pauling, for example, became convinced in the 1970s that Vitamin C was a wonder drug. He advocated taking mega-doses of the supplement to ward off the common cold and any number of other ailments. There was no actual evidence for Pauling's claims, but Pauling had a Nobel in chemistry, and so his conclusions about the effect of vitamins seemed to many people to be a reasonable extension of his expertise.

In fact, Pauling failed to apply the scientific standards of his own profession at the very start of his advocacy for vitamins. He began taking Vitamin C in the late 1960s on the advice of a self-proclaimed doctor named Irwin Stone, who told Pauling that if he took three thousand milligrams of C a day—fifty times the recommended daily amount—that he would live twenty-five years longer. "Doctor" Stone's only degrees, however, were two honorary awards from a nonaccredited correspondence school and a college of chiropractic medicine.[18]

Pauling wanted to believe in the concept, and he started gobbling the vitamin. Immediately, he felt its miraculous effects. A more impartial observer might suspect a "placebo effect," in which telling someone a pill will make them feel better makes them think they feel better, but because of Pauling's illustrious contributions to science, his colleagues took him seriously and tested his claims.

None of these examinations of Vitamin C panned out, but Pauling would not hear of it. As Dr. Paul Offit, a pediatrician and a specialist in infectious diseases at the University of Pennsylvania, later wrote, "Although study after study showed that he was wrong, Pauling refused to believe it, continuing to promote vitamin C in speeches, popular articles, and books. When he occasionally appeared before the media with obvious cold symptoms, he said he was suffering from allergies."

Throughout the 1970s Pauling expanded his claims. He argued that vitamins could treat everything, including cancer, heart disease, leprosy, and mental illness, among other maladies. He later went on to suggest looking into the uses of Vitamin C in the fight against AIDS. Vitamin manufacturers, of course, were happy to have a Nobel Laureate as their patron saint. Soon, vitamin supplements (including "antioxidants," a term that became the "gluten-free" and "non-GMO" of its day) were big business.

Except, as it turns out, big doses of vitamins can actually be dangerous, including increasing the chance of certain kinds of cancers and strokes. Pauling, in the end, hurt not only his own reputation but also the health of potentially millions of people. As Offit put it, a "man who was so spectacularly right that he won two Nobel Prizes" was "so spectacularly wrong that he was arguably the world's greatest quack." To this day, there are people who still think a vitamin-laden horse pill can ward off illness, despite the fact that science worked exactly the way it's supposed to work by testing and falsifying Pauling's claims.

Pauling himself died of cancer at age ninety-three. Whether he got the extra twenty-five years "Doctor" Stone promised him, we'll never know.

Sometimes, experts use the luster of a particular credential or achievement to go even further afield of their area, in order to influence important public policy debates. In the fall of 1983, a New York City radio station broadcast a program about the nuclear arms race. The early 1980s were tense years in the Cold War, and 1983 was one of the worst. The Soviet Union shot down a civilian Korean airliner, talks between the United States and the USSR about nuclear arms broke down in Geneva, and ABC's docudrama on a possible nuclear war, *The Day After*, debuted as the most-watched television program up until that time. It was also soon to be an election year.

I was one of the listeners, as a young graduate student in New York at the time studying the Soviet Union and looking ahead to a career in public policy. "If Ronald Reagan is re-elected," the voice on my radio said in a sharp Australian accent, "nuclear war is a mathematical certainty." The declaration that nuclear war was inescapable got my attention, especially as there were no serious predictions that Reagan was in any electoral danger in 1984. Who was this person who was so definite—to the point of *mathematical certainty*—that we were therefore headed for Armageddon?

The speaker was a woman named Dr. Helen Caldicott. She was not a doctor of physics or government or international affairs, but a pediatrician from Australia. Her concern about nuclear weapons, by her own recollection, stemmed from reading Nevil Shute's 1956 postapocalyptic novel *On the Beach* (which was set in her native country). As she later put it, she saw no point in treating children for their illnesses when the world around them could be reduced to ashes at any moment. In short order, she became a prominent voice in debates on arms control and nuclear policy, despite her almost complete lack of credentials or experience with the subject matter.

Caldicott was prone to making definitive statements about highly technical matters. She would discourse confidently on things like the resilience of US missile silos, civil defense measures, and the internal workings of the Soviet foreign policy apparatus. She resided in the United States for almost a decade, and she became a regular presence in the media representing the antinuclear activist community.

She reached the apex of her cross-expertise influence when she published her 1985 book *Missile Envy*, a book replete with medical terminology as a "diagnosis" of the arms race. (The chapters include "Etiology," "Physical Examination," "Case Study," and so on.) The title of the book is a spoiler: the pediatrician found a psychological grounding for the Cold War in the psyches of old Soviet and American men. She noted that American women, having won the right to vote, "have done virtually nothing with it"; women in government like then-British prime minister Margaret Thatcher, Caldicott said, did not "represent the true attributes of the large majority of sensible, wise women."[19] (When I heard Caldicott on New York radio, she was even more blunt: "Margaret Thatcher," the doctor declared, "is not a woman.") Caldicott went back to Australia in the late 1980s to run for political office. She was defeated.

The expert community is full of such examples. The most famous, at least if measured by impact on the global public, is the MIT professor Noam Chomsky, a figure revered by millions of readers around the world. Chomsky, by some counts, is the most widely cited living American intellectual, having written a stack of books on politics and foreign policy. His professorial post at MIT, however, was actually as a professor of linguistics. Chomsky is regarded as a pioneer, even a giant, in his own field, but he is no more an expert in foreign policy than, say, the late George Kennan was in the origins of human language. Nonetheless, he is more famous among the general public for his writings on politics than in his area of expertise; indeed, I have often encountered college students over the years who are familiar with Chomsky but who had no idea he was actually a linguistics professor.

Like Pauling and Caldicott, however, Chomsky answered a need in the public square. Laypeople often feel at a disadvantage challenging traditional science or socially dominant ideas, and they will rally to outspoken figures whose views carry a patina of expert assurance. It may well be that doctors should look closely at the role of vitamins in the human diet. It is certain that the public should be involved in an ongoing reconsideration of the role of nuclear weapons. But a degree in chemistry or a residency in pediatrics does not make advocates of those positions more credible than any other autodidact in those esoteric subjects.

The public is remarkably tolerant of such trespasses, and this itself is a paradox: while some laypeople do not respect an expert's actual area of knowledge, others assume that expertise and achievement are so generic that experts and intellectuals can weigh in with some authority on almost anything. The same people who might doubt their family physician about the safety of vaccines will buy a book on nuclear weapons because the author's title includes the magic letters "MD."

Unfortunately, when experts are asked for views outside their competence, few are humble enough to remember their responsibility to demur. I have made this mistake, and I have ended up regretting it. In a strange twist, I have also actually argued with people who have insisted that I am fully capable of commenting on a subject when I have made plain that I have no particular knowledge in the matter at hand. It is an odd feeling indeed to assure a reporter, or especially a student, that despite their faith in me, it would be irresponsible of me to answer their question with any pretense of authority. It is an uncomfortable admission, but one we can only wish linguistics professors, pediatricians, and so many others would make as well.

I PREDICT!

In the early 1960s, an entertainer known as "The Amazing Criswell" was a regular guest on television and radio shows. Criswell's act was to make outrageous predictions, delivered with a dramatic flourish of "I predict!" Among his many pronouncements, Criswell warned that New York would sink into the sea by 1980, Vermont would suffer a nuclear attack in 1981, and Denver would be destroyed in a natural disaster in 1989. Criswell's act was pure camp, but the public enjoyed it. What Criswell did not predict, however, was that his own career would fizzle out in the late 1960s and end with a few small roles in low-budget sexploitation films made by his friend, the legendarily awful director Edward D. Wood, Jr.[20]

Prediction is a problem for experts. It's what the public wants, but experts usually aren't very good at it. This is because they're not supposed to be good at it; the purpose of science is to explain, not to predict. And yet predictions, like cross-expertise transgressions, are catnip to experts.

Experts and laypeople alike believe that because experts have a better handle on a subject than others, they will have a better track record of prediction. For experts in the hard sciences, this is always a stronger claim, because they use experimental methods to determine the conditions under which the physical world will behave as they would expect. When unpredictable things happen, scientists have a new starting point for investigation. As the late science-fiction writer (and professor of biochemistry) Isaac Asimov said, the words that have spurred the greatest scientific breakthroughs are probably not "Eureka," but "Gee, that's funny."

Some experts, however, embrace prediction and even charge a handsome fee for it. Pollsters, for example, sell their services to political candidates and to media subscribers, while marketing experts test the waters for new services and products. Polling has come a long way since 1936, when *Literary Digest* predicted that Alf Landon would defeat Franklin Roosevelt (mostly by surveying its own readers). Today, research on public opinion is a science, with its own experts and journals. Some pollsters are partisans who slant their results toward a preferred outcome, but most have an academic background in statistics and methods that allows them, in the main, to make reasonably accurate calls.

When polls and market research get something wrong, however, they can get it very wrong. The Coca-Cola Corporation's introduction of "New Coke" in the mid-1980s was such a disaster that the term "New Coke" itself has become a meme for a failure to read public opinion accurately. More recently political pollsters and experts missed several important calls in the early twenty-first century, including the results of the 2014 midterm election in the United States and the 2015 general election in the United Kingdom.

In fact, a survey of pollsters in 2015 found that they believed their reputations had been tarnished by this string of misses. Some felt that this was a result of media bias (which favors covering failure more than success), while others admitted that technological and demographic changes were making accurate polling a more challenging endeavor. "Polls are wrong is a more interesting story than when the polls do well," the polling expert Barbara Carvalho told FiveThirtyEight (itself a site dedicated to polling). But the pollster Matthew Towery admitted in 2015 that, "obviously, there were several high-profile calamities in the past three years."[21]

The problem here is not so much with polling—whose accuracy is limited by the involvement of actual human beings—as it is with what people expect from polling. Polls are not a written guarantee of future results. Many things, from unforeseeable events to advertising, can change minds. As in every other expert endeavor, the measure of competence is in the overall trend and in whether the experts examine their own failures carefully. Likewise, for every New Coke, there are thousands of successful product launches and accurate campaign forecasts. As is always the case, however, people tend to remember the bad calls—especially if they didn't like the results—while ignoring the more numerous successes.

People expect too much from expert prediction, but at least some experts are also willing to stand on their clairvoyance strongly enough to sell it. For decades, the political science professor Bruce Bueno de Mesquita has been using "proprietary software" to make predictions about world events for both public and private customers. His firm's clients over some thirty years have included the US Central Intelligence Agency, which in a 1993 study said that in hundreds of predictions he "hit the bullseye" twice as often as its own analysts did.

Other experts have not been able to test Bueno de Mesquita's claims, since his methods and models are protected as business property rather than presented in published studies. As a *New York Times* profile noted in 2009,

> While Bueno de Mesquita has published many predictions in academic journals, the vast majority of his forecasts have been done in secret for corporate or government clients, where no independent academics can verify them. "We have no idea if he's right 9 times out of 10, or 9 times out of a hundred, or 9 times out of a thousand," [Harvard professor Stephen] Walt says.
>
> Walt also isn't impressed by [the] C.I.A. study showing Bueno de Mesquita's 90 percent hit rate. "It's one midlevel

C.I.A. bureaucrat saying, 'This was a useful tool,'" Walt says. "It's not like he's got Brent Scowcroft saying, 'Back in the Bush administration, we didn't make a decision without consulting Bueno de Mesquita.' "[22]

While Bueno de Mesquita's accuracy is unknowable, the more important point is that there is a healthy market for his predictions. Organizations with a great deal at stake—lives, money, or both—inevitably embark on voracious searches for information before taking risks. An expert who says he or she can peek into the future will always be more in demand than one who offers more limited advice.

Pollsters and consultants like Bueno de Mesquita are paid to predict things, and the value of their work is up to their clients. But other experts and public intellectuals make predictions, too, and the many failures of expert predictions have done much to undermine public confidence in scholars and professionals. When people who didn't foresee the end of the Soviet Union—or who promised that a major war with Iraq would be an easy win—return to provide yet more advice on life-and-death decisions, the public's skepticism is understandable.

If we leave aside the issue of whether experts *ought* to predict, we're still left with the problem that they *do* predict, and their predictions often are startlingly bad. In a widely read study on "black swan" events—the unforeseeable moments that can change history—Nassim Nicholas Taleb decried the "epistemic arrogance" of the whole enterprise of prediction.

But we act as though we are able to predict historical events, or, even worse, as if we are able to change the course of history. We produce 30-year projections of social security deficits and oil prices without realizing that we cannot even predict these for next summer—our cumulative prediction errors for political and economic events are so monstrous that every time I look at the empirical record I have to pinch myself to verify that I am not dreaming.[23]

Taleb's warning about the permanence of uncertainty is an important observation, but his insistence on accepting the futility of prediction is impractical. Human beings will not throw their hands up and abandon any possibility of applying expertise as an anticipatory hedge.

The question is not whether experts should engage in prediction. They will. The society they live in and the leaders who govern it will ask them to do so. Rather, the issue is when and how experts should make predictions, and what to do about it when they're wrong.

In 2005, the scholar Philip Tetlock gathered data on expert predictions in social science, and he found what many people suspected: "When we pit experts against minimalist performance benchmarks—dilettantes, dart-throwing chimps, and assorted extrapolation algorithms—we find few signs that expertise translates into greater ability to make either 'well-calibrated' or 'discriminating' forecasts."[24] Experts, it seemed, were no better at predicting the future than spinning a roulette wheel. Tetlock's initial findings confirmed for many laypeople a suspicion that experts don't really know what they're doing.

But this reaction to Tetlock's work was a classic case of laypeople misunderstanding expertise. As Tetlock himself noted, "radical skeptics welcomed these results, but they start squirming when we start finding patterns of consistency in who got what right. Radical skepticism tells us to expect nothing. . . . But the data revealed more consistency in forecasters' track records than could be ascribed to chance."[25]

Tetlock, in fact, did not measure experts against everyone in the world, but against basic benchmarks, especially the predictions of other experts. The question wasn't whether experts were no better than anyone else at prediction, but why *some* experts seemed better at prediction than *others*, which is a very different question. Or as James Surowiecki (the "wisdom of crowds" writer) pointed out, saying that "cognitive diversity" is important—meaning that many views can be better than one—it does *not* mean that if "you assemble a group of diverse but thoroughly uninformed people, their collective wisdom will be smarter than an expert's."[26]

What Tetlock actually found was not that experts were no better than random guessers, but that certain kinds of experts seemed better at applying knowledge to hypotheticals than their colleagues. Tetlock used the British thinker Isaiah Berlin's distinction between "hedgehogs" and "foxes" to distinguish between experts whose knowledge was wide and inclusive ("the fox knows many things") from those whose expertise is narrow and deep ("the hedgehog knows but one"). Tetlock's study is one of the most important works ever written on how experts think, and it deserves a full reading. In general, however, one of his more intriguing findings can be summarized by noting that while experts ran into trouble when trying to move from explanation to prediction, the "foxes" generally outperformed the "hedgehogs," for many reasons.

Hedgehogs, for example, tended to be overly focused on generalizing their specific knowledge to situations that were outside of their competence, while foxes were better able to integrate more information and to change their minds when presented with new or better data. "The foxes' self-critical, point-counterpoint style of thinking," Tetlock found, "prevented them from building up the sorts of excessive enthusiasm for their predictions that hedgehogs, especially well-informed ones, displayed for theirs."[27]

Technical experts, the very embodiment of the hedgehogs, had considerable trouble not only with prediction but with broadening their ability to process information outside their area in general. People with a very well-defined area of knowledge do not have many tools beyond their specialization, so their instinct is to take what they know and generalize it outward, no matter how poorly the fit is between their own area and the subject at hand.[28] This results in predictions that are made with more confidence but that tend to be more often wrong, mostly because the scientists, as classic hedgehogs, have difficulty accepting and processing information from outside their very small but highly complicated lane of expertise.

There are some lessons in all this, not just for experts, but for laypeople who judge—and even challenge—expert predictions.

The most important point is that failed predictions do not mean very much in terms of judging expertise. Experts usually cover their predictions (and an important part of their anatomy) with caveats, because the world is full of unforeseeable accidents that can have major ripple effects down the line. History can be changed by contingent events as simple as a heart attack or a hurricane. Laypeople tend to ignore these caveats, despite their importance, much as they ignore their local weather forecaster when told there is a 70 percent chance of rain. If the three in ten possibility of a sunny day arrives, they think the forecaster was wrong.

This isn't to let experts, especially expert communities, off the hook for massive failures of insight. While no one Soviet expert in the 1970s could predict the fall of the USSR by 1991, the hardening of expert opinion around the opposite view—that the collapse of the Soviet state was practically impossible—is a sizable error in judgment that should haunt that field. (Unfortunately, it does not; for twenty years, most Russia specialists have shied away from examining each other's mistakes.)

Predictive failure, however, does not retroactively strip experts of their claim to know more than laypeople. Laypeople should not jump to the assumption that a missed call by the experts therefore means all opinions are equally valid (or equally worthless). The polling expert Nate Silver, who made his reputation with remarkably accurate forecasts in the 2008 and 2012 presidential elections, has since admitted that his predictions about Republican presidential nominee Donald Trump in 2016 were based on flawed assumptions.[29] But Silver's insights into the other races remain solid, even if the Trump phenomenon surprised him and others. As the columnist Noah Rothman later wrote, "Trump has demonstrated that so many of the rules that political professionals spent their careers studying were not predictive this year. But 'everything we knew about politics was wrong' does not yield to 'we know nothing about politics.'"[30]

Calling experts to account for making worse predictions than other experts is a different matter. But to phrase questions as raw yes-or-no predictions, and then to note that laypeople can be right as often as experts, is fundamentally to misunderstand the role of expertise itself. Indeed, to ask such undifferentiated questions is also to let experts off the hook. There's an old joke about a British civil servant who retired after a long career in the Foreign Office spanning most of the twentieth century. "Every morning," the experienced diplomatic hand said, "I went to the Prime Minister and assured him there would be no world war today. And I am pleased to note that in a career of 40 years, I was only wrong twice." Judged purely on the number of hits and misses, the old man had a pretty good record.

The goal of expert advice and prediction is not to win a coin toss, it is to help guide decisions about possible futures. To ask in 1980 whether the Soviet Union would fall before the year 2000 is a yes-or-no question. To ask during the previous decades how best to bring about a peaceful Soviet collapse and to alter the probability of that event (and to lessen the chances of others) is a different matter entirely.

Given my own background in Russian studies, an alert reader at this point might be wondering if I was part of the community of Soviet experts who got it wrong, and whether I am just throwing spitballs from the back of the classroom. It's a fair question.

I did not get the Soviet collapse wrong—but only because I never had the chance to be wrong in the first place. I finished graduate school in late 1988, when it was already clear that the fissioning of the USSR was under way. Instead, I waited another ten years before making my own howlingly wrong prediction about Russian politics. I know the dangers of making bad predictions, because I have my own for which I must answer.

In early 2000 I wrote that the emergence of a new Russian leader, an unknown bureaucrat named Vladimir Putin, might actually be a step along the way toward further democracy in Russia. I could not have been more wrong, of course; Putin turned out to be a dictator and he remains a continuing threat to global peace. *Why* I was wrong is still a question that absorbs my own work and my discussions with my colleagues, especially those who shared my view. Were we fooled by Putin in 2000? Or were we right to be optimists, but Putin himself changed along the way and we missed it? Or did something happen inside the Kremlin, so far invisible to outsiders, that took the entire Russian leadership down the path of autocracy and international aggression?

To a layperson, this does not matter much—nor should it. When pressed to reach a judgment about Putin (as many of us in Russian affairs were), I rendered a definite opinion rather than taking the more patient, but less interesting, view that it was too early to tell. In trying to unravel today's Russia, however, does my trainwreck of a prediction nearly twenty years ago now invalidate my analysis and advice? Am I no more capable of discussing Putin's motivations than a well-read layperson?

I was wrong about Putin, but the fact remains that the average person would be in over his or her head trying to explain the complexity of Russian politics, or even to teach an introductory course on the subject. Why I and others were wrong is an important question, not least because it forces us to revisit our assumptions and engage in the debate and self-correction that is the duty of an expert community. A great many people were pessimistic about Putin, but some of that was no more than reflexive Russophobia or a mere guess, neither of which is useful in policymaking. An uninformed judgment, even when right, is often less useful than a reasoned view, even when wrong, that can then be dissected, examined, and corrected.

REPAIRING THE RELATIONSHIP

Both experts and laypeople have responsibilities when it comes to expert failure. Professionals must own their mistakes, air them publicly, and show the steps they are taking to correct them. Laypeople, for their part, must exercise more caution in asking experts to prognosticate, and they must educate themselves about the difference between failure and fraud.

In general, experts do examine their mistakes but not in places the public is likely to look. The average person is not going to read a medical journal or a statistical analysis of an article in sociology. To be honest, I suspect that most experts and scholars would probably prefer that laypeople avoid doing so, because they would not understand most of what they were reading and their attempt to follow the professional debate would likely produce more public confusion than enlightenment.

This is where public intellectuals, the people who can bridge the gap between experts and laypeople, might shoulder more responsibility. The public is poorly served if the only people talking about a new medical treatment are doctors who have a hard time translating their knowledge into basic English (and who may be invested in a position), or journalists who have no scientific background cannot evaluate complicated scientific claims. This leaves a wide open space—usually on the Internet—for amateurs, hucksters, charlatans, and conspiracy theorists.

Public intellectuals are often derided within their own fields as mere "popularizers," and there's some truth to the charge. The world probably does not need another Bill Nye ("The Science Guy") weighing in on global climate change. Nor does the foreign policy community need one more former bureaucrat or relatively junior retired military officer crowding the airwaves with deep thoughts merely because there is now too much time and bandwidth to fill. But if the gulf between the public and the experts gets too wide, the experts will talk only to each other, and the public will end up excluded from decisions that will later affect their lives.

Citizens, however, have the most important role here. They must educate themselves not only about issues that matter to them but about the people to whom they're listening. Tetlock, for one, has advocated looking closely at the records of pundits and experts as a way of forcing them to get better at giving advice, so that they will have "incentives to compete by improving the epistemic (truth) value of their products, not just by pandering to communities of co-believers."[31]

Outing the track records of bad pundits, however, will only matter if people bother to pay attention. If they remain passive recipients of information on a television screen, or if they actively search only for information they want to believe, nothing else will matter very much. Instead, laypeople have to ask themselves some important questions, including how much they want to learn about a subject, and whether they're really willing to encounter facts that undermine their own beliefs. They have to ask better questions about the sources of their information, and they must consider the background of the experts to whom they listen.

If a layperson really wants to believe that Vitamin C can cure cancer, experts with sterling records of research and prediction will have less effect than a website with a picture of a pill on it. If an uninformed citizen really believes that invading a foreign country (or building a wall with one) will solve America's problems, reams of expert writings will not matter to them. Laypeople must take more responsibility for their own knowledge, or lack of it: it is no excuse to claim that the world is too complicated and there are too many sources of information, and then to lament that policy is in the hands of faceless experts who disdain the public's views.

The public also needs to approach expert advice with a certain combination of skepticism and humility. As the philosopher Bertrand Russell wrote in a 1928 essay, laypeople must evaluate expert claims by exercising their own careful logic as well.

> The skepticism that I advocate amounts only to this: (1) that when the experts are agreed, the opposite opinion cannot be held to be certain; (2) that when they are not agreed, no opinion can be regarded as certain by a non-expert; and (3) that when they all hold that no sufficient grounds for a positive opinion exist, the ordinary man would do well to suspend his judgment.

It is not enough to know what the experts agree upon. It is equally important to accept the limits of that agreement and not to draw more conclusions than the weight of expert views can support.

Moreover, laypeople must accept that experts are not policy-makers. Experts advise national leaders and their voices carry more impact than those of laypeople, but they do not make the final decisions. In a democracy, even a highly regulated and bureaucratized republic like the United States, few experts are sole policymakers. Politicians, from city councils up through the White House, have the final say on many of the most important decisions in our lives, from drugs to deterrence. If laypeople refuse to take their duties as citizens seriously, and do not educate themselves about issues important to them, democracy will mutate into technocracy. The rule of experts, so feared by laypeople, will grow by default.

For laypeople to use expert advice and to place professionals in their proper roles as servants, rather than masters, they must accept their own limitations as well. Democracy cannot function when every citizen is an expert. Yes, it is unbridled ego for experts to believe they can run a democracy while ignoring its voters; it is also, however, ignorant narcissism for laypeople to believe that they can maintain a large and advanced nation without listening to the voices of those more educated and experienced than themselves.

How to find that balance, and thus to mitigate the increasingly worrisome collisions between experts and their clients in society, is the subject of the next and final chapter.

Conclusion

Experts and Democracy

> A people who mean to be their own Governors must arm them-
> selves with the power which knowledge gives.
>
> James Madison

> I reserve the right to be ignorant. That's the Western way of life.
>
> *The Spy Who Came In from the Cold*

"THE EXPERTS ARE TERRIBLE"

During the 2016 "Brexit" debate over whether the United Kingdom
should leave the European Union, advocates of leaving the EU specifically identified experts—most of whom were warning that Brexit
was a terrible idea—as enemies of the ordinary voter. A leader in
the Brexit movement, Michael Gove, argued that facts were not as
important as the feelings of the British voter. "I think people in this
country," he sniffed, "have had enough of experts." Interrupted mid-
sentence, Gove tried to clarify, adding that he was referring to experts
from "organizations with acronyms, saying that they know what is
best and getting it consistently wrong."

But as an American writer and foreign policy expert, James Traub,
later noted about Gove's sniping,

The word "expert" is, of course, the pejorative term for someone who knows what he or she is talking about—like Gove, I imagine, who graduated from Oxford and spent years as a minister in Conservative Party governments. What Gove was actually saying was that people should be free to build gratifying fantasies free from unpleasant facts.[1]

Nigel Farage, the leader of the nativist United Kingdom Independence Party, even suggested that the "experts" were actually on the take, working for the British government or in the pay of the European Union itself.[2] In June 2016, the "leave" vote won with just under 52 percent of the vote in a national referendum.

The attack on the experts was part of a strategy meant to capitalize on the political illiteracy of a fair number of British voters and their instinctive mistrust of the intellectual elites who overwhelmingly opposed Brexit. Within days—but with the votes safely counted—the Brexiteers admitted that many of their claims had been either exaggerated or even wrong. "Frankly," the British politician and Brexit advocate Daniel Hannan said on British television, "if people watching think that they have voted and there is now going to be zero immigration from the EU, they are going to be disappointed." Hannan's comments provoked a backlash from voters who, apparently, thought that such a policy was exactly what they had chosen. "There really is no pleasing some people," Hannan said, and he then announced that he would "take a month off Twitter."[3]

Britain's actual exit from the EU is still years in the future. Anti-intellectualism and the consequent distrust of expertise, however, played a more immediate and central role in the United States during the 2016 presidential campaign. At a Wisconsin rally in early 2016, Republican candidate Donald Trump unleashed an attack on experts. In earlier debates, Trump had often been caught at a loss for words over basic issues of public policy, and now he was striking back. "They say, 'Oh, Trump doesn't have experts,'" he told the crowd. "You know, I've always wanted to say this. . . . The experts are terrible. They say, 'Donald Trump needs a foreign policy adviser.'. . . But supposing I didn't have one. Would it be worse than what we're doing now?"[4]

Trump's sneering at experts tapped into a long-standing American belief that experts and intellectuals are not only running the lives of ordinary people, but also doing a lousy job of it. Trump's rise in 2016 was the result of many factors, some of them (like a crowded field that produced only a plurality winner) purely matters of circumstance. Trump's eventual victory, however, was also undeniably one of the most recent—and one of the loudest—trumpets sounding the impending death of expertise.

Consider the various ways in which Trump's campaign represented a one-man campaign against established knowledge. He was one of the original "birthers" who demanded that Barack Obama prove his American citizenship. He quoted the *National Enquirer* approvingly as a source of news. He sided with antivaccine activism. He admitted that he gets most of his information on foreign policy from "the shows" on Sunday morning television. He suggested that Supreme Court Justice Antonin Scalia, who died from natural causes in early 2016, might have been murdered. And he charged that the father of one of his opponents (Ted Cruz) was involved in the Mother of All Conspiracy Theories, the assassination of John F. Kennedy.

Outright mistakes in stump speeches are an occupational hazard for political candidates—as when then-senator Barack Obama claimed to have visited all fifty-seven states—but Trump's ignorance during the campaign was willful and persistent. He had no idea how to answer even rudimentary questions about policy; rather than be shamed by his lack of knowledge, he exulted in it. Asked about the nuclear triad, the massive arsenal that would be at his disposal as president of the United States, Trump said, "We have to be extremely vigilant and extremely careful when it comes to nuclear. Nuclear changes the whole ballgame." Pressed about what he meant, he added, "I think—I think, for me, nuclear is just the power, the devastation is very important to me."

These were not missteps. Asked to clarify Trump's comments later, one of Trump's spokespeople waved away the entire matter as irrelevant. Trump, Katrina Pierson told Fox News, was tough, and that's all that mattered. "What good does it do to have a good nuclear triad if you're afraid to use it?" she asked. Pierson's fellow guest was the attorney and political commentator Kurt Schlichter, a retired Army colonel whose military specializations included chemical and nuclear issues, and who by any standard is an ultra-conservative. Schlichter was visibly astonished. "The point of the nuclear triad is to be afraid to use the damn thing," he said emphatically.

Trump survived all of this, seized the Republican nomination, and won, because in the end, he connected with a particular kind of voter who believes that knowing about things like America's nuclear deterrent is just so much pointy-headed claptrap.

Worse, voters not only didn't care that Trump is ignorant or wrong, they likely were unable to recognize his ignorance or errors. The psychologist David Dunning—who along with his colleague Justin Kruger discovered the Dunning-Kruger Effect, in which uninformed or incompetent people are unlikely to recognize their own lack of knowledge or incompetence—believes that the dynamic they describe was at work among the electorate and perhaps even central to understanding the bizarre nature of the 2016 election:

> Many commentators have pointed to [Trump's] confident missteps as products of Trump's alleged narcissism and egotism. My take would be that it's the other way around. Not seeing the mistakes for what they are allows any potential narcissism and egotism to expand unchecked.

In voters, lack of expertise would be lamentable but perhaps not so worrisome if people had some sense of how imperfect their civic knowledge is. If they did, they could repair it. But the Dunning-Kruger Effect suggests something different. It suggests that some voters, especially those facing significant distress in their life, might like some of what they hear from Trump, but they do not know enough to hold him accountable for the serious gaffes he makes.[5]

In other words, it's not that Trump's supporters were excusing him when he blurted out his most ignorant claims, but rather, as Dunning says, "They fail to recognize those gaffes as missteps."

Trump's strongest support in 2016, unsurprisingly, was concentrated among people with low levels of education. "I *love* the poorly educated," Trump exulted after winning the Nevada caucuses, and that love was clearly reciprocated.[6] In Trump, Americans who believe shadowy forces are ruining their lives and that any visible intellectual ability is itself a suspicious characteristic in a national leader found a champion. But where would people get such ideas, such as believing that the political elite and their intellectual allies are conspiring against them?

In part, they get these ideas by observing the behavior of the political elite and their intellectual allies. A month after Trump decried the uselessness of experts, for example, one of President Obama's top foreign policy advisers validated exactly the kind of suspicions that fuel attacks on expert participation in national policy. Describing the Obama administration's press for Congress and the American public to accept a deal with Iran on its nuclear weapons program, Deputy National Security Adviser Ben Rhodes told the *New York Times Magazine* that the administration knew it would have to "discourse the [expletive] out of this."

Rhodes gave the interview to a *Times* reporter, David Samuels, whose own objectivity (on the Iran deal as well as about some of the people named in the piece) was called into question when the story appeared.[7] Still, the Rhodes admissions were remarkably blunt: he proudly identified think tanks, experts, and journalists who he claimed were part of the administration's press for the deal.

> "We created an echo chamber," he admitted, when I asked him to explain the onslaught of freshly minted experts cheerleading for the deal. "They were saying things that validated what we had given them to say."
>
> When I asked whether the prospect of this same kind of far-reaching spin campaign being run by a different administration is something that scares him, he admitted that it does. "I mean, I'd prefer a sober, reasoned public debate, after which members of Congress reflect and take a vote," he said, shrugging. "But that's impossible."[8]

It is not unusual for senior government officials to assert that some matters, especially in national security, are too important and complicated to be left to uninformed public debate. Secret diplomacy and campaigns to win public opinion are part and parcel of the history of every democratic government, including the United States.

What Rhodes said, however, was different, and far more damaging to the relationship between experts and public policy. In effect, he bragged that the deal with Iran was sold by warping the debate among the experts themselves, and by taking advantage of the fact that the new media, and especially the younger journalists now taking over national reporting, wouldn't know any better. "The average reporter we talk to is 27 years old, and their only reporting experience consists of being around political campaigns," Rhodes said. "That's a sea change. They literally know nothing."

Rhodes's implication was clear. Not only did he think the public was too stupid to understand the deal—which was not wrong, although Rhodes did nothing to make them any smarter—but that everyone else, including Congress, was too stupid to get it as well. For Rhodes, contaminating the debate with misinformation was just a requirement for the greater good.

Trump and Rhodes, in different ways, used the public's ignorance to serve their own interests. They differed only in tactics: Trump sought power during the 2016 election by mobilizing the angriest and most ignorant among the electorate, while Rhodes stage-managed the Iran deal by throwing a fictional narrative out for public consumption and bypassing the electorate entirely while he and others did as they thought best in secret.

Both of these situations are intolerable. There is plenty of blame to go around for the parlous state of the role of expertise in American life, and this book has apportioned much of it. Experts themselves, as well as educators, journalists, corporate entertainment media, and others have all played their part. In the end, however, there is only one group of people who must bear the ultimate responsibility for this current state of affairs, and only they can change any of it: the citizens of the United States of America.

EXPERTISE AND DEMOCRACY: THE DEATH SPIRAL

Expertise and government rely upon each other, especially in a democracy. The technological and economic progress that ensures the well-being of a population requires the division of labor, which in turn leads to the creation of professions. Professionalism encourages experts to do their best in serving their clients, to respect their own boundaries, and to demand their boundaries be respected by others, as part of an overall service to the ultimate client: society itself.

Dictatorships, too, demand this same service of experts, but they extract it by threat and direct its use by command. This is why dictatorships are less efficient and less productive than democracies, despite the historical myths many Americans continue to believe about the putative efficiency of Nazi Germany and other such regimes.[9] In a democracy, the expert's service to the public is part of the social contract. Citizens delegate the power of decision on myriad issues to elected representatives and their expert advisers, while experts, for their part, ask that their efforts be received in good faith by a public that has informed itself enough to make reasoned judgments.

The relationship between experts and citizens, like almost all relationships in a democracy, is built on trust. When that trust collapses, experts and laypeople become warring factions. And when that happens, democracy itself can enter a death spiral that presents an immediate danger of decay either into rule by the mob or toward elitist technocracy. Both are authoritarian outcomes, and both threaten the United States today.

This is why the collapse of the relationship between experts and citizens is a dysfunction of democracy itself. The abysmal literacy, both political and general, of the American public is the foundation for all of these problems. It is the soil in which all of the other dysfunctions have taken root and prospered, with the 2016 election only its most recent expression. As the writer Daniel Libit described it, the nation's public policy experts found the 2016 presidential race "an increasingly demoralizing lesson in the imperviousness of the American voter."[10] The warning signs, however, were present long before then.

As the writer Susan Jacoby put it in 2008, the most disturbing aspect of the American march toward ignorance is "not lack of knowledge per se but arrogance about that lack of knowledge."

The problem is not just the things we do not know (consider the one in five American adults who, according to the National Science

Foundation, thinks the sun revolves around the Earth); it's the alarming number of Americans who have smugly concluded that they do not need to know such things in the first place. . . . The toxic brew of anti-rationalism and ignorance hurts discussions of U.S. public policy on topics from health care to taxation.[11]

Ordinary Americans might never have liked the educated or professional classes very much, but until recently they did not widely disdain their actual learning as a bad thing in itself. It might even be too kind to call this merely "anti-rational"; it is almost reverse evolution, away from tested knowledge and backward toward folk wisdom and myths passed by word of mouth—except with all of it now sent along at the speed of electrons.

This plummeting literacy and growth of willful ignorance is part of a vicious circle of disengagement between citizens and public policy. People know little and care less about how they are governed, or how their economic, scientific, or political structures actually function. Yet, as all of these processes thus become more incomprehensible, citizens feel more alienated. Overwhelmed, they turn away from education and civic involvement, and withdraw into other pursuits. This, in turn, makes them into less capable citizens, and the cycle continues and strengthens, especially when the public appetite for escape is easily fed by any number of leisure industries.

Awash in gadgets and conveniences that were once unimaginable even within their own lifetimes, Americans (and many other Westerners, if we are to be fair about it) have become almost childlike in their refusal to learn enough to govern themselves or to guide the policies that affect their lives. This is a collapse of functional citizenship, and it enables a cascade of other baleful consequences.

In the absence of informed citizens, for example, more knowledgeable administrative and intellectual elites do in fact take over the daily direction of the state and society. In a passage often cited by Western conservatives and especially loved by American libertarians, the Austrian economist F. A. Hayek wrote in 1960: "The greatest danger to liberty today comes from the men who are most needed and most powerful in modern government, namely, the efficient expert administrators exclusively concerned with what they regard as the public good."[12]

Even the most intellectually minded thinkers across the American spectrum would agree with Hayek. Unelected bureaucrats and policy specialists in many spheres exert tremendous influence on the daily lives of Americans. Today, however, this situation is by default rather than by design. Populism actually reinforces this elitism, because the celebration of ignorance cannot launch communications satellites, negotiate the rights of US citizens overseas, or provide for effective medications, all of which are daunting tasks even the dimmest citizens now demand and take for granted. Faced with a public that has no idea how most things work, experts likewise disengage, choosing to speak mostly to each other rather than to laypeople.

Meanwhile, Americans have increasingly unrealistic expectations of what their political and economic system can provide. This sense of entitlement is one reason they are continually angry at "experts" and especially at "elitists," a word that in modern American usage can mean almost anyone with any education who refuses to coddle the public's mistaken beliefs. When told that ending poverty or preventing terrorism is a lot harder than it looks, Americans roll their eyes. Unable to comprehend all of the complexity around them, they choose instead to comprehend almost none of it and then sullenly blame experts, politicians, and bureaucrats for seizing control of their lives.

THE KNOWERS AND THE DECIDERS

This underscores another problem motivating the death spiral in which democracy and expertise are caught: citizens do not understand, or do not choose to understand, the difference between experts and elected policymakers. For many Americans, all elites are now just an undifferentiated mass of educated, rich, and powerful people. This is patent silliness. Not all rich people are powerful, and not all powerful people are rich. Intellectuals and policy experts are seldom rich *or* powerful. (Trust me on that one.)

Whatever else George W. Bush may have gotten wrong during his presidency, he was right when he reminded Americans that when it came to the actions of his administration, he was "the decider." Experts can only propose; elected leaders dispose. In fact, policymaking experts and elected leaders are almost never the same group, and it cannot be otherwise: there are simply not enough hours in the day for a legislator, even in a city council or a small US state (and much less for a president) to master all of the issues modern policymaking requires. This is why policymakers engage experts—the knowers—to advise them.

Sometimes, this partnership between advisers and policymakers fails. Experts get things wrong, and they counsel political leaders to take courses of action that can result in disaster. Critics of the role of expertise point to national traumas like the Vietnam War as one such example. With the benefit of hindsight, these criticisms are often made as though such painful choices could have been avoided by consulting the wisdom of the common citizen.

This call to fall back on the knowledge and virtue of laypeople, however, is romanticized nonsense. Evan Thomas, a journalist and biographer of Richard Nixon, admitted that the "best and the brightest," among them academics like Henry Kissinger and "corporate titans" like Secretary of Defense Robert S. McNamara, "were far from perfect" and that they "bear the blame for Vietnam and the 58,000 American soldiers who died there, not to mention the millions of Vietnamese."[13] But as Thomas points out, those same experts and elites "strengthened a world order balanced precariously on the edge of nuclear war. They expanded trade, deepened alliances and underwrote billions in foreign aid."

None of these policies would have been popular in and of themselves, but they helped the United States and the West to survive the Cold War and to reach its peaceful end. More important, what kinds of policies would nonexperts or populists have chosen? Thomas challenged readers to "contrast the mistakes of the 1960s to times when Washington allowed foreign policy to be set by public consensus."

> In the 1930s, Congress closed off free trade to protect American industry and listened to voters who wanted a smaller, less costly military with no entangling alliances. The results? The Smoot-Hawley tariff contributed to the Great Depression, and the failure of the League of Nations allowed the rise of fascism and global war.

This illustrates an important point: then as now, Americans tend to think about issues like macroeconomic policy or foreign affairs only when things go wrong. The rest of the time, they remain happily unaware of the policies and processes that function well everyday while the nation goes about its business.

The question nonetheless remains whether America really needs all these experts, especially when their advice becomes so spread out over so many people that no one seems responsible when disaster strikes. Andrew Bacevich, for one, has called for vanquishing the modern expert class, at least in public policy:

> Policy intellectuals—eggheads presuming to instruct the mere mortals who actually run for office—are a blight on the republic. Like some invasive species, they infest present-day Washington, where their presence strangles common sense and has brought to the verge of extinction the simple ability to perceive reality.

A benign appearance—well-dressed types testifying before Congress, pontificating in print and on TV, or even filling key positions in the executive branch—belies a malign impact. They are like Asian carp let loose in the Great Lakes.[14]

The irony here is that Bacevich himself is a prolific author, a former senior military officer, and a retired professor who regularly proposes very specific instructions for the same group of mortals. Still, he has a point: in addition to the five or six hundred visible policymakers at the top levels of the US government, there are thousands of experts behind them who may, in fact, not be very good at what they do.

Experts cannot dodge their own responsibilities here. The Knowers cannot merely hide behind elected officials every time something goes wrong, telling the public to leave them alone and instead to go and punish the Deciders. When the experts screw up, the leaders who trusted their advice on behalf of the public need to adjudicate their failures and to decide what kind of correction is needed.

Sometimes, the remedy for expert failure is the time-honored blue-ribbon panel and its recommendations. Sometimes the answer is just to fire somebody. In his seminal work on expertise, however, Philip Tetlock suggests other ways in which experts might be held more accountable without merely trashing the entire relationship between experts and the public. There are many possibilities, including more transparency and competition, in which experts in any field have to maintain a record of their work, come clean about how often they were right or wrong, and actually have journals, universities, and other gatekeepers hold their peers responsible more often for mistakes. Whether this would work is another matter, and Tetlock acknowledges the many barriers to such solutions.

The most daunting barrier, however, is the public's own laziness. None of these efforts to track and grade experts will matter very much if ordinary citizens do not care enough to develop even a basic interest in such matters. Tetlock points out that laypeople, unfortunately, are not usually interested in finding experts with excellent track records: they are mostly interested in experts who are accessible without much effort and who already agree with their views. As Tetlock rightly notes, it is not enough to encourage accountability among the "providers of intellectual products" if the "consumers are unmotivated to be discriminating judges of competing claims and counterclaims." These consumers may well be less interested in "the dispassionate pursuit of truth than they are in buttressing their prejudices," and when this happens, laypeople approach the role of expertise with "the psychology of the sports arena, not the seminar room."[15]

Experts need to own their advice and to hold each other accountable. For any number of reasons—the glut of academic degrees, the lack of interest on the part of the public, the inability to keep up with the production of knowledge in the Information Age—they have not lived up to this duty as conscientiously as their privileged position in society requires. They can do better, even if those efforts might, in the main, go unnoticed.

There are measures that experts can take to improve their accountability. There are other issues in the relationship with the public, however, that are beyond their control. Laypeople need to think about the ways in which they misunderstand the role of expert advice in a democratic republic. Among the many misconceptions the public has about experts and policymakers, five are especially worth considering.

First, experts are not puppeteers. They cannot control when leaders take their advice. Even in the closest relationships between an elected politician and an expert adviser, there is not a complete fusing of beliefs. Whether Nixon and Kissinger—or Obama and Rhodes— no leader is merely the vessel by which experts implement ideas.

Any expert worth his or her salt has stories of defeat in the policy game. I was many years ago an aide to a senior US senator who treated me as a trusted adviser but who also once threw me out of his office in a fusillade of curses during a principled disagreement in the tense days leading up to the 1991 Gulf War. While there is usually a close identity of interests and views between a political leader and the expert staff, the policymaker or elected official has pressures and responsibilities the expert will never feel, and conflict is inevitable.

Second, experts cannot control how leaders implement their advice. There is a kind of "monkey's paw" problem here for experts. ("The Monkey's Paw," readers might recall, is a famous early twentieth-century story about a magic talisman that granted wishes in the worst way: when the main character in the tale wishes for money, it comes in the form of compensation for the death of his son.) Experts can advise policymakers on what to do, but they may find their advice taken in ways that were never intended. An economist who is also an environmentalist might believe that lowering taxes is a good idea, for example, only to find later that her advice was indeed taken—by a Congress wanting to lower taxes on *gasoline*.

Third, no single expert guides a policy from conception through execution, a reality that the public often finds bewildering and frustrating. This is why policy analysis is an entire scholarly discipline in itself, especially in the study of large organizations like governments and businesses. The Knowers and the Deciders may have settled on what they want, but the institutions below them, like players in a huge game of "telephone," can mangle intended policies and turn them into something else, with perverse effects, by the time the whole project comes to fruition.

Fourth, experts cannot control how *much* of their advice leaders will take. Experts can offer advice, but often political leaders will often hear only the parts they want to hear—specifically, the parts that will be popular with their respective constituencies. They will then mobilize experts that emphasize the message they prefer. Some experts might, for example, advocate cutting taxes; others might call for increased spending on pet projects ranging from the social safety net to national defense. Both positions—cutting taxes and increasing spending—may have a logical foundation, but they cannot usually be adopted at the same time. The experts, however, cannot control the fact that politicians might well choose all of the options anyway, even if they conflict with each other. (The next set of experts called in will then be asked to help solve the mystery of a massive budget deficit.)

The public, unfortunately, is much the same way. When nutritional scientists took eggs off the list of dietary culprits, they did not intend for people to order fast-food egg sandwiches every morning as part of a healthy breakfast. People hear what they want to hear and then stop listening. And when their incomplete adoption of an expert's advice produces poor results, they blame the experts for being incompetent, because everybody has to blame somebody.

Finally, experts can only offer alternatives. They cannot, however, make choices about *values*. They can describe problems, but they cannot tell people what they should want to do about those problems, even when there is wide agreement on the nature of those challenges.

Is the earth's climate changing? Most experts believe it is, and they believe they know why. Whether their models, extrapolated out for decades and centuries, are accurate is a legitimate area for debate. What experts cannot answer is what to *do* about climate change. It might well be that Boston or Shanghai or London will be underwater in fifty years, but it might well also be that voters—who have the right to be wrong—will choose to shift that problem to later generations rather than to risk jobs (or comfort) now.

Experts can tell the voters what is likely to happen, but voters must engage those issues and decide what they value most, and therefore what they want done. Letting Boston slide into the harbor is not my preferred outcome, but it is not a failure of expertise if people ignore the experts and let it happen anyway: it is instead a failure of civic engagement. If Boston is to become Venice, it should be by choice, not by accident. When voters remain utterly unwilling to understand important issues because they are too difficult or discomfiting, it is unsurprising that experts will give up talking to them and instead rely on their positions in the policy world to advocate for their own solutions.

Experts sometimes give poor advice or make mistakes, but an advanced society and its government cannot do without them, no matter what an increasing number of Americans seem to believe. To ignore expert advice is simply not a realistic option, not only due to the complexity of policymaking, but because to do so is to absolve citizens of their responsibilities to learn about issues that matter directly to their own well-being. Moreover, when the public no longer makes a distinction between experts and policymakers and merely wants to blame everyone in the policy world for outcomes that distress them, the eventual result will not be *better policy* but more *politicization of expertise*. Politicians will never stop relying on experts; they will, however, move to relying on experts who will tell them—and the angry laypeople banging on their office doors—whatever it is they want to hear.

This is the worst of all worlds, in which both democracy and expertise are corrupted because neither democratic leaders nor their expert advisers want to tangle with an ignorant electorate. At that point, expertise no longer serves the public interest, but the interest of whatever political clique is taking the temperature of the public at any given moment. We are already perilously close to this outcome in modern America.

A REPUBLIC, IF YOU KNOW WHAT ONE IS

The challenges of expert accountability are compounded by the fact that most Americans do not seem to understand their own system of government. The United States is a *republic*, not a *democracy*. One hardly ever hears the word "republic" anymore, which reveals, in a small way, the degree to which modern Americans confuse "democracy" as a general political philosophy with a "republic" as its expression in a form of government. In 1787, Benjamin Franklin was supposedly asked what would emerge from the Constitutional Convention being held in Philadelphia. "A republic," Franklin answered, "if you can keep it." Today, the bigger challenge is to find anyone who knows what a republic actually is.

This is crucial because laypeople too easily forget that the republican form of government under which they live was not designed for mass decisions about complicated issues. Neither, of course, was it designed for rule by a tiny group of technocrats or experts. Rather, it was meant to be the vehicle by which an informed electorate— *informed* being the key word here—could choose other people to represent them and to make decisions on their behalf.

Classical American thought might be rooted in the glory that was Athens, but the United States is not, nor was it ever meant to be, anything like the Athenian marketplace. And for that, Americans should be grateful. As the writer Malcolm Gladwell pointed out in 2010, large organizations do not make decisions by polling everyone in them, no matter how "democratic" it might seem.

> Car companies sensibly use a network to organize their hundreds of suppliers, but not to design their cars. No one believes that the articulation of a coherent design philosophy is best handled by a sprawling, leaderless organizational system. Because networks don't have a centralized leadership structure and clear lines of authority, they have real difficulty reaching consensus and setting goals. They can't think strategically; they are chronically prone to conflict and error.

How do you make difficult choices about tactics or strategy or philosophical direction when everyone has an equal say?[16]

This is one of many challenges republican government was designed to overcome. Even when most people know what they're doing in their own area of competence, they cannot agglomerate their decisions into coherent public policy the same way as if they are guessing the weight of a bull or trying to pin down the target price of a stock. The republican solution allows a smaller group of people to aggregate the public's often irresolvable demands.

Determining what the public actually wants, however, is exponentially more difficult when the electorate is not competent in any of the matters at hand. Laypeople complain about the rule of experts and they demand greater involvement in complicated national questions, but many of them only express their anger and make these demands after abdicating their own important role in the process: namely, to stay informed and politically literate enough to choose representatives who can act on their behalf. In the words of Ilya Somin, "When we elect government officials based on ignorance, they rule over not only those who voted for them but all of society. When we exercise power over other people, we have a moral obligation to do so in at least a reasonably informed way."[17]

This is not the place for a meditation on the American form of representative democracy, especially since there are already plenty of copies of *The Federalist Papers* still available. But the death of expertise and its associated attacks on knowledge fundamentally undermine the republican system of government. Worse, these attacks are campaigns conducted by those least capable of supplanting that system. The most poorly informed people among us are those who seem to be the most dismissive of experts and are demanding the greatest say in matters about which they have exerted almost no effort to educate themselves.

Consider the fact that people change what they say they want based on who they think is advocating a position. The comedian Jimmy Kimmel was once again the prankster here: he stopped people on the street, and asked them which of the tax plans offered by Hillary Clinton and Donald Trump they preferred. The interviewees, however, did not know that Kimmel had switched the details of each plan. As *The Hill* newspaper later reported, the answers depended on whom people thought they were supporting: "Sure enough, one by one, the Clinton voters were stunned to discover that they were vouching for the proposal of her archrival." One man, when told he was supporting Trump's plan rather than Clinton's, decided to go for broke: "Well, I support Donald Trump, then."[18]

As it turns out, Kimmel's hijinks actually illustrated a truth long known to pollsters and campaign experts: voters are often more interested in candidates and their personalities than in their ideas or policies. The *Huffington Post*'s polling director, Ariel Edwards-Levy, put it this way:

> Americans, regardless of their political views, don't have a solid opinion about every single issue of the day, particularly when it concerns a complicated or obscure topic. People tend, reasonably, to rely on partisan cues—if a politician they support is in favor of a bill, they're likely to think it's a good idea, or vice versa.[19]

When Levy and her colleagues conducted a more formal version of the Kimmel ambush, they found the same thing: Republicans who strongly disagree with Democratic Party positions on health care, Iran, and affirmative action objected far less if they thought the same policies were those of Donald Trump. Democrats, for their part, went in the other direction: they were less supportive of their own party's policies if they thought they were Trump's positions.

At least tax policy and health care are real issues with real positions attached to them. In 2015, Public Policy Polling, a liberal polling group, asked both Republicans and Democrats whether they would support bombing the country of Agrabah. Nearly a third of Republican respondents said they would support such action. Only 13 percent were opposed, and the rest were unsure. Democrats were less inclined to military action: only 19 percent of self-identified Democrats supported bombing while 36 percent decisively voiced their opposition.

Agrabah doesn't exist. It's the fictional country in the 1992 animated Disney film *Aladdin*. Liberals crowed that this poll was evidence of the ignorance and aggressiveness of Republicans, while conservatives countered that it only showed how Democrats were reflexively against military action no matter how little they knew about the situation. For experts, however, there was no way around the overall reality captured in the poll, even if only accidentally: 43 percent of Republicans and 55 percent of Democrats had an actual, defined view on bombing a place in a cartoon.[20]

Some of these games are unfair to the public. Ordinary people are busy living their lives, not trying to figure out if they're being manipulated by pollsters or pranked by comedians like Kimmel (or the Fox News personality Jesse Watters, who conducts similar pop quizzes on the street). This is especially true when voters are presented with "all sides" of the issues in the media without any indication of which views are more authoritative than another. As the psychologist Derek Kohler put it,

> Government action is guided in part by public opinion. Public opinion is guided in part by perceptions of what experts think. But public opinion may—and often does—deviate from expert opinion, not simply, it seems, because the public refuses to acknowledge the legitimacy of experts, but also because the public may not be able to tell where the majority of expert opinion lies.[21]

A talk show, for example, with one scientist who says genetically modified organisms (GMOs) are safe and one activist who says they are dangerous looks "balanced," but in reality that is ridiculously skewed, because nearly nine out of ten scientists think GMOs are safe for consumption. At some point, in the midst of all the bickering, the public simply gives up and goes back to relying on simpler sources of information, even if it is a meme on Facebook.

This is no excuse, however, for citizen ignorance and disengagement—and especially for hyper-partisan attachments that make people change their minds about policy only because of who advocated them. If the public has no idea about the substance of an issue, and will vote based on who they *like* rather than what they *want*, it is difficult to put too much blame on policymakers and their expert advisers for being confused themselves. How can a republic function if the people who have sent their representatives to decide questions of war and peace cannot tell the difference between Agrabah, Ukraine, or Syria?

Put another way, when the public claims it has been misled or kept in the dark, experts and policymakers cannot help but ask, "How would you know?"

When laypeople disregard expertise and declare themselves fed up with everything and everyone, they forget that the people they elected still have to make decisions, every day, about an ongoing blizzard of issues. These officials do not have the luxury of casting a pox upon the experts and the polls and then retreating to their televisions and computer screens and game controllers. They have to make commitments, sometimes of lives and always of money, on everything from navigation rights to child care. These decisions, and how they are implemented, will affect the lives of all citizens, the informed as well as the ignorant, the involved and the detached.

The breakdown of trust between the public, experts, and elected officials in a republic goes in all directions. The public, especially, needs to be able to trust leaders and their expert advisers. This relationship becomes impossible to sustain, however, when laypeople have no idea what they're talking about or what they want.

When that trust breaks down, public ignorance can be turned by cynical manipulation into a political weapon. Anti-intellectualism is itself a means of short-circuiting democracy, because a stable democracy in any culture relies on the public actually understanding the implications of its own choices. Most laypeople, already suspicious of the educated classes, need little prodding to rebel against experts—even when such rebellions are cynically led by other intellectuals.

In 1942, President Franklin D. Roosevelt asked radio listeners to go and purchase maps so they could follow along as he narrated the progress of World War II. Maps quickly sold out across the country. In 2006, fewer than sixty-five years later, a national study found that nearly half of Americans between the ages of eighteen and twenty-four—that is, those most likely to have to fight in a war—did not think it was necessary to know the location of other countries in which important news was being made.[22] A decade later, during the 2016 election, Donald Trump raised cheers when he summed up his approach to terrorists in the Middle East: "I would bomb the shit out of them. I'd blow up the pipes, I'd blow up the refineries, I'd blow up every single inch, there would be nothing left."

A republic, if you can keep it. Or if you can find it on a map.

I'M AS GOOD AS YOU

Finally, and most disturbing, citizens of the Western democracies, and Americans in particular, no longer understand the concept of democracy itself. This, perhaps more than anything, has corroded the relationship between experts and citizens. The relationship between experts and citizens is not "democratic." All people are not, and can never be, equally talented or intelligent. Democratic societies, however, are always tempted to this resentful insistence on equality, which becomes oppressive ignorance if given its head.

And this, sadly, is the state of modern America. Citizens no longer understand democracy to mean a condition of political equality, in which one person gets one vote, and every individual is no more and no less equal in the eyes of the law. Rather, Americans now think of democracy as a state of actual equality, in which every opinion is as good as any other on almost any subject under the sun. Feelings are more important than facts: if people *think* vaccines are harmful, or if they *believe* that half of the US budget is going to foreign aid, then it is "undemocratic" and "elitist" to contradict them.

This problem is not new, nor is it unique to the United States. The British writer C. S. Lewis warned long ago of the danger to democracy when people no longer recognize any difference between political equality and actual equality, in a vivid 1959 essay featuring one of his most famous literary creations, a brilliant and evil demon named Screwtape.

As one of the Inferno's most senior bureaucrats, Screwtape is invited to give the commencement address at Hell's training college for new tempters. During his speech, Screwtape leaves aside what, for him, is the dull business of individual temptation and instead surveys the global landscape. While he is repulsed by human progress (including the French and American revolutions, and the abolition of slavery, among other moments), he sees great hope—for Hell, not for human beings—in capturing the concept of democracy and wresting it away from its noble meaning.

"*Democracy* is the word with which you must lead them by the nose," Screwtape gleefully advises the graduates, and he then promises that by use of the word "purely as an incantation," human beings can be fooled not only into believing an obvious lie, but led to nurture that lie as a cherished feeling:

The feeling I mean is of course that which prompts a man to say *I'm as good as you.*

No man who says *I'm as good as you* believes it. He would not say it if he did. The St. Bernard never says it to the toy dog, nor the scholar to the dunce, nor the employable to the bum, nor the pretty woman to the plain. The claim to equality, outside the strictly political field, is made only by those who feel themselves to be in some way inferior. What it expresses is precisely the itching, smarting, writhing awareness of an inferiority which [a human being] refuses to accept.

And therefore resents. Yes, and therefore resents every kind of superiority in others; denigrates it; wishes its annihilation.[23]

This was the same warning José Ortega y Gasset gave when he wrote *Revolt of the Masses* in 1930: "The mass crushes beneath it everything that is different, everything that is excellent, individual, qualified and select. Anybody who is not like everybody, who does not think like everybody, runs the risk of being eliminated."[24]

"*I'm as good as you,*" Screwtape chortles at the end of his address, "is a useful means for the destruction of democratic societies."

And so it is. When resentful laypeople demand that all marks of achievement, including expertise, be leveled and equalized in the name of "democracy" and "fairness," there is no hope for either democracy or fairness. Everything becomes a matter of opinion, with all views dragged to the lowest common denominator in the name of equality. An outbreak of whooping cough because an ignoramus would not vaccinate a child is a sign of tolerance; the collapse of a foreign alliance because a provincial isolationist can't find other nations on an atlas is a triumph of egalitarianism.

Democracy, as practiced in the United States in the early twenty-first century, has become a resentful, angry business. The fragile egos of narcissistic college students jostle against the outraged, wounded self-identity of talk-radio addicts, all of whom demand to be taken with equal seriousness by everyone else, regardless of how extreme or uninformed their views are. Experts are derided as elitists, one of many groups putatively oppressing "we the people," a term now used by voters indiscriminately and mostly to mean "me." Expert advice or any kind of informed deliberation by anyone whom laypeople perceive as an elite—which is to say almost everyone but themselves—is rejected as a matter of first principles. No democracy can go on this way.

THE REVOLT OF THE EXPERTS

I do not intend to end this book on such a note of pessimism, but I am not sure I have much choice. Most causes of ignorance can be overcome, if people are willing to learn. Nothing, however, can overcome the toxic confluence of arrogance, narcissism, and cynicism that Americans now wear like full suit of armor against the efforts of experts and professionals.

Traditional solutions no longer work. Education, instead of breaking down barriers to continued learning, is teaching young people that their feelings are more important than anything else. "Going to college" is, for many students, just one more exercise in personal self-affirmation. The media, mired in competition at every level, now asks consumers what they'd like to know instead of telling them what's important. The Internet is a mixed blessing, a well of information poisoned by the equivalent of intellectual sabotage.

Faced with the public's resolute ignorance, experts are defeated. "Many of us feel powerless against it," said David Autor, a labor economist at MIT. "We feel we can train our students, but our students aren't the public and we don't know how to school the public." A Yale professor, Dan Kahan, was more pessimistic: "Bombarding people with knowledge doesn't help," he said in 2015. "It doesn't do anything to explain things to people, but here I am just explaining the facts over and over again. Maybe the joke's on me."[25]

One hopeful sign is that experts seem to be rebelling against attacks on their expertise. In decrying the Brexit outcome, for example, James Traub bluntly said that it was time for the defenders of classical Western liberalism "to rise up against the ignorant masses."[26] Of course, to do so is to risk the dread accusation of "elitism," a charge that has always had more impact in egalitarian America than in more stratified cultures in Europe and elsewhere, as Traub himself recognized: "It is necessary to say that people are deluded and that the task of leadership is to un-delude them. Is that 'elitist'? Maybe it is; maybe we have become so inclined to celebrate the authenticity of all personal conviction that it is now elitist to believe in reason, expertise, and the lessons of history."

Nonetheless, professionals across a spectrum of fields in a number of countries seem fed up. Anecdotally, I was struck that after my original article on the "death of expertise" appeared, I was contacted by scientists, doctors, lawyers, teachers, and many other professionals in America and around the world. They told me not only of their frustration, but of their anger and sadness over ruptured relationships with patients, clients, and students, and even the cooling of close personal friendships, all because they are finally demanding an end to ill-informed lectures about their own area of competence.

Medical doctors, especially, seem to have had enough. To take a humorous recent example, in 2015, Kimmel—yet again—ran a satirical public service announcement in which actual doctors engaged in expletive-filled rants against recalcitrant patients who feared vaccinations. "Remember that time you got polio?" asked one of the physicians. "No, you don't. Because your parents got you [expletive] vaccinated." Another said, "I have to use my only day off to talk to you idiots about vaccines?" as another chimed in: "Because you listened to some moron who read a forwarded email?"

The Kimmel spot went viral, reported in major media and replayed (as of this writing) more than eight million times on YouTube alone. The reaction, of course, was swift. Sites like Infowars.com and a host of antivaccination bloggers (of course) called the doctors ignorant, tools of a corrupt system, and the other usual insults. But the antivaccination wave seems to have crested for now, in part because professionals and their supporters have decided to use the media and the Internet in the same way as the conspiracy theorists.

These kinds of efforts in the media will save the lives of some children, but they are not enough to defeat the campaign against established knowledge or to reverse its effects on American democracy. In the end, experts cannot demand that citizens pay attention to the world around them. They cannot insist people eat healthy meals or exercise more. They cannot drag citizens by the neck away from the latest reality television show and make them look at a map instead. They cannot cure narcissism by fiat.

Tragically, I suspect that a possible resolution will lie in a disaster as yet unforeseen. It may be a war or an economic collapse. (Here, I mean a major war that touches America even more deeply than the far-away conflicts fought by brave volunteers, or a real depression, rather than the recession of the early twenty-first century.) It may be in the emergence of an ignorant demagoguery, a process already underway in the United States and Europe, or the rise to power of a technocracy that finally runs out of patience and thus dispenses with voting as anything other than a formality.

The creation of a vibrant intellectual and scientific culture in the West and in the United States required democracy and secular tolerance. Without such virtues, knowledge and progress fall prey to ideological, religious, and populist attacks. Nations that have given in to such temptations have suffered any number of terrible fates, including mass repression, cultural and material poverty, and defeat in war.

I still have faith in the American system, and I believe the people of the United States are still capable of shrugging off their self-absorption and isolation and taking up their responsibilities as citizens. They did it in 1941, and again after the trials of Vietnam and Watergate, and yet again after the attacks of 9/11. Each time, however, they slid back into complacency, and each time, the hole of ignorance and disaffection they dug for themselves got deeper. At some point, they might no longer see daylight.

We can only hope that before this happens, citizens, experts, and policymakers will engage in a hard (and so far unwelcome) debate about the role of experts and educated elites in American democracy. Recoiling from Donald Trump's march to the GOP nomination, the writer Andrew Sullivan warned in 2016 that "elites still matter in a democracy."

> They matter not because they are democracy's enemy but because they provide the critical ingredient to save democracy from itself. The political Establishment may be battered and demoralized, deferential to the algorithms of the web and to the monosyllables of a gifted demagogue, but this is not the time to give up on America's near-unique and stabilizing blend of democracy and elite responsibility.
>
> It seems shocking to argue that we need elites in this democratic age—especially with vast inequalities of wealth and elite failures all around us. But we need them precisely to protect this precious democracy from its own destabilizing excesses.[27]

Democracy, as Lewis's Screwtape knew, denotes a system of government, not an actual state of equality. Every single vote in a democracy is equal to every other, but every single opinion is not, and the sooner

American society reestablishes new ground rules for productive engagement between the educated elite and the society they serve, the better.

Experts need to remember, always, that they are the servants and not the masters of a democratic society and a republican government. If citizens, however, are to be the masters, they must equip themselves not just with education, but with the kind of civic virtue that keeps them involved in the running of their own country. Laypeople cannot do without experts, and they must accept this reality without rancor. Experts, likewise, must accept that their advice, which might seem obvious and right to them, will not always be taken in a democracy that may not value the same things they do. Otherwise, when democracy is understood as an unending demand for unearned respect for unfounded opinions, anything and everything becomes possible, including the end of democracy and republican government itself.

That, at least, is my expert opinion on the matter. I could be wrong.

NOTES

Introduction

1. Pride Chigwedere et al., "Estimating the Lost Benefits of Antiretroviral Drug Use in South Africa," *Journal of Acquired Immune Deficiency Syndromes* 49 (4), December 1, 2008.
2. Kyle Dropp, Joshua D. Kertzer, and Thomas Zeitzoff, "The Less Americans Know about Ukraine's Location, the More They Want U.S. to Intervene," *Monkey Cage* Blog, *Washington Post* online, April 7, 2014.

Chapter 1

1. José Ortega y Gasset, *The Revolt of the Masses* (New York: W. W. Norton, 1993), 16–18.
2. Richard Hofstadter, *Anti-Intellectualism in American Life* (New York: Vintage, 1963), 34.
3. Ilya Somin, "Political Ignorance in America," in Mark Bauerlein and Adam Bellow, eds., *The State of the American Mind* (West Conshohocken, PA: Templeton, 2015), 163–164.
4. Dana Goodyear, "Raw Deal: California Cracks Down on an Underground Gourmet Club," *New Yorker,* April 30, 2012.
5. Olga Khazan, "27% of Surgeons Still Think Obamacare Has Death Panels," *Atlantic* online, December 19, 2013.

6. Kaiser Family Foundation, 2013 Survey of Americans on the US Role in Global Health.

7. Henry Blodget, "Here's What Day Traders Don't Understand," *Business Insider*, March 29, 2010.

Chapter 2

1. See David Dunning, "We Are All Confident Idiots," *Pacific Standard* online, October 27, 2014.

2. Justin Kruger and David Dunning, "Unskilled and Unaware of It: How Difficulties in Recognizing One's Own Incompetence Lead to Inflated Self-Assessments," *Journal of Personality and Social Psychology* 77(6), December 1999, 1121–1122.

3. Dunning, "We Are All Confident Idiots."

4. John Allen Paulos, *Innumeracy: Mathematical Illiteracy and Its Consequences* (New York: Hill and Wang, 2001), 9.

5. Michael Crichton, "Panic in the Sheets," *Playboy*, December 1991; archived at MichaelCrichton.com.

6. There's an entire subject in statistics, called "Bayesian analysis," named for an eighteenth-century English mathematician, which deals with this question.

7. Social scientists, no less than any other, are aware of this problem. See Charles O. Jones, "Doing before Knowing: Concept Development in Political Research," *American Journal of Political Science* 18(1), February 1974.

8. Maria Konnikova, "How a Gay-Marriage Study Went Wrong," *New Yorker* online, May 22, 2015.

9. Jonathan Kay, "Has Internet-Fueled Conspiracy Mongering Crested?," in Mark Bauerline and Adam Bellow, eds., *The State of the American Mind* (West Conshohocken, PA: Templeton, 2015), 138–139.

10. Indeed, the scholar Ross E. Cheit has argued that the poorly handled cases in the 1980s and 1990s backfired tragically, as the pendulum of public opinion swung from always believing small children to being highly skeptical of any claims of abuse at all. Still, the Satanic element was part of a hysteria, and later studies by academics and law enforcement found no evidence of such networks in day-care centers or anywhere else. See Ross E. Cheit, *The Witch-Hunt Narrative* (New York: Oxford University Press, 2014).

11. Jef Rouner, "Guide to Arguing with a Snopes-Denier," *Houston Press*, April 2, 2014.

12. Ali Mahmoodi et al., "Equality Bias Impairs Collective Decision-Making across Cultures," *Proceedings of the National Academy of Sciences*, March 24, 2015.

13. Chris Mooney, "The Science of Protecting People's Feelings: Why We Pretend All Opinions Are Equal," *Washington Post* online, March 10, 2015.

14. Karl Taro Greenfield, "Faking Cultural Literacy," *New York Times* online, May 24, 2014.

15. Quoted in Chris Mooney, "Liberals Deny Science, Too," *Washington Post* online, October 28, 2014.

16. The one difference was that conservatives reacted more intensely to data that contradicted their beliefs, but the researchers suggest that this is because "issues that challenge conservatives are the issues currently more polarizing in society today." The authors made these and the following comments in a press release from Ohio State University titled "Both Liberals, Conservatives Can Have Science Bias," February 9, 2015.

Chapter 3

1. Daniel W. Drezner, "A Clash between Administrators and Students at Yale Went Viral," *Washington Post* online, November 9, 2015.

2. A study by the Educational Testing Service, the group that administers the Scholastic Aptitude Test, or SAT, to college-bound students, found that there was no associated increase in ability connected to the explosion of college attendance. See Educational Testing Service, *America's Skills Challenge: Millennials and the Future* (Princeton, NJ: Educational Testing Service, 2015).

3. Ben Casselman, "Shut Up about Harvard," FiveThirtyEight.com, March 30, 2016.

4. James Piereson and Naomi Schaefer Riley, "Remedial Finance: The Outsized Cost of Playing Academic Catch-Up," *Weekly Standard* online, May 9, 2016.

5. Robert Hughes, *Culture of Complaint* (New York: Time Warner, 1993), 68.

6. Valerie Strauss, "I Would Love to Teach, But . . .," *Washington Post* online, December 31, 2013.

7. Emma Brown, "Former Stanford Dean Explains Why Helicopter Parenting Is Ruining a Generation of Children," *Washington Post* online, October 16, 2015.

8. Megan McArdle, "Sheltered Students Go to College, Avoid Education," BloombergView.com, August 13, 2015.

9. Jeffrey J. Selingo, "Helicopter Parents Are Not the Only Problem. Colleges Coddle Students, Too," *Washington Post*, October 21, 2015.

10. Robby Soave, "Yale Students Tell English Profs to Stop Teaching English: Too Many White Male Poets," Reason.com, June 1, 2016.

11. Jonathan D. Glater, "To: Professor@University.edu Subject: Why It's All about Me," *New York Times* online, February 22, 2006.

12. James V. Schall, *Another Sort of Learning* (San Francisco: Ignatius, 1988), 30–37.

13. David Dunning, "We Are All Confident Idiots," *Pacific Standard* online, October 27, 2014.

14. Tiny Castleton State College in Vermont, now a "university," is one of many examples in New England alone. Lisa Rathke, "Switching from a College to a University Could Mean More Money, More Students," *Huffington Post*, July 12, 2015.

15. Catherine Rampell, "The Rise of the 'Gentleman's A' and the GPA Arms Race," *Washington Post* online, March 28, 2016.

16. Richard Arum, "College Graduates: Satisfied, but Adrift," in Mark Bauerlein and Adam Bellow, eds., *The State of the American Mind* (West Conshohocken, PA: Templeton, 2015), 68.

17. The 2016 data were an extension of studies previously done by Professors Stuart Rojstaczer and Chris Healy, who continued to gather data on grades after writing papers on the subject in 2010 and 2012. They maintain a database of their work at www.gradeinflation.com.

18. For just two of many reports and reactions from both conservatives and liberals, see Katy Waldman, "Yale Students Erupt in Anger over Administrators Caring More about Free Speech Than Safe Spaces," *Slate*, November 7, 2015; and Shoshanna Weismann, "How Babies Are Made," *Weekly Standard*, November 10, 2015.

19. Mará Rose Williams, "Race Protests at Mizzou Could Stunt Freshmen Enrollment," *Kansas City Star* online, January 13, 2016.

20. Conor Friedersdorf, "The New Intolerance of Student Activism," *Atlantic* online, November 9, 2015.

21. Glenn Reynolds, "After Yale, Mizzou, raise the voting age—to 25," *USA Today* online, November 16, 2015.

Chapter 4

1. Adrienne LaFrance, "Raiders of the Lost Internet," *Atlantic* online, October 14, 2015.

2. Nicholas Carr, "Is Google Making Us Stupid?," *Atlantic* online, July/August 2008.

3. Caitlin Dewey, "What Was Fake on the Internet This Week: Why Do We Even Bother, Honestly?," *Washington Post* online, October 30, 2015.

4. Caitlin Dewey, "What Was Fake on the Internet This Week: Why This Is the Final Column," *Washington Post* online, December 18, 2015.

5. Damian Thompson, *Counterknowledge* (New York: W. W. Norton, 2008), 11.

6. Allen West, "Obama's America: Look What Our Troops Are Being FORCED to Do for Islam's Holy Month," allenbwest.com, June 29, 2015.

7. Michael Miller, "Gwyneth Paltrow's No Vagina Expert, Doctors Say," *People* online, January 29, 2015. Dr. Gunter's blog is at drjengunter.wordpress.com.

8. Laura Hooper Beck, "I Went to a Spa for My Uterus and This Is My Story," FastCompany.com, January 27, 2015.

9. Frank Bruni, "California, Camelot and Vaccines," *New York Times* online, July 4, 2015.

10. "'Stop Googling Your Symptoms,' Teenage Cancer Victim Told before Death," *Daily Telegraph,* June 16, 2015.

11. Matthew Fisher et al., "Searching for Explanations: How the Internet Inflates Estimates of Internal Knowledge," *Journal of Experimental Psychology* 144(3), June 2015, 674–687.

12. Tom Jacobs, "Searching the Internet Creates an Illusion of Knowledge," *Pacific Standard* online, April 1, 2015.

13. This and subsequent references are from the University College of London CIBER Briefing Paper "The Google Generation: The Information Behaviour of the Researcher of the Future," January 11, 2008.

14. Robert Epstein, "How Google Could Rig the 2016 Election," *Politico*, August 19, 2015.

15. James Surowiecki, *The Wisdom of Crowds* (New York: Anchor, 2005), xii–xiii.

16. Quoted in Tom Simonite, "The Decline of Wikipedia," *MIT Technology Review*, October 22, 2013.

17. Ibid.

18. Andrea Peterson, "Liberals Are More Likely to Unfriend You over Politics— Online and Off," *Washington Post* online, October 21, 2014.

19. A. O. Scott, "Everybody's a Critic. And That's How It Should Be," *New York Times Sunday Review* online, January 30, 2016.

20. Andrew Sullivan, "Democracies End When They Are Too Democratic," *New York* online, May 1, 2016.

21. A Dartmouth College researcher, Brendan Nyhan, among others, has been leading investigations for some years into why people double-down in the face of being proven wrong. Joe Keohane, "How Facts Backfire: Researchers Discover a Surprising Threat to Democracy: Our Brains," *Boston Globe* online, July 11, 2010.

22. David Dunning, "We Are All Confident Idiots," *Pacific Standard* online, October 27, 2014.

23. Megan McArdle, "Your Assessment of the Election Is Way Off," *Forbes* online, April 14, 2016.

Chapter 5

1. Sarah Kaplan, "How, and Why, a Journalist Tricked News Outlets into Thinking Chocolate Makes You Thin," *Washington Post* online, May 28, 2015.

2. Mollie Hemingway, "*Vox*'s Motto Should Be 'Explaining the News Incorrectly, Repeatedly,'" TheFederalist.com, July 17, 2014.

3. Elisabetta Povoledo, "Pope Calls for 'Peace in All the World' in First Easter Message," *New York Times* online, March 31, 2013.

4. Pew Research Center, "The Age of Indifference: A Study of Young Americans and How They View the News," June 28, 1990, 1.

5. Richard Arum, "College Graduates: Satisfied, but Adrift," in Mark Bauerlein and Adam Bellow, eds., *The State of the American Mind* (West Conshohocken, PA: Templeton, 2015), 73.

6. James E. Short, "How Much Media? Report on American Consumers." 2013. Institute for Communication Technology Management, Marshall School of Business, University of Southern California, http://classic.marshall.usc.edu/assets/161/25995.pdf.

7. Jan Zverina, "U.S. Media Consumption to Rise to 15.5 Hours a Day—Per Person—by 2015," UC San Diego News Center, November 6, 2013.

8. Quoted in Benjamin Mullen, "Buyouts Hit the *Dallas Morning News*," Poynter. org, July 7, 2015.

9. Quoted in Jeremy Peters, "Some Newspapers, Tracking Readers Online, Shift Coverage," *New York Times* online, September 5, 2010.

10. Peters, "Some Newspapers, Tracking Readers Online, Shift Coverage."

11. National Journal Group, *Washington in the Information Age*, 2015, Washington, DC.

12. Steven Metz, "As Celebrity Pundits Rise, U.S. National Security Policy Suffers," *World Politics Review*, August 14, 2015.

13. Mindich in Bauerlein and Bellow, *State of the American Mind*, 101.

14. R. R. Reno, "Trumpageddon!," *First Things* online, February 20, 2016.

15. Eliot Cohen, "The Age of Trump," *American Interest* online, February 26, 2016.

16. Anne Pluta, "Trump Supporters Appear to Be Misinformed, Not Uninformed," FiveThirtyEight.com, January 7, 2016.

17. Justin McCarthy, "Trust in Mass Media Returns to All-Time Low," Gallup.com, September 17, 2014.

18. Paul Farhi, "How Biased Are the Media, Really?," *Washington Post* online, April 27, 2012.

19. Dale Maharidge, "People's Stories: What Happens When No One Wants to Print Their Words Anymore?," *Nation* online, March 2, 2016.

20. Michael Nunez, "Want to Know What Facebook Really Thinks of Journalists? Here's What Happened When It Hired Some," Gizmodo.com, May 3, 2016.

21. Will Saletan, "Unhealthy Fixation," Slate.com, July 15, 2015.

22. John Bohannon, "I Fooled Millions into Thinking Chocolate Helps Weight Loss. Here's How," io9.Gizmodo.com, May 27, 2015.

23. Joshua Foust, "The Birth (and Death) of a Meme: Embedded Reporters Don't Always Get the Story," *Columbia Journalism Review* online, September 10, 2008.

24. Sheila Coronel, Steve Coll, and Derek Kravitz, "*Rolling Stone's* Investigation: 'A Failure That Was Avoidable,'" *Columbia Journalism Review* online, April 5, 2015.

25. Emily Yoffe, "The College Rape Overcorrection," Slate.com, December 7, 2014.

26. Quoted in Greg Jaffe, "VA Study Finds More Veterans Committing Suicide," *Washington Post* online, February 1, 2013.

27. Brandon Friedman, "Military Suicides Top Combat Deaths—But Only Because the Wars Are Ending," *TIME* online, January 16, 2013.

Chapter 6

1. Helen Thompson, "Teen Schools Professor on 'No Irish Need Apply' Signs," Smithsonian.com, August 5, 2015.

2. Geoffrey Norman, "Do I Dare to Eat an Egg," *The Weekly Standard* online, March 16, 2015.

3. Peter Whoriskey, "The Science of Skipping Breakfast: How Government Nutritionists May Have Gotten It Wrong," *Washington Post* online, August 10, 2015.

4. Seweryn Bialer and Joan Afferica, "Reagan and Russia," *Foreign Affairs*, Winter 1982–1983, 263.

5. Stephen M. Meyer, "Testimony before the Senate Foreign Relations Committee," in Theodore Karasik, ed., *Russia and Eurasia Armed Forces Review Annual* 15, 1991 (Gulf Breeze, FL: Academic International Press, 1999), 348.

6. Richard Ned Lebow and Thomas Risse Kappen, "Introduction," in Richard Ned Lebow and Thomas Risse Kappen, eds., *International Relations Theory and the End of the Cold War* (New York: Columbia University Press, 1995), 2.

7. The ten are the United States, Russia, the United Kingdom, France, the People's Republic of China, India, Pakistan, North Korea, Israel (undeclared), and South Africa (renounced). The South African arsenal was dismantled when the apartheid regime that created it fell from power.

8. W. Ian Lipkin, "Anti-Vaccination Lunacy Won't Stop," *Wall Street Journal* online, April 3, 2016.

9. See Richard Van Noorden, "Political Science's Problem with Research Ethics," *Nature* online, June 29, 2015; Brian C. Martinson, Melissa S. Anderson, and Raymond de Vries, "Scientists Behaving Badly," *Nature* 435 (June 9, 2005): 737–738.

10. Carl Zimmer, "A Sharp Rise in Retractions Prompts Calls for Reform," *New York Times* online, April 16, 2012.

11. Benedict Carey, "Many Psychology Findings Not as Strong as Claimed, Study Says," *New York Times* online, August 27, 2015.

12. Quoted in Rachel Gross, "Psychologists Call Out the Study That Called Out the Field of Psychology," Slate.com, March 3, 2016.

13. Daniel Engber, "Cancer Research Is Broken," Slate.com, April 19, 2016.

14. Garret Epps, "Genuine Christian Scholars Smack Down an Unruly Colleague," *Atlantic* online, August 10, 2012.

15. "Actresses' Role in Farm Issue Stirs Criticism," *Los Angeles Times* online archive, May 3, 1985.

16. Jessica Goldstein, "Is Gwyneth Paltrow Wrong about Everything? This Scientist Thinks So," ThinkProgress.com, April 21, 2016.

17. Alexandra Petri, "Dr. Carson, This Is Not Brain Surgery," *Washington Post* online, November 5, 2015.

18. This account is drawn from Paul Offit, "The Vitamin Myth: Why We Think We Need Supplements," *Atlantic* online, July 19, 2013.

19. Helen Caldicott, *Missile Envy* (New York: Bantam, 1985), 235; Helen Caldicott, *If You Love This Planet* (New York: W. W. Norton, 1992), 156.

20. There is a claim that has circulated in various articles about Criswell over the years that he got one prediction within shouting distance of something like creepy accuracy. He apparently told the television host Jack Paar in March 1963 that President Kennedy would not run for reelection in 1964 because of something that would happen to him in November 1963. This, however, might yet be an urban legend, at least until someone turns up an old videotape or kinescope (if any exists).

21. Carl Bialik, "Most Pollsters Say Their Reputations Have Worsened," FiveThirtyEight.com, December 28, 2015.

22. Clive Thompson, "Can Game Theory Predict When Iran Will Get the Bomb?" *New York Times Magazine* online, August 12, 2009.

23. Nassim Nicholas Taleb, *The Black Swan* (New York: Random House, 2010), xxiv–xxv.

24. Philip E. Tetlock, *Expert Political Judgment* (Princeton, NJ: Princeton University Press, 2005), 20.

25. Tetlock, *Expert Political Judgment*, 20.

26. James Surowiecki, *The Wisdom of Crowds* (New York: Anchor, 2005), 31.

27. Tetlock, *Expert Political Judgment*, 21.

28. See Tetlock, *Expert Political Judgment*, 101–103.

29. See, for example, Tina Nguyen, "How Nate Silver Failed to Predict Trump," *Vanity Fair*, February 1, 2016.

30. Noah Rothman, "Why They Think Trump Can Win in Nov?," *Commentary* online, April 27, 2016.

31. Tetlock, *Expert Political Judgment*, 23.

Conclusion

1. See James Traub, "First, They Came for the Experts," *Foreign Policy*, July 7, 2016.

2. Quoted in Michael Deacon, "Michael Gove's Guide to Britain's Greatest Enemy . . . the Experts," *Telegraph* online, June 10, 2016.

3. Quoted in Stephen Castle, "Having Won, Some 'Brexit' Campaigners Begin Backpedaling," *New York Times* online, June 26, 2016.

4. Quoted in Nick Gass, "Trump: 'The Experts Are Terrible,' " Politico.com, April 4, 2016.

5. David Dunning, "The Psychological Quirk That Explains Why You Love Donald Trump," Politico.com, May 25, 2016.

6. See, for example, Jennifer Kerr, "Educational Divide in GOP White House Race: What's behind It," Associated Press, April 3, 2016; Max Ehrenfreund, "The Outlandish Conspiracy Theories Many of Donald Trump's Supporters Believe," *Washington Post* online, May 5, 2016; Scott Clement, "Donald Trump Is Splitting the White Vote in Ways We've Never Seen Before," *Washington Post* online, May 31, 2016.

7. The journalist Jeffrey Goldberg, for one, claimed that Samuels was using the piece to settle a personal score with him. See Jeffrey Goldberg, "Ben Rhodes and the 'Retailing' of the Iran Deal," *Atlantic* online, May 9, 2016.

8. David Samuels, "The Aspiring Novelist Who Became Obama's Foreign-Policy Guru," *New York Times Sunday Magazine* online, May 5, 2016.

9. A classic episode of the original *Star Trek* series, first aired in 1968, featured a misguided attempt by a well-meaning professor—of course—to base an entire planet on the Nazi experience. It all ends in disaster, but the dying professor still calls Nazi Germany "the most efficient state Earth ever knew," with the show's voice of reason, Mr. Spock, chiming in to say, "Quite true." In reality, Nazi Germany was deeply corrupt and inefficient, and many of its leading scientists and intellectuals fled the country after 1933. Many Americans, however, still believe in the myth of Nazi efficiency.

10. Daniel Libit, "How the Expert Class Got Trumped and Berned," CNBC.com, May 12, 2016.

11. Susan Jacoby, "The Dumbing of America," *Washington Post* online, February 17, 2008.

12. Friedrich Hayek, *The Constitution of Liberty: The Definitive Edition* (Chicago: University of Chicago Press, 2011), 378.

13. Evan Thomas, "Why We Need a Foreign Policy Elite," *New York Times* online, May 8, 2016.

14. Andrew Bacevich, "Rationalizing Lunacy: The Intellectual as Servant of the State," *Huffington Post*, May 8, 2015.

NOTES TO PAGES 222-237

15. Philip E. Tetlock, *Expert Political Judgment* (Princeton, NJ: Princeton University Press, 2005), 231–232.

16. Malcolm Gladwell, "Small Change: Why the Revolution Will Not Be Tweeted," *New Yorker*, October 4, 2010.

17. Ilya Somin, "Political Ignorance in America," in Mark Bauerlein and Adam Bellow, eds., *The State of the American Mind* (West Conshohocken, PA: Templeton, 2015), 166.

18. Neetzan Zimmerman, "Kimmel Fools Hillary Supporters into Backing Trump's Tax Plan," *The Hill*, September 30, 2015.

19. Ariel Edwards-Levy, "Republicans Like Obama's Ideas Better When They Think They're Donald Trump's," *Huffpost Politics*, September 1, 2015.

20. Nick Saffran, "Wipe That Grin Off Your Smug Faces, Progressive Pollsters," TheFederalist.com, December 29, 2015.

21. Derek Kohler, "Why People Are Confused about What Experts Really Think," *New York Times* online, February 14, 2016.

22. Jacoby, "Dumbing Of America."

23. C. S. Lewis, *The Screwtape Letters with Screwtape Proposes a Toast* (New York: Image, 1981), 136–139 (emphases in the original).

24. José Ortega y Gasset, *The Revolt of the Masses* (New York: W. W. Norton, 1993), 18.

25. See Libit, "How the Expert Class Got Trumped and Berned"; and Julie Beck, "Americans Believe in Science, Just Not Its Findings," *Atlantic* online, January 29, 2015.

26. James Traub, "It's Time for the Elites to Rise Up against the Ignorant Masses," *Foreign Policy*, June 28, 2016.

27. Andrew Sullivan, "Democracies End When They Are Too Democratic," NYMag.com, May 1, 2016.

INDEX

9/11 *see* United States of America, 2001 terrorist attacks

Abagnale, Frank, 179
Adams, Scott, 14
Affleck, Ben, 38
Affordable Care Act (United States legislation), 26
Afghanistan, 162
Agnew, Spiro, 146
AIDS, 1, 2, 49, 50, 181, 192
  denial of HIV as cause, 1, 2, 181
Ailes, Roger, 153
Animal House (1978 film), 188
Arizona State University, 81
Armstrong, Neil, xxii
Asimov, Isaac, 1, 196
Assad, Bashar, 128
Australia, 2, 48, 114, 193, 194

Bacevich, Andrew, 220, 221
Barton, David, 186, 187
Bayesian analysis, 240n
Beck, Glenn, 148
Bellesiles, Michael, 186
Bialer, Seweryn, 172, 173
blogging, 3, 108, 114, 160, 236
Bohannon, John, 135

Brown University, 73
Brown, Henry Billings, 31
Bruni, Frank, 105, 117
Bueno de Mesquita, Bruce, 198, 199
Bush, George W., 57, 113, 123, 219

Cable News Network, 144, 151, 152, 154, 155, 156
Caldicott, Helen, 193–195
Carrey, Jim, 3, 117
Carter, Jimmy, 34, 151
Casey Anthony trial (2011), 152
Centers for Disease Control, 22, 117
Challenger disaster (1986), 10
Chancellor, John, 151
Cheers (television show), 13, 106
China, 62, 65, 245n
Chomsky, Noam, 39, 194, 195
Christopher, Warren, 19
Churchill, Ward, 180, 181
Clinton, Bill, 146
Clinton, Hillary, 147, 228
CNN *see* Cable News Network
Coelho, Tony, 189
Colbert, Stephen, 156
Cold War, xxi, 2, 28, 193, 194, 220
Columbia University, 34, 51, 52, 161, 163, 181, 186
  Harriman Institute, 34

confirmation bias, 8, 47, 50–55, 60–68, 118, 123, 157
conspiracy theories, 55–60, 108, 112
Cornell University, 43, 45
Court TV, 152
Crichton, Michael, 49
Criswell (Jeron Criswell Konig), 196
    possibly predicts JFK assasination, 246n
Cronkite, Walter, 141, 156
cultural literacy, 66

Damon, Matt, 38
Dartmouth College, 82, 84, 243
Dawkins, Richard, 102
democracy, xx, 1, 5, 6, 11, 17, 19, 20, 28, 30, 69, 114, 122, 129, 158, 174, 204–208, 215–218, 225–238
    republic as a form of, 225–238
Denmark, 65
Dewey, Caitlin, 112, 113
Drezner, Dan, 73
Duesberg, Peter, 1, 2, 181
Dunning, David, 43–46, 64, 67, 87, 131, 212, 213
Dunning-Kruger Effect, 43, 44, 64, 119, 212, 213
    "metacognition" as a crucial aspect, 45

Ebola, 50
eggs, debate over, 10, 22, 23, 171, 172, 175, 224
Erdeley, Sabrina, 163, 168
experts and expertise, xx–xxv, 3–20, 22–24, 27–37, 39, 40, 42, 45–48, 51, 54, 58, 60–70, 71, 72, 82, 84, 106, 107, 110, 115, 118, 121–128, 131–137, 139, 144, 145, 147–159, 166–179, 184, 188–238
    acting outside their competence, 150, 167, 188–195
    defined, 28–37
    prediction, 196–204

Facebook, 115, 129, 130–132, 142, 160, 161, 230
Fleming, Ian, 58
Fonda, Jane, 189

Fox News, 147, 151–155, 212, 229
France, 245n
Franklin, Benjamin, 191, 226

generalization, 61–63
Genetically Modified Organisms see GMOs
Georgetown University, 85, 86
Germany, 107, 175, 216, 247n
GMOs, 161, 162, 192, 230
Goldberg, Jeffrey, 247n
Good Will Hunting (1997 film), 38
Google, xix, 3, 84, 102, 105, 118, 121, 170, 191
Gorbachev, Mikhail, 173
Gove, Michael, 209, 210
Gvosdev, Nick, 173

Harvard University, 2, 24, 31, 95, 96, 184, 198
    Extension School, 96
    Medical School, 24
    School of Public Health, 2
Heinlein, Robert, 14
higher education, 42, 71, 72, 76, 80, 88, 90, 95
    as a client service, 71–82
    grade inflation, 93, 95, 98
Hill, Anita, 151
Hofstadter, Richard, 18, 19
Holdren, John, 148
House, MD (television show), 51
Hughes, Robert, 5, 78
human immunodeficiency virus (HIV), 1, 2

Internet, xxii, 6, 9, 15, 41, 42, 105–133, 137, 139, 142–146, 148, 149, 154, 155, 171, 206, 234, 236
Iran, 65, 149, 213–215, 228
    1979 revolution, 149
    nuclear agreement with, 213–215
Iraq, 199, 223
Isaiah Berlin, 201
Israel, 245n

Jastrow, Robert, 82, 83
Jefferson, Thomas, 70, 186, 187

journalists, 9–11, 102, 123, 133, 135, 137, 140, 143, 150, 154, 159, 160–163, 166, 167, 168, 205, 214, 215

Kaszeta, Dan, 83, 84, 127
Keillor, Garrison, 44
Kennan, George, 195
Kennedy, John F., 59, 177, 211
Kennedy, Robert F., Jr., 117
Kerry, John, 123
Kimmel, Jimmy, 45, 228, 229, 235, 236
Konnikova, Maria, 52, 67
Koppel, Ted, 150
Krauthammer, Charles, 153
Kruger, Justin, 43–46, 64, 212, 213

Landon, Alfred, 197
Lange, Jessica, 189
law of parsimony, 56, 57
lawyers, 4, 30, 33, 235
League of Nations, 220
Lewis, Clive Staples, 40, 232
    literary creation "Screwtape," 232, 233, 238
Lewis, Jeffrey, 83
Limbaugh, Rush, 146–148, 153
Lincoln, Abraham, 31, 43, 105
low-information voter, 25–28

Madison, James, 209
Mbeki, Thabo, 1, 2
McCarthy, Jenny, 3, 190
McNamara, Robert, 219
moral panics, 60, 240n
MSNBC, 153, 156, 161

Nightline (television news program), 149–151
Nixon, Richard, 219, 222
North Korea, 3, 245n
Norway, 63
nuclear weapons, 2, 27, 173, 177, 193, 195, 211–213, 245n
Nye, Bill, 206
Nyhan, Brendan, 243n

O'Reilly, Bill, 110
Obama, Barack, 57, 113, 114, 132, 148, 211, 213, 222
Occam's Razor, 56, 171
OJ Simpson trial (1995), 152
On the Beach (1956 novel), 193
Ortega y Gasset, Jose, 17, 233

Pakistan, 245n
Palin, Sarah, 26
Paltrow, Gwyneth, 115, 116, 117, 190, 191
Pauling, Linus, 191–195
Paulos, John Allen, 48
peer review, 35, 52, 53, 135, 183
Pelosi, Nancy, 26
physicians, 1, 2, 4, 21–24, 29, 49, 118, 122, 165, 174, 177, 179, 195, 205, 235
plagiarism, 179, 181, 183, 188
polling and public opinion, 138, 158, 197, 198, 202, 214, 226, 228, 229, 240
Princeton University, 52, 95
Putin, Vladimir, 204, 205

Rain Man (1988 film), 47
Rather, Dan, 123, 124
raw milk movement, 21, 22
Reagan, Ronald, 82, 151, 190, 193
Reasoner, Harry, 141
Reddit, 131
Reynolds, Frank, 151
Rhodes, Ben, 213, 222
Rolling Stone, 163
Roosevelt, Franklin D., 57, 197, 231
Russell, Bertrand, 170, 207
Russian Federation, 2, 22, 59, 63, 92, 173, 202–204, 245n
Rwanda, 19

Safire, William, 146
Saletan, Will, 161, 162
Sanders, Bernie, 76
Saturday Night Live (television show), 149
Schall, James, 86, 87
Scholastic Aptitude Test, 241n
scientific method, 53
Shulman, Marshall, 34

Silver, Nate, 202
So I Married an Axe Murderer (1993 film), 134
social media, xxii, 15, 40, 41, 66, 81–85, 112, 114, 128, 129, 130, 132, 142, 146, 160
South Africa, 1, 2, 177, 245*n*
Spacek, Sissy, 189
Star Trek (television series), 247*n*
stereotypes, 20, 61, 62
Stern, Howard, 147
Stewart, Jon, 156
Sturgeon, Theodore, 107
Sturgeon's Law, 105, 107, 108, 119, 140
superstitions, 54, 55
Surowiecki, James, 122, 201
Syria, 127, 128, 230

Taleb, Nassim, 199, 200
talk radio, 145–148, 153, 154
Ted Turner, 151
Tetlock, Philip, 200, 201, 206, 221, 222
thalidomide, 10, 23, 24
Thatcher, Margaret, 3, 194
The Big Lebowski (1998 film), 40
The Brothers Karamazov, 58
The Graduate (1967 film), 70
The Spy Who Came In From from the Cold (1965 film), 209
Thomas, Clarence, 151
Thucydides, 16
Tocqueville, Alexis, 17, 18
Trump, Donald, 203, 210–213, 228, 231, 237
Twitter, 3, 83, 84, 102, 129, 131, 132, 142, 161, 189, 210

Ukraine, 2, 230
Union of Soviet Socialist Republics, 28, 34, 137, 141, 172, 173, 193, 194, 199, 202–204
    1991 collapse, 173, 202–204
United Kingdom, 59, 181, 197, 209, 210, 245*n*
    2015 Brexit debate, 209, 210, 235
    Conservative Party, 210

UKIP (United Kingdom Independence Party), 210
United States of America, ii, xix, xxiv, 1, 2, 4, 11, 16, 17, 18, 27, 48, 60, 62, 72, 74, 94, 98, 137, 140, 141, 146, 158, 171, 173, 174, 176, 189, 193, 194, 197, 207, 210, 211, 214–216, 220, 226, 232, 233, 236, 237, 245*n*
    2001 terrorist attacks, 57, 113, 180, 237
    2014 midterm election, 197
    2016 election, 14, 212, 216, 231, 236
    Central Intelligence Agency, 198
    Congress, 26, 43, 158, 159, 213–215, 220–223
    Democratic Party, 28, 228, 229
    Food and Drug Administration, 22
    foreign aid, 27, 220, 232
    Republican Party, 28, 228, 229
    Veteran's Administration, 165
United States Naval War College, 37, 96
University College of London, 120
University of California at Berkeley, 182
University of Chicago, 94, 138
University of Colorado, 180
University of Missouri, 101, 102
University of Southern California, 92
University of Virginia, 163
urban legends, 16, 112, 113, 170

vaccines, 3, 13, 21, 28, 117, 161, 181, 195, 232, 235, 236
Vietnam War, xxiii, 10, 100, 145, 149, 219, 237
Vox.com, 135, 171, 243

Wakefield, Andrew, 181
Waugh, Evelyn, 136, 159
Wellesley College, 95
West, Allen, 114
Wikipedia, 3, 124–127
Wood, Edward D., 196

X-Files (television show), 57, 59